MASTERING
POWERPOINT 97

MASTERING POWERPOINT® 97
THIRD EDITION

Katherine Murray

SYBEX®

San Francisco • Paris • Düsseldorf • Soest

Associate Publisher: Amy Romanoff
Acquisitions Manager: Kristine Plachy
Acquisitions & Developmental Editor: Melanie Spiller
Project Editor: Doug Robert
Technical Editor: Beth Shannon
Book Designers: Patrick Dintino, Catalin Dulfu
Electronic Publishing Specialist: Bob Bihlmayer
Production Coordinator: Amy Eoff
Indexer: Nancy Guenther
Cover Designer: Design Site
Cover Photographer: Mark Johann

Screen reproductions produced with Collage Complete.

Collage Complete is a trademark of Inner Media Inc.

SYBEX is a registered trademark of SYBEX Inc.

Mastering is a trademark of SYBEX Inc.

TRADEMARKS: SYBEX has attempted throughout this book to distinguish proprietary trademarks from descriptive terms by following the capitalization style used by the manufacturer.

The author and publisher have made their best efforts to prepare this book, and the content is based upon final release software whenever possible. Portions of the manuscript may be based upon pre-release versions supplied by software manufacturer(s). The author and the publisher make no representation or warranties of any kind with regard to the completeness or accuracy of the contents herein and accept no liability of any kind including but not limited to performance, merchantability, fitness for any particular purpose, or any losses or damages of any kind caused or alleged to be caused directly or indirectly from this book.

Earlier versions of this book were published under the titles *Mastering PowerPoint 4* and *Mastering PowerPoint for Windows 95*, copyright ©1994 and 1996 respectively, SYBEX Inc.
Copyright ©1997 SYBEX Inc., 1151 Marina Village Parkway, Alameda, CA 94501. World rights reserved. No part of this publication may be stored in a retrieval system, transmitted, or reproduced in any way, including but not limited to photocopy, photograph, magnetic or other record, without the prior agreement and written permission of the publisher.

Library of Congress Card Number: 97-69204
ISBN: 0-7821-2154-3

Manufactured in the United States of America

10 9 8 7 6 5 4 3 2 1

*To Kelly, Christopher,
and Cameron,
and our upcoming
adventure in Alaska.
Love, Mom*

Acknowledgments

Say you're standing in front of a large group of people. You've just given your presentation, and a huge rush of relief washes over you. You look around the room and see several of the people who helped you prepare this important work. A computer book is a lot like a presentation in that regard: it takes quite a number of people to make sure everything goes smoothly—from the first idea to the last period. Special thanks to Melanie Spiller, developmental editor, who is always together, insightful, fast-acting, and fun to work with; to Beth Shannon, who not only played the role of technical editor to ensure the accuracy of my examples and procedures, but also wrote the updated sections for some of the later chapters in the book; and to all the editors, project editors, tech editors, and production coordinators who have worked on this book through three editions now, for pulling together any wayward pieces and making sure I said what I meant to say.

Contents at a Glance

Introduction xvii

PART ONE: POWERPOINT ESSENTIALS — 1

1 PowerPoint Possibilities — 3
2 The Quick and Easy Presentation — 29

PART TWO: THE RIGHT TOOL FOR THE JOB — 62

3 Entering, Editing, and Enhancing Text — 65
4 Creating and Enhancing Graphs — 115
5 Picture This! Custom and Clip Art — 151
6 Adding Sound — 191
7 Ready, Set, Video! — 213
8 Finishing the Slide Show — 239

PART THREE: QUINTESSENTIAL POWERPOINT — 274

9 Coloring Your Presentation — 277
10 Printing Slides and Handouts — 305
11 Web Publishing with PowerPoint — 325
12 Working with Multimedia Files — 339
13 You're On! Giving the Presentation — 357

APPENDICES — 367

A Installing PowerPoint 97 — 367
B Modifying Program Defaults — 373
C Tips for the First-Time Presenter — 383
D High-End PowerPoint — 387

Glossary 389

Index 398

Table of Contents

Introduction . . . .*xvii*

PART I • POWERPOINT ESSENTIALS

1 PowerPoint Possibilities   3

Why Presentations? And Why PowerPoint? 5
    How Are Presentations Used? 6
    What Do I Need to Present? 6
Getting Started with PowerPoint 7
Important PowerPoint Elements 11
    PowerPoint Views 13
    The AutoContent Wizard 18
    Masters 19
    Templates 19
    ValuPack 20
    PowerPoint Central 21
    Color Schemes 23
Tips for Creating a Good Presentation 24
    Considering the Audience 25
    Considering the Tone 25
    Considering the Tools 26
    The Big C: Continuity 27
What's Next? 28

2 The Quick and Easy Presentation   29

Starting PowerPoint 32
Getting Help 34
    Working with the Office Assistant 35
    Microsoft on the Web 36
Creating a Simple Presentation 36
    Working with Wizards and Templates 37
    Exploring the PowerPoint Menus 44
    Understanding Toolbars 45
    Adding Text 49
Starting a New Slide 53
    Changing Views 56
    Starting a Slide Show 57
    Saving Presentations 58
    Printing the Presentation 59
What's Next? 60

PART II • THE RIGHT TOOL FOR THE JOB

3 Entering, Editing, and Enhancing Text — 65

Text Rules 68
    Too Much Is Too Much 68
    The Clearer, the Better 68
    Know Where You're Going 69
    Use Text to Highlight, Not Narrate 70
    Color and Contrast Are Important 70
    Think about Your Audience 71
    Timing Is Everything 71
Before You Add Text... 71
Entering Text 72
    Adding Text in Slide View 73
    Adding New Text Boxes 75
    Adding Text in Outline View 76
    Working with Text Levels 80
Using the AutoContent Wizard 81
Editing Text 83
    Simple Text Editing 83
    Selecting Text for Editing 84
    Using the Spelling Checker to Catch Spelling Errors 85
    Using AutoCorrect 86
    Using the Style Checker to Catch Style Inconsistencies and Problems 86
    Editing in Outline View 90
    Collapsing the Outline 90
    Editing in Slide Sorter View 95
    Expanding Slides 96
Formatting Text 98
    Applying a New Design 98
    Changing Format with a New Layout 98
    Displaying the Ruler 100
    Changing Indents 101
    Working with Tabs 102
    Enhancing Text 106
What's New? 113

4 Creating and Enhancing Graphs — 115

A Few Graph Ideas 117
Is This PowerPoint or Microsoft Graph? 118
    Using Excel Graphs in Your PowerPoint Presentations ... 118
An Overview of Graph Types 119

Creating a Graph 119
    Starting the Graph 121
    Working with the Datasheet 121
Choosing the Graph Type 124
    Importing Chart Data 128
What Data Can You Import? 129
    Importing Files 130
Editing Graphs 130
    Basic Procedures: Cutting, Copying, Pasting, and Resizing Graphs 131
    Modifying Graph Elements 132
    Changing the Data Arrangement 134
    Creating a Data Table 136
    Changing the X and Y Axes 136
Enhancing Graphs 138
    Changeable Chart Elements 139
    Working with Graph Text 139
    Adding Gridlines 143
    Hiding and Displaying the Legend 145
    Adding a Text Box 146
    Specifying Color 146
    Changing Patterns 147
    Animating Charts 148
Chapter Summary 149

5   Picture This! Custom and Clip Art   151

Checking Out PowerPoint's Clip Art 154
    Letting AutoClipArt Make the Choice 154
    Adding New Clip Art Slides 156
    Finding Specific Clip Art 159
    Organizing Clip Art 159
Importing Art 162
Drawing Art 165
    The Difference between Drawing and Painting 165
Planning the Art You Want 166
Displaying the Drawing Tools 167
Using AutoShapes 171
    Choosing AutoShape Groups 172
    Setting AutoShape Options 173
    Modifying Art 175
Basic Art Editing 175
    Editing an Image with Format Picture 176
Grouping and Ungrouping Objects 178
Layering Art Objects 180
Animating Art Objects 187
Chapter Summary 189

6 Adding Sound — 191

- Sound Basics 194
  - A Sound Glossary 195
  - WAV and MID Sound Files: Which Do You Need? 197
- The Multimedia-Ready PC 198
  - What You Need for Sound 199
  - Upgrading for Sound 200
- Using PowerPoint's Sound Effects 202
  - Choosing Transitional Sound Effects 202
  - Adding Sound from Other Sources 202
- Adding Sound to Animations 205
- Inserting Sound Objects 206
- Recording Your Own Sound 206
  - Recording Narration 208
  - Using Sound Recorder 210
- Reviewing Different Sound Choices 211
- Some Sound Advice for Presenting 211
- Chapter Review 212

7 Ready, Set, Video! — 213

- Getting Started 216
  - Why Use Video Clips in Your Presentations? 216
  - What You Need to Use Video 217
  - Where Do You Get Video? 217
  - Understanding Video Formats 218
- Adding Movies to PowerPoint Slides 220
  - Making Movie Posters 220
  - Adding a Movie Icon 222
- Resizing and Moving Movie Objects 224
  - Playing Movies 224
- Editing Movies 227
  - Simple Editing 228
  - Advanced Editing: Using Media Player 228
  - Cropping the Movie Object 235
  - Recoloring Images 236
- Chapter Review 237

8 Finishing the Slide Show — 239

- What Is a Slide Show? 242
- Adding the Finishing Touches 242
  - PowerPoint "Polishing" Tools 243
  - Setting Slide Transitions 243
  - Choosing the Transition 244

Choosing Transition Speed 249
Choosing Manual or Automatic Slide Advance 250
Adding Sound Effects 253
Creating Hidden Slides 255
Hiding a Slide 256
Displaying a Hidden Slide 257
Rehearsing Slide Display Timing 258
Starting a Screen Show 260
Working with the Set Up Show Dialog Box 261
Moving through a Slide Show 262
Using the Slide Navigator 262
Presentation Special Features 265
Drawing On-Screen 266
Creating On-the-Spot Notes with Meeting Minder 267
Presentation Comments and Review 271
Presentation Conferencing 272
Chapter Review 273

PART III • QUINTESSENTIAL POWERPOINT

9   Coloring Your Presentation   277

How Do You Use Color? 280
A Shortcut to Color Choices: Templates 281
Making a Fast Color Change 282
Changing Text Color 282
Changing Object Color: Inside 283
Changing Object Color: Outside 284
What If You Want More Colors? 285
Creating Custom Colors 285
Changing Entire Color Schemes 287
Viewing and Changing the Current Color Scheme 288
Creating a Custom Color Scheme 289
Using Apply to All to Globally Replace a Color 290
Working in Black and White 291
Setting Black-and-White Options 292
Do I Need a Black-and-White Color Scheme or Just a Black-and-White View? 294
Recoloring Clip Art 295
Working with Slide Backgrounds 297
Shaded Backgrounds 299
Textured Backgrounds 300
Patterned Backgrounds 301
Picture Backgrounds 302
Chapter Review 303

10 Printing Slides and Handouts — 305

- Why Print Your Presentations? ...308
- Getting Started ...309
  - Printing Decisions You Need to Make ...309
  - A Few Printing Ideas ...310
  - Checking Page Setup for Slides ...310
  - Choosing Page Size ...311
  - Changing Slide Width and Height ...312
  - Choosing Orientation ...312
  - Numbering Slides ...313
  - Adding Headers and Footers ...315
- Printing the Presentation ...317
  - Selecting Your Printer ...318
  - Choosing Print Options ...319
  - What Do You Want to Print? ...319
  - Printing to a File ...322
  - Finally...Printing! ...322
  - How Did It Turn Out? ...323
- Chapter Summary ...323

11 Web Publishing with PowerPoint — 325

- Web Basics ...327
  - Web Terms ...328
  - What Does a Web Page Look Like? ...328
- Creating Links ...331
- Displaying the Web Toolbar ...333
- Saving the Presentation as an HTML File ...334
  - The Internet Assistant ...335
- Posting Your Web Page ...335
- Chapter Summary ...337

12 Working with Multimedia Files — 339

- The Big File ...341
  - Windows 95 Compression ...342
  - Compression Techniques ...343
- Working with Files ...344
  - Planning File Organization ...345
  - What Kind of Files Will You Use? ...346
- Linking and Embedding Files ...349
  - Linking vs. Embedding ...349
  - Linking Objects ...350
  - Embedding Objects ...352
- Importing and Exporting Files ...353
  - Importing Presentations ...353
  - Exporting Presentations ...353

Running a Presentation on a Computer without PowerPoint .354
    Using the Pack and Go Wizard 354
    Running the Presentation 356
Chapter Review 356

13 You're On! Giving the Presentation   357

What Is a Finished Presentation? 359
What Are Your Options for Presenting? 360
Effective Rehearsal Techniques 362
    Even If It's Informal, Practice 362
    Choose a Diverse Trial Audience 362
    Include Setup in the Trial Run 363
    Go Straight through, from Start to Finish 363
    When You're Finished Giving the Trial Presentation, Evaluate 363
PowerPoint Case Studies 364
    The Small Group 364
    On the Road 364
    The Corporate Meeting 365
Chapter Summary 366

APPENDICES

A   Installing PowerPoint 97   367

The Installation Process 368
Adding and Removing Options 370

B   Modifying Program Defaults   373

General Options 374
Edit Options 376
View Options 376
Printing Options 378
Save Options 379
Spelling Options 380
Advanced Options 381

C   Tips for the First-Time Presenter   383

D   High-End PowerPoint   387

Glossary   389

Index . . . . *.398*

Introduction

Two things are certain about that next presentation you're going to give: (1) It's going to include the best ideas you can come up with, and (2) It will be better than your last one, because this time you're using Microsoft PowerPoint 97.

If you're a professional who doesn't have much time to devote to learning new programs, PowerPoint is the program you need. This popular presentation graphics program has been designed with one thing in mind: to help *you*, the harried professional, assemble all the pieces that comprise an effective presentation, with a minimum of time and trouble.

Whether you want a simple presentation with no-nonsense bulleted lists, or an entertainment feature with built in narrations, sound, video, and special slide-show effects, PowerPoint 97 can help you create the biggest effect for the least hassle, making sure your message is communicated in the clearest possible way.

How to Use This Book

Mastering PowerPoint 97 introduces you to the kernels of knowledge all users need when exploring a program for the first time. Like the software it presents, this book takes you through the process of creating presentations in a sequence of logical, what-do-I-do-next steps.

Beyond the basics, however, *Mastering PowerPoint 97* adds depth and breadth, by providing tips for creating both quick and more detailed presentations. Additionally, Part Two includes side discussions that give a professional spin to the topic at hand. For example, in Chapter 4, "Creating and Enhancing Graphs," the discussion "The Four Most Effective Charts" tells you which charts are used most often by professional presenters when displaying different types of information.

Pictures of the what you should expect to see on your computer's monitor illustrate important steps within each section. Additionally, tables are used to organize and highlight information in a quick-look format. Bulleted lists call attention to items in each section, and each chapter begins with a list of the major topics covered in that chapter.

Throughout the book, you'll find tips, notes, and warnings, as well as sidebars that give you information above and beyond the basic procedures and examples.

Feel free to use this book in the most logical way for you: if you're pressed for time or need a simple reminder on a task you've tried before, look up the task you need in the index or the in table of contents and use the book as a reference. When you have a few minutes to spare and want to experiment with some of PowerPoint's new features, use this book as a guide and follow along with some of the examples—you will learn the hows and whys behind different operations and you'll find that you've sped through the learning curve in no time at all.

Who Should Read This Book?

This book will help you concentrate on the process of creating your presentations as quickly and cleanly as possible. You'll find the organization, examples, and illustrations of this book helpful if you fit any of these descriptions:

- You are responsible for creating weekly production charts used in the departmental meeting.
- You are new to presentation graphics and need a straightforward, no-frills guide to creating effective slides and going a few steps beyond the ordinary.
- You hope to learn more about multimedia and want to master PowerPoint in order to produce professional-looking slide shows.
- You are looking for a way to make professional-looking presentations easily.
- You want to create and publish Web pages using PowerPoint for your company or personal use.
- You have a lot of work to fit into an already filled-to-bursting day and you want a guide that will help you cut the time and effort you would usually need to invest in learning a new program.

Highlights of Microsoft PowerPoint

You'll see one of the biggest benefits of Microsoft PowerPoint 97 from the first moment you start the program. Recognize the general layout? If you've worked with other Microsoft programs, you'll be able to find your way through PowerPoint easily. Other features that help you create your presentations include the following:

- Professionally designed templates, some with animation, that you can use to create presentations quickly

- An AutoContent wizard that actually helps you write the content of your presentation (it doesn't just proffer advice)
- An Outline view in which you can enter the text for your presentation and organize your thoughts before adding artwork
- A wide array of charting features (including the ability to create 3-D charts in a variety of styles), which gives you almost unlimited capacity to display data
- A large palette of preset color schemes that are consistent with Office 97 color palettes, providing you with color sets that work effectively together (or you can create your own)
- Full drawing capabilities, which give you the freedom to either add hand-drawn art to your slide show or use one of the many clip art files included with PowerPoint
- Four different views—Slide, Outline, Notes Pages, and Slide Sorter—which allow you to see your presentation in all possible perspectives
- Full text support, including such enhancement options as font, size, style, and color selections, as well as special effects like shading and shadowing
- The ability to print collateral materials—handouts, speaker notes, slide printouts—in either full color or black and white
- The option of easily publishing your presentation to the World Wide Web
- Seamless compatibility with other Microsoft Office programs so that you can use data from other programs in your presentations with a minimum of hassle

The designers of Microsoft PowerPoint had a two-pronged goal: to create an easy-to-use presentation graphics program that gives you all the help you want, and to give you the freedom to be creative. PowerPoint's flexibility and wide variety of features will help you make your points powerfully—right from the first time you use the program.

What's New in Microsoft PowerPoint?

PowerPoint 97 builds on the easy-to-use features of its predecessor. If you used the previous version of PowerPoint, you'll notice the number of features added to make your job of creating easier and more accurate; you'll also find several additional tools that help you at the point of presentation. PowerPoint 97 introduces these additional or enhanced features:

- **The ValuPack CD-ROM,** which includes numerous templates, graphics, sounds, and even movies you can use in your own presentations

- **PowerPoint Central,** a utility that takes you to a Web site that is run specifically for PowerPoint users, with numerous resources for objects you can add to your slides
- **The Office Assistant,** an interactive help utility that "watches" what you're trying to do and offers help when you need it
- **Multiple undos,** so you can undo (reverse) many operations—not only your last one
- **An Expand Slide feature,** which enables you to divide one slide into several slides
- **Voice narration,** so you can do a voice-over of a presentation and have it play while the presentation runs
- **The ability to add "sticky notes"** to presentations so others can review and make suggestions on the presentation as you're developing it
- **An Action Settings dialog box** that enables you to control the various actions for a selected object. For example, you may want the presentation to advance to a different page, run another presentation, or go to a Web page when the user clicks an object in your presentation.
- **Save as HTML,** a feature that enables you to save your presentation as a Web file, ready for publishing on the World Wide Web
- **New chart types,** including bubble charts, cylinders, and pyramid charts. You can also animate chart elements to show data trends in your presentations
- **Music tracks** (included on the program's CD-ROM) can add impact to your animations or can be used as background sound throughout your entire presentation
- **An image editor** that enables you to fine-tune graphics and scanned images
- **A Web animation feature** that enables you to easily save your presentation as a Web animation, to be played as an animated object on your Web site
- **New levels of programmability** are available with the VBA component in almost all of the Office 97 applications, including, of course, PowerPoint. Now you can create your own forms, add-on utilities, and more, using Visual Basic for Applications.

How This Book Is Organized

Mastering PowerPoint 97 consists of three parts, and each will add to your repertoire of PowerPoint skills. If you have some experience with presentation graphics or with PowerPoint in particular, you may want to skip some of the early sections and go right to more complex operations. Overall, this book is presented in a sequential, process-oriented manner to ensure that you'll learn everything you need to know about PowerPoint from the ground up. Information is provided for both the exploring beginner and the stretching enthusiast. The following sections explain each of the parts of *Mastering PowerPoint*.

Part One: PowerPoint Essentials

This first part sets up the groundwork for the rest of your PowerPoint experience.

- *Chapter 1* tells you what's possible with PowerPoint. You'll find out what you need in order to present effectively and explore the variety of features PowerPoint includes to help you get going quickly on your first presentation. This chapter gives you the basics of all the important PowerPoint elements you'll encounter throughout the program and finishes up with tips for creating effective presentations.

- *Chapter 2* gives you a quick PowerPoint once-over. If you're in a hurry—"The meeting starts in 20 minutes. Can you whip up a quick presentation?"—you can use the techniques in this chapter to help you produce a professional presentation quickly. You'll learn about all the basic facets of the program and see how it all fits together in this fast bird's-eye-view of program features.

Part Two: The Right Tools for the Job

Part Two gives you the information you need for working with the various components in your PowerPoint presentations.

- *Chapter 3* lets you jump right in and start on the text of your presentation. Whether you choose to let PowerPoint direct you (the AutoContent Wizard will walk you through the process of creating the slide text) or go solo, you'll quickly discover how simple text entry, editing, and enhancement is in PowerPoint. Additional features like AutoCorrect help you make sure you've got the right word in the right place, and Outline view gives you an easy way to scan the content of your presentation at a glance.

- *Chapter 4* explains the ins and outs of creating and working with graphs. From learning what graph type best represents what data to working with the datasheet, modifying entries, adding labels, and enhancing the graph, you'll uncover ways to display your information graphically using the best of PowerPoint's graphing capabilities.
- *Chapter 5* takes you into the world of graphic arts—PowerPoint style. Whether you choose to use the new AutoClipArt feature PowerPoint offers (the program will suggest what pieces of clip art fit the text in your presentation), make your selection from the ClipArt Gallery, or draw it yourself, you'll find the information you need to add art to your slides.
- *Chapter 6* is all about sound. From beeps to soundtracks, sound adds an element unavailable just a few years ago on most PCs. Today, you can easily add sound to your PowerPoint presentation. This chapter helps you add sound to single objects or slide transitions and play the sound either once or repeatedly to produce the desired effect.
- *Chapter 7* explores the basics of adding video to your multimedia presentation. Where can you find video and how do you set it up to run in your PowerPoint presentation? Learn how to add video objects to your PowerPoint presentation and use the Windows 95 Media Player to select, edit, and save the video you want without ever leaving PowerPoint.
- *Chapter 8* takes you one step closer to presenting by helping you add the finishing touches to your presentation. This chapter focuses on things like setting automatic or manual timing, choosing slide transitions, and working with build and hidden slides. You'll also learn to start a slide show, rehearse the timing of your presentation, and use PowerPoint's special presentation features like the Slide Navigator, the Meeting Minder, and Presentation Conferencing.

Part Three: Quintessential PowerPoint

Now that you've got the basics (and then some), this part concentrates on those features of PowerPoint that go above and beyond creating the traditional presentation.

- *Chapter 9* explores the wealth of color options available in Microsoft Power-Point. Professional designers have created a large number of color schemes that work together effectively; you can use their expertise to help you design the best presentation possible. Or, if you prefer, you can mix and match your own colors—whether you're recoloring a single item or an entire presentation.

- *Chapter 10* shows you how to best print the slides you've created. You can print a variety of other materials as well, including audience handouts, speaker notes, and slide printouts. Also in this chapter, you'll learn to add headers and footers to your slides and evaluate the printouts you produce.
- *Chapter 11* tells you about another output option for your presentation files: the Internet. You can become an Internet or intranet publisher simply by preparing Web pages from your presentations. You can use animations, ActiveX controls, and more, to make your site interesting and functional. And you can use the commands in PowerPoint to prepare the pages so they are ready to be uploaded to your Internet Service Provider.
- *Chapter 12* gives you information on working with multimedia files—which ones you're most likely to be working with, how to store them, and what you can do to manage them most effectively.
- *Chapter 13* completes the book by opening the curtain on your actual presentation. Are you ready? Tips for presenting before the fact, practice advice, evaluation sheets, and practical considerations in this chapter are included to help you make the best statement possible. The chapter concludes with case studies of presentations used in different settings.
- *Appendix A* may turn out to be the first resource you need, because it covers the procedures for installing PowerPoint. *Appendix B* tells you how to change some of the program defaults once you are comfortable with the basic workings of the program. *Appendix C* provides a number of tips for the first-time presenter. Look here before you get up in front of that crowd. *Appendix D* identifies programmability issues—customizing PowerPoint presentations using VBA, macros, and more.
- *A glossary* provides you with a key to presentation graphics terms that may be new to you.

Now that you know the overall game plan for the book, it's time we got started. In just a few short minutes, you could be making points—powerfully—with PowerPoint.

PART I

PowerPoint Essentials

LEARN TO:

- Discover presentation possibilities with PowerPoint

- Get started using PowerPoint

- Learn about PowerPoint's important elements

- Create your first presentation

- Use templates to create presentations quickly

- Save your presentation file

Chapter 1

PowerPoint Possibilities

FEATURING

Why presentations? And why PowerPoint?

Getting started with PowerPoint

Important PowerPoint elements

Tips for creating a good presentation

PowerPoint Possibilities

C*ommunication* is everything. Whether you are trying to win board approval for that new product you're designing or you're getting up in front of a group of potential clients for the first time, the way that you present your message—and yourself—is the most important factor determining whether or not you hit your mark.

PowerPoint is a presentation graphics program that helps you create simple, yet slick and even stunning presentations that are limited only by the capability of the computer equipment you use and your imagination.

Why Presentations? And Why PowerPoint?

If you're a Microsoft Office user, you may have stumbled across PowerPoint on your way from Word to Excel. PowerPoint is the presentation part of the Microsoft Office suite of programs, giving you the ability to present data created in the other applications in your PowerPoint presentations.

For example, suppose that you've been writing an annual report for a client. You use Microsoft Word and create a professional, four-color report with photos and a sophisticated layout. The client is pleased. "You know," he says, "Our annual meeting is coming up. Do you think you could do a presentation to go along with the report?"

"Sure," you answer, thinking to yourself, "But *how*?"

PowerPoint gives you the answer. With PowerPoint, you can easily adapt the text from your Word document to fit your PowerPoint presentation. You can use the photos; you can design a similar layout. And then you can go several steps farther and add multimedia, including elements like a video of the CEO talking about his vision for the future, sound capsules of happy employees, or even animation showing the changes in the production line.

As new technological standards become the norm, people are creating presentations in more varied settings and with better tools than ever before. Never again must you face a roomful of twenty expressionless faces, armed only with two weak visual aids and note-cards dog-eared from hours of nervous practice. Now the small business owner trying to drum up financial support for his endeavors can take a laptop into the potential investor's office, fire up PowerPoint, and show the investor an animated slide show with striking color and design and even music—a hard thing to resist if you're accustomed to an open hand and an apologetic gaze. PowerPoint helps you make a strong statement, even when making statements isn't your strong point.

How Are Presentations Used?

Presentations are used in all kinds of settings, all over the globe. In large corporations and small, one-person businesses and volunteer organizations, presentations are used to inspire ("Look what a great job we did this quarter! Let's do it again next time!"), educate ("Here's how you apply for financial aid..."), and inform ("Statistics show that 38 percent of all households currently own computers equipped with CD-ROM drives").

What Do I Need to Present?

Before you begin exploring PowerPoint on your own, you may be wondering what type of system you'll need in order to present these eye-opening, pulse-quickening presentations you'll be creating.

Years ago, a presentation was a pretty bland affair. An instructor type stood in front of the room with a wax pencil and an overhead projector. The acetate sheets may have been created by a typesetter—if you were lucky and got a "professional" presentation; otherwise, you may have seen hand-written slides or images dummied up with press-on letters.

When the PC came into the picture, the support for on-screen display was minimal. Presentation programs need lots of memory, lots of RAM, and lots of pieces like sound cards, video cards, and interfaces that must be compatible for everything to work together smoothly. In the old days, this was a rare thing.

With the introduction of Windows 3.1, multimedia—the mixing of a variety of media to create a presentation that includes music, video, graphics, text, and sound effects—was officially recognized. That version of Windows included multimedia capabilities, acknowledging to the world that multimedia was here to stay.

Today, with the advent of Windows 95, we see overwhelming support for multimedia features. Plug-and-Play means that you can easily add components to expand your system's capabilities. With the incredible range of CD-ROM titles and multimedia experiences available to us on a daily basis (even America Online says "Hello!" when you log on), we are riding the wave into an ever-more interactive future. And as we see the 97 generation of programs (such as Office 97 and PowerPoint 97), the focus is on ease of use, seamless Internet access, and point-and-click Web page creation.

Hardware-wise, to run presentations you need a computer capable of running Windows 95 comfortably, including at least 8MB of RAM (16 or more is better), plenty of hard disk space, a sound system, and a good video system.

For presenters, this embracing of multimedia means that the choices you have available in terms of how you will present have greatly improved. You might make your presentation on your laptop that you position on a client's desk. You may stand in front of a crowd of 200 people, projecting the presentation on a screen. You may send your presentation over the airwaves as part of an infomercial, upload it to an online service to be accessed by thousands of interested potential clients, or incorporate it into a shareware CD-ROM given to subscribers of industry magazines.

When you use the technology and the tools available to you, each presentation you create is a potential masterpiece—you are limited only by your own imagination and your willingness to use it.

Getting Started with PowerPoint

No matter who you are and what you work with, chances are that PowerPoint will not be something you'll use every day. Your need for it will come and go. You'll use it every day for a week while you prepare a special presentation, and then perhaps not use it again until the following month—or year.

Foreseeing this, Microsoft created PowerPoint to be easy to use in a short period of time. You won't need lengthy refresher courses or spend hours retaking tutorials or scanning the documentation. The features in the following list are part of this easy-to-return-to design:

- When you first start PowerPoint, you can access the AutoContent Wizard shown in Figure 1.1, which will actually create the basic content of your presentation for you. If words aren't your strong point, you can choose the type of message you've got to convey and let PowerPoint assemble the outline for you. Then just plug in your text, add sound and video if you like, and present.

FIGURE 1.1
PowerPoint includes an AutoContent Wizard that will suggest topics for your presentation's content.

- PowerPoint Presentations—as you'll see in Chapter 2, they have their own tab in the New Presentation dialog box—have been designed, from start to finish, with all the necessary colors, text choices, and slide layouts. You simply choose the presentation you want and enter your own information.
- Presentation Designs are slides that contain basic color, style, text, and alignment choices for your presentation. You choose the look you want and then create the rest of the presentation—slide layouts and all—the way you want it.
- A new tab for Web Pages lets you keep your Web designs separate from traditional presentations. And you can use the two samples as the basis for your own Web pages.

- The PowerPoint screen is organized so that everything you need is visible at all times (see Figure 1.2). Once you've had a few minutes to get oriented, you won't have any trouble remembering where things are and how you move from one view to the next. From the Window-style toolbars and on-screen buttons to the status bar and work area, everything will become familiar quickly.

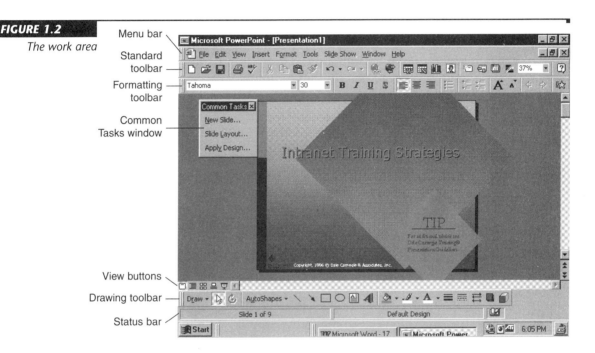

FIGURE 1.2
The work area

- ToolTips appear when you position the mouse pointer above a specific tool, telling you the name of the tool you're about to select. This way, you don't need to remember which tool does what, because PowerPoint will tell you what you need to know when you need to know it.
- Automated features—special tools such as AutoCorrect, Auto-ClipArt, and Style Checker—keep an eye on you as you create the presentation and provide additional tips and suggestions to help you stay on track. Without prompting, AutoCorrect automatically changes things like mistakes in capitalization (two capitalized letters in a row or days of the week in lowercase letters). AutoCorrect

can also be used to change your "shorthand" into longer phrases you don't want to spend the time typing out (see Figure 1.3). For more information on using AutoCorrect, see Chapter 5, "Entering and Editing Text."

FIGURE 1.3

AutoCorrect changes capitalization and can substitute your shorthand for longer words that you teach it.

- PowerPoint's great help system takes you in and out of PowerPoint processes easily. The Office Assistant is an interactive "helper" that monitors what you are trying to do and offers help when you seem stuck (see Figure 1.4). For more about working with PowerPoint help, see Chapter 2, "The Quick and Easy Presentation."

FIGURE 1.4
You can elect to get help in a variety of ways with PowerPoint, letting you learn as you go along.

Important PowerPoint Elements

Before you start creating your first presentation with PowerPoint, you need to know a little more about the tools that are available to you. This section gives you a basic introduction to some of the features and tools unique to PowerPoint, like the choices you have for displaying slides and the various toolbars, templates, palettes, and such. Table 1.1 introduces the new highlights of PowerPoint 97, giving you an overview of the features newest to the program.

TABLE 1.1: POWERPOINT 97 HIGHLIGHTS	
Feature	Description
ValuPack	On your PowerPoint CD-ROM, a folder called ValuPack includes many different multimedia elements—sound, video, graphics, and templates—that you can use in your own presentations.
PowerPoint Central	A utility that takes you online to a PowerPoint Web site where you can download items for your presentations, read about industry news, learn about creating presentations, and more.
Office Assistant	An interactive, animated help assistant that pops up over the work area to offer how-to procedures for the current task you are performing.
Enhanced AutoContent Wizard	The AutoContent Wizard has been improved to include new ideas, formats, designs, and suggestions. Ideas from Dale Carnegie help you become a better presenter.
Multiple undo	Now you can reverse numerous operations—not simply the last task you performed.
Summary Slide	In Outline or Slide Sorter view, you can create a Summary Slide from slides you select.
Expand Slide	The Expand Slide feature divides one slide into smaller slides, based on text content.
New Chart Styles	Now PowerPoint includes bubble charts, cylinder charts, cone charts, pyramid charts, and various other new chart styles.
Image editing	You can change the color, shading, contrast, and brightness of graphics you select or import.
Voice narration	Your presentation can include voice-over narration that plays while your presentation runs.
Music tracks	The sound samples on the PowerPoint CD-ROM can be used as special sound effects or a running soundtrack behind your presentation.
Web features	PowerPoint includes a number of Web features that turn you into a Web publisher, right from your presentation. You can save your presentation as an HTML document, post it to the Web, and create animations for use on your Web pages.
Custom Shows	The Custom Shows feature makes it easy for you to create different customized shows based on a single presentation.
VBA support	Programmability is a big feature in Office 97, and PowerPoint includes support for Visual Basic applications that you can design to increase PowerPoint's functionality and better fit the program to your company's needs.

PowerPoint Views

With PowerPoint, you can look at your presentation five different ways. Depending on what you're doing, different views will be helpful at different times. Table 1.2 explains the different views and gives you an idea of when you might use each.

TABLE 1.2: POWERPOINT 97 VIEWS

View	Description	Use To
Slide View	Displays the current slide in the work area.	Add text or objects to a single slide or format only one slide.
Outline View	Displays the presentation text only, in outline form.	Enter text quickly, following a format provided by PowerPoint or your own; move, copy, or cut text; spell-check text; read through for consistency; or print a script for your presentation.
Slide Sorter View	Displays multiple slides in reduced size on the screen.	Add transitional effects, set timing, move or delete slides, or check presentation continuity.
Notes Pages View	Displays the current slide in a reduced size with room for notes at the bottom of the page.	Add a memo, notation, or instruction for a slide or slides. You can also use Notes Pages View to design explanatory handouts for your audience.
Slide Show	Presents the slides in a slide show, using the entire screen.	Check the timing, transition, and multimedia effects of a show before you present it, see what you've done so far, or show a client the presentation you've been working on.

After you make your initial choices about your presentation in the New Slide dialog box (whether you want to use the AutoContent Wizard or a Presentation Design, start from scratch, etc.), you can choose the layout of the first slide you want. After you click on OK, the first slide of your presentation appears in the work area, displayed in what's known as Slide View (see Figure 1.5).

FIGURE 1.5

When you display a new presentation, it appears in Slide View.

In subsequent work sessions, PowerPoint will open an existing file to wherever you were when you saved and closed the file. If you were working in another view, for example, or had used the Zoom command to enlarge the display, those settings will be in effect the next time you open the file.

Slide View

Slide View shows you the slide you're creating as it will appear in final display. Years ago, Slide View would have been comparable to the desktop, where you put together this piece of text, that clip art (manually clipped out of an art set), and that piece of acetate to come up with the most professional slide you possibly could.

In Slide View, you work on slides one at a time, adding the various elements of your presentation. You will do most of your up-close work here. While in Slide View, you'll also choose colors, perhaps add text, create charts, add clip art, insert movies, add sound, and copy, cut, and paste slides. To select Slide View, click on the Slide View button.

MASTERING THE OPPORTUNITIES

A Matter of Perspective

Different views appeal to different people, and as your experience with PowerPoint grows, you'll settle into using the views you like best. In general, when I'm creating presentations I use the views as follows:

1. I start in Slide View to design the basic look of the page. I choose colors, add background elements, and make decisions about text color, font, and alignment.
2. Then I go to Outline View. It's here that I brainstorm ideas for the content of the presentation, jotting down roughly what I plan to cover and then cleaning it up into a recognizable outline.
3. I go back to Slide View to look at each page individually, change formats, move text, and add charts and clip art.
4. When I've got the basic elements in place, I go to Slide Sorter View and take a look at the whole presentation in thumbnail size. Here I can see whether I've been consistent with certain elements and varied enough with others. Did I use the same headline font all the way through? Did I break up the slides so I don't have four charts in a row? Slide Sorter View helps me see patterns I might not see in Slide View.
5. Next I practice the presentation in Slide Show view. I make notes of anything I need to remember at the point of presentation and add those notes in Notes Pages view.
6. Then, after practicing a few times, I'm ready to give the presentation to my best and most critical friends, so they can help me identify spots I still need to work on.

Outline View

Outline View looks like a scrap of notebook paper on which you might jot down ideas between meetings. Instead of scribbling notes and using them (or losing them), you can enter the notes directly into PowerPoint's Outline View, using them as the basis for your presentation.

To select Outline View, click the Outline View button in the bottom left corner of the work area. Your presentation appears in outline form, as shown in Figure 1.6. Note that an existing presentation is displayed in the figure; if you are creating a new presentation from scratch, when you display Outline View, the page will be blank. If you are creating a presentation based on one of PowerPoint's templates, however, sample text appears in the outline.

FIGURE 1.6

Outline View makes it easy for you to write down your thoughts quickly and coherently.

[Figure 1.6: Screenshot of PowerPoint Outline View showing "Internet Training Strategies" presentation with labeled callouts: Slide miniature, Slide title, Bullet text, Slide View button, Outline View button, Slide Sorter View button, Notes Pages View button, Slide Show button]

Entering the text for your presentation in Outline View is simple; just position the text cursor and start typing. Commands in the toolbar let you start new slides and indent points easily, and text control settings help you get the look you want. A new feature in PowerPoint 97 is a miniature image of the current page shown in Slide View in the upper right corner of Outline View.

You can do anything—except add art—in Outline View. If you think better on paper, you'll find the Outline View comforting, as you can just type in your thoughts and worry about the graphics later. PowerPoint lets you print your outline and create an Outline Master for objects that repeat from slide to slide.

Slide Sorter View

Have you ever spent an afternoon arranging scraps of paper on your desk, trying to decide the order in which you should present your information? We all know there's more than one way to present a good idea—but searching for the best way is sometimes an exhausting experience.

Slide Sorter View lets you experiment with different page orders by moving pages around on the screen. While you're at it, you can check out the way your colors look and decide whether you like the overall effect of the text, transition, and timing settings you've chosen. Slide Sorter View itself resembles a big light table (remember those?) on which you can arrange a number of slides (see Figure 1.7). One new feature of PowerPoint 97 is the Summary Slide tool, on the right side of the Slide Sorter toolbar. Using the Summary Slide tool, you can create a slide that provides a summary of your presentation, including only those slides you select.

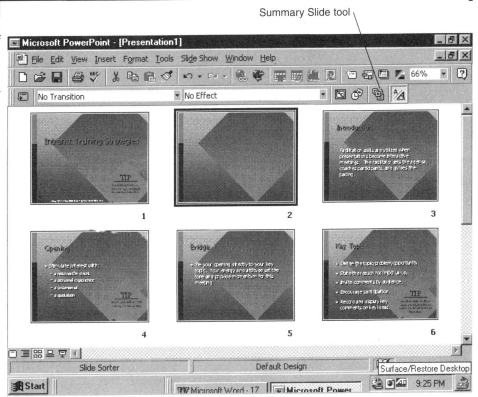

FIGURE 1.7

Slide Sorter View displays a number of slides on the screen at one time so you can rearrange them and change their settings if necessary.

Notes Pages View

Trying to use ordinary notes while giving a presentation can be pretty risky. Papers get shuffled and fall out of your folder or even get stuck to the back of other documents.

PowerPoint helps you create notes that will stay with your presentation—and with you. Notes Pages View provides you with an area for speaker notes, along with a reduced picture of the slide. You enter the notes in a text box beneath the slide so that when you print the page, the slide and your notes are printed on the same sheet.

Figure 1.8 shows an example of Notes Pages View. The small image of the slide appears in the top half of the page; your notes go in the bottom half. You can type—or add artwork, if you like—in the notes section.

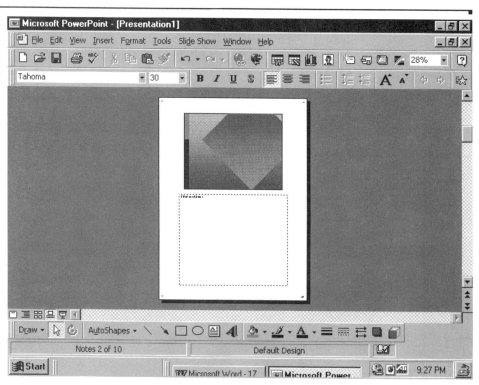

FIGURE 1.8
In Notes Pages View, you can enter notes that correspond to the displayed slide, producing self-documenting slides and handouts.

The AutoContent Wizard

A wizard is an automated utility that walks you through a particular process so you don't have to figure it out from scratch. By asking you a series of questions, the wizard interactively assembles the presentation for you. The AutoContent Wizard that appears when you first start PowerPoint will, if you like, help you develop the basic content of your presentation. In Chapter 2, "The Quick and Easy Presentation," you'll use the AutoContent Wizard to create a fast presentation of your own. Although PowerPoint 95 first introduced the AutoContent Wizard, PowerPoint 97 gives it a new level of helpfulness. Now you'll find new ideas, more content, and suggestions from the experts—like Dale Carnegie—on how to make your presentations the best they can be.

Masters

One of the keys to a good presentation is consistency—you want your presentation to have a certain look and feel so readers or viewers can follow your ideas easily.

PowerPoint Masters can help you get and keep that consistency throughout your presentation. A master is like a piece of your company's letterhead—it has the same basic information on every sheet. On the Slide Master, for example, which serves as the background for all slides in your presentation, you might want to include the following things:

- Your company's logo
- Your company's name
- Your department
- The date the presentation was prepared

PowerPoint includes masters for slides, titles, handouts, and notes. In addition to adding different objects to masters, you can control the way the text appears by choosing a certain typeface, size, and style for text. The master "remembers" your text selections and displays the text in your slides in the specified style. The same thing applies to color—you can assign a certain color scheme to the master and PowerPoint will apply the color you've chosen to your developing presentation.

Templates

PowerPoint knows that you aren't always sure how you want your presentation to look before you start. For that reason, the developers included a number of presentation templates you can use as the basis for the presentations you create. PowerPoint divides its templates into two groups, both of which are available when you choose New from the File menu.

In the New Presentation dialog box, you can choose templates from either the Presentation Designs tab or the Presentations tab (see Figure 1.9). Both include a number of templates. The difference is that a Presentation Design includes only a single slide with all the color, background, and text options already set; you then build the rest of your presentation based on those choices. The Presentations tab, on the other hand, displays templates of entire presentations, complete with various slide layouts, as well as color, background, and text choices.

FIGURE 1.9
Choose the template you want in the Presentation Designs or Presentations tab of the New Presentation dialog box.

If you want a pre-done presentation in which you need only plug in text and art, select the Presentations tab. If you want to make your own slide layout selections and build the presentation based on preset color and design choices, click on the Presentation Designs tab instead.

ValuPack

On your Microsoft Office 97 CD-ROM, or on your PowerPoint program CD, you'll find a folder called ValuPack. Inside this folder are all kinds of "extras" you can use in Office 97 or PowerPoint. Specifically for PowerPoint, you'll find clip art, sounds, videos, even complete sound tracks. There're also tips on presenting, a tutorial, and more. You can see what's in the ValuPack by opening the file OVERVIEW.PPT in PowerPoint. Figure 1.10 shows the first slide of the Overview presentation.

FIGURE 1.10

The ValuPack, on your program CD-ROM, includes all kinds of elements you can use in your own presentations.

PowerPoint Central

Another special feature new to PowerPoint 97 is PowerPoint Central, your central resource for PowerPoint information. Similar to the ValuPack, PowerPoint Central includes links to additional presentation elements—sound files, animations, video, clip art, photos, templates, and more. You'll also find a Frequently Asked Questions file (called a FAQ), interviews with experts, and other tidbits of useful information. The coolest thing about PowerPoint Central is that it is part program feature, part Web site. Periodically, PowerPoint will tell you it's been awhile since your version of PowerPoint Central has been updated and ask whether you want to check the Web for updates. You can simply click Yes, and PowerPoint will do the rest, updating the files and taking you into the realm of new PowerPoint goodies. To get to PowerPoint Central, choose Tools ➤ PowerPoint Central. Your screen will look similar to the one shown in Figure 1.11.

FIGURE 1.11

PowerPoint Central is part program feature, part Web site. PowerPoint will update the feature via the Web on a regular basis.

MASTERING TROUBLESHOOTING

Help! I'm Webless!

Do you need Internet access to use PowerPoint 97? No. But you'll find that the capabilities of the program and the resources you can tap into to make your presentations the best they can be will be limited if you don't have access to the World Wide Web. PowerPoint Central plugs into the Web to get updates on a regular basis. You can also scour Web sites all over the globe to find backgrounds, clip art, sounds, video, and more—items that are offered as freeware or shareware.

How do you get Web access? First you need a modem, of course. A fast modem. 33.6 Kbps is currently the fastest modem standard, but 14.4 or 28.8 will do. (The numbers refer to the speed at which the modem sends and receives data—the higher the number, the faster the transmission.)

> **MASTERING TROUBLESHOOTING CONTINUED**
>
> Next, you need an account with an Internet Service Provider or an online service that offers Internet access. Information services like CompuServe, America Online, and The Microsoft Network all have Internet components in addition to their own offerings. Internet Service Providers are available in your local area (check your phone book or call a local library or university to find out where).
>
> Finally, you need a *Web browser*, which is a program that enables you to "surf" or browse the World Wide Web. Your Internet Service Provider may provide you with one, or you can download Internet Explorer 3.0 or the soon-to-be-released version 4.0 from Microsoft's Web site at http://www.microsoft.com.
>
> Not only will having Internet access expand your computer horizons, but it will add ideas to your storehouse of things you'd like to try, and significantly increase your resources for doing new and unusual presentations. And who knows? You might wind up becoming a Web publisher yourself. Publishing presentations to the Web is easy to do with PowerPoint. (See Chapter 11 in Part III for details.)

Color Schemes

Choosing the right color scheme often determines whether your presentation works or not. With effective color, you can turn a boring, no-one's-going-to-pay-attention-anyway presentation into something everybody talks about for weeks.

But many people have trouble mixing and matching colors. What looks good together, and why? What colors fit the tone of your presentation? What colors should you use under different lighting conditions?

Color-wise, PowerPoint knows what's hot and what's not. Simply select the Slide Color Scheme command from the Format menu and then choose the basic color scheme you want. You can choose from several preset palettes in the Standard tab or create your own by selecting the Custom tab. Figure 1.12 shows the Standard tab of the Color Scheme dialog box.

The color schemes are coordinated to work together on-screen, in print, and on slides. You control whether you want the color scheme applied only to the current slide or to every slide in the presentation. With over 16 million colors to choose from, this takes an enormous worry off the shoulders of presentation graphics neophytes.

FIGURE 1.12

PowerPoint makes choosing a collection of colors for your presentation a simple process.

Now in PowerPoint 97, the color schemes you use can be easily applied to other Office applications, as well. When you copy and paste shapes and text from one program to another, you can be sure that the color in one program will be consistent with the color in another.

In this section, you've seen some of the elements that make PowerPoint easy to use and master. Throughout the book, you'll find many more features to help you on your way through your PowerPoint experience.

Tips for Creating a Good Presentation

With some careful planning, adequate time, and the right tools, anyone using PowerPoint can create a stunning presentation. But, especially if this is your first time creating a presentation, how do you know what makes a good presentation good? This section gives you some basic guidelines you can use while creating your own presentations. Remember, however, that you can always rely on the expertise in the templates to make design choices, and the AutoContent Wizard can lead you through the process of writing the text in an organized fashion.

When you are ready to create your own presentation without the help of a template or wizard, you can use these guidelines to help you hit the mark:

- Consider your audience.
- Consider the tone of your presentation.
- Consider your tools for presentation.

Let's look at each of these considerations and ask some important questions as you begin planning your presentation.

Considering the Audience

Before you even start planning your project, you need to know about the audience that will be seeing your work. Are you going up before a board of directors for a large firm? A small non-profit organization? Stockholders? Advertising executives? Prospective clients?

Knowing the audience for your presentation will help you tailor the content and tone of your work. You wouldn't give an equipment training session to a group of high-level managers; similarly, you won't spend a large amount of time analyzing financial matters for personnel more involved with employee productivity.

The audience will also have some bearing on the type of presentation you create. Are you teaching a class? Title and bullet charts will help reinforce your points better than a series of complex charts. If you hope to motivate a roomful of salespeople by explaining sales trends, colorful attention-grabbing charts may convey in a glance what could take quite a bit longer verbally.

Before you actually begin creating your presentation, think about the best way to reach your audience. And remember that once you've reached them, you need to hold their attention.

Considering the Tone

The tone of your presentation is much like the personality of your work. After you've figured out who the audience is and what kind of presentation they may be expecting to see, think about the way you'll present the information. Is the meeting hurried, with only a few moments allotted to each presenter? Or do you have plenty of time, with more time left over for questions and answers? The answers to these questions will affect whether your presentation must be quick and to the point or can be more relaxed in style and content.

In a typical business, the corporate identity is important. Logos run rampant throughout presentations, and bulleted lists highlighting goals and productivity requirements are a staple. With PowerPoint, you can add some "serious" graphics by adding a picture of the world, international maps and flags, landmarks, or other far-reaching symbols that add a sense of importance to the background of your work. If you need to lighten things up a little, you can choose from PowerPoint's many cartoon illustrations to give your presentation a more relaxed look.

PowerPoint's new AutoClipArt feature actually makes suggestions about the type of clip art you may want to use in your presentation. The clip art packaged with PowerPoint includes standard icons, foreign symbols, international landmarks, cartoons, and a variety of hand and landscape drawings.

Considering the Tools

As you create your presentation, daydream a little about how you envision it being presented. Will you be standing before a large crowd? Sitting at a board room table? Will you have access to a large-screen monitor (or to a computer at all)? Will you be confined to a slide or overhead projector? Will you be giving the presentation over the Internet?

Think about the tools you'll have for delivering the presentation and how effective those tools will be, given the type of audience you're presenting to. If you are speaking to a large crowd and have only a small-screen monitor on which to display, you will either need to arm-wrestle the AV department for a data panel (a device that plugs into your computer and allows you to project the contents of your display onto a screen) or you'll have to make do with the small screen and print handouts for your audience. If you won't be present in person—for example, if you're giving the presentation on your company's Intranet or sending it via e-mail to a client in another country—think about the tools you need to get the file where it's going.

Giving members of the audience something to take with them after a presentation—notes or printed graphs—is good for reinforcing your message. Be careful not to simply repeat your presentation in print, however; that's a good way to make sure your printed materials wind up in the recycling bin.

The Big C: Continuity

When you get down to the nitty-gritty of on-screen composition, having a few simple design ideas in mind will help you create a usable and successful presentation.

This sounds like something out of fourth-grade English class, but it's important: Continuity makes sure your presentation hangs together as a whole, presents your message clearly, and gives that sense of "Aha!" that clicks inside people when they've just witnessed a well thought out and presented plan.

Continuity helps your audience understand the "big picture" of your presentation. Suppose, for example, that your presentation is about new products your toy company is manufacturing for the upcoming holiday season. The overall tone is one of excitement and anticipation, as your company has done very well in the last year. You put quite a bit of money into research and development and created a new line of top-quality toys. Hold onto that enthusiasm—it should carry through your entire presentation.

Continuity in tone is sometimes a difficult goal to achieve, especially when you've got both good and bad news to communicate to your audience. If you need to talk about both the phenomenal success of your new line of Slimeballs and the screeching halt of sales of Godzilla-tron, talk about Godzilla-tron first. That way, the good news washes the bad news off the palate.

Visual continuity is much easier to achieve. With visual continuity, your presentation holds together with the help of a series of design elements repeated from page to page or from section to section. Simple items you can use to add visual continuity to your presentation include the following:

- Company name and/or logo
- The project name
- Date and page information
- The background color used throughout
- A project symbol or logo
- Background design elements like custom art, shadows, maps, flags, etc.

Suppose, in a different example, you are creating a presentation that highlights the two best-selling products in your insurance agency. One, a life insurance policy, has been doing very well in sales to individuals and business owners. The other, a health policy, targets businesses and has seen a whopping increase in the last 12 months. For each of these products, you want to show three charts: last year's sales, this year's sales, and projected sales for the next 12 months.

A presentation without visual continuity might use a different chart type for each chart—leaving viewers unsure what you're saying and wondering why you chose the charts you did. A visually continuous presentation, on the other hand, would parallel the two products and use the same type of graph to show similar data relationships. The continuity helps viewers understand your points and remember more of your presentation later.

What's Next?

This chapter introduced you to PowerPoint 97 and explored the benefits the program has to offer. You learned about many of the important elements you'll work with as you begin your hands-on experience with presentation graphics, and also picked up a few pointers that will help you create your own presentations. In the next chapter, you get to work creating a fast and easy PowerPoint presentation.

Chapter 2

The Quick and Easy Presentation

FEATURING

Starting PowerPoint

Getting Help

Creating a Simple Presentation

Starting a New Slide

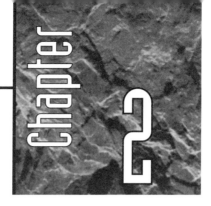

Chapter 2
The Quick and Easy Presentation

If you, like many people, are responsible for putting together a presentation on short notice, you don't want to wade through lengthy academic descriptions of procedures you may never use just to find the few important pieces of information you need. Instead, this chapter is designed around a "ready, set, go!" approach. You'll learn only what you need to start up PowerPoint, make some choices for starting your presentation, add text and graphics, save, show, and print the file. The procedures described in this chapter will walk you through your first presentation in 30 minutes or less.

If you have not yet installed PowerPoint 97, take the time to do it now. Appendix A tells you how to install PowerPoint.

Starting PowerPoint

You can start PowerPoint two ways. Double-click the My Computer icon on your desktop, then navigate to the folder in which you installed PowerPoint 97, and double-click the program icon, as shown in Figure 2.1. If the menu bar of your My Computer window looks different, don't worry—I have Internet Explorer 4.0 installed on my system, and it makes all the windows look like Web browsers. (You get used to it.)

FIGURE 2.1
You can start PowerPoint by navigating to the program icon and double-clicking it.

The other way to start PowerPoint is via a menu command. Choose Start ➤ Programs ➤ Microsoft PowerPoint. (Figure 2.2 shows the submenu that appears after you open the Programs menu.)

With either approach, after you click Microsoft PowerPoint to start the program, you'll see the screen shown in Figure 2.3.

STARTING POWERPOINT   33

FIGURE 2.2

Choosing PowerPoint from the Programs menu

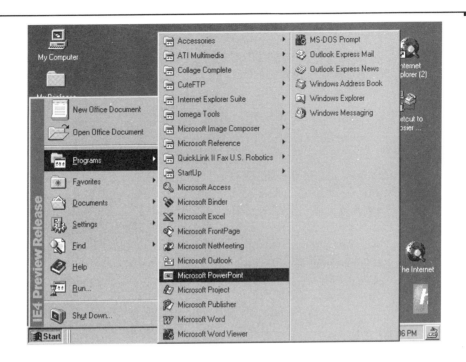

FIGURE 2.3

The PowerPoint screen

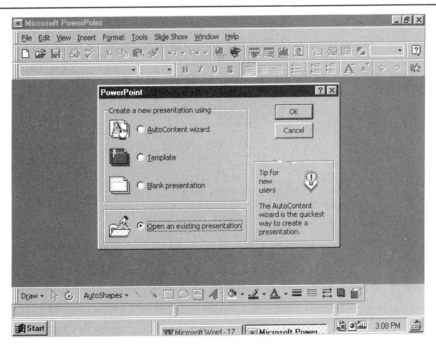

In the center of the PowerPoint work area, the PowerPoint dialog box appears. This dialog box gives you the choice of starting a new presentation (several different ways) or opening an existing presentation. You can choose from the following options:

- AutoContent wizard
- Template
- Blank presentation
- Open an existing presentation

Choosing *AutoContent wizard* takes you to an automated utility that helps you create the content of your presentation. You'll learn how to create a simple presentation using this feature in the next section. If you choose *Template*, you will be given the option of choosing a basic presentation design on which you can build your own presentation. *Blank presentation* takes you to a blank presentation screen, where you can create all your own elements for your presentation. Finally, the *Open an existing presentation* option displays the Open dialog box so you can open a PowerPoint file you have already created. After you make your choice, click OK to start working with PowerPoint.

Getting Help

When you begin learning anything new, it's a good idea to know what tools are available to you in times of trouble. PowerPoint has a comprehensive help system that enables you to ask for and get help in whatever form is most comfortable for you. If you've worked with Windows programs before, you won't find any surprises in the PowerPoint help interface—the Help Topics dialog box enables you to search for help by topic or keyword, and the Answer Wizard enables you to enter plain-English questions and plain-English answers.

You'll also find help buttons in the upper right corner of dialog boxes (click on the small question mark and then on any option or setting you don't understand).

The Annotate help option enables you to make notes about the help topic in your own words. You might then want to copy and paste your notes into another document.

Working with the Office Assistant

New with Office 97 is the Office Assistant, an animated little fellow who pops up in the lower right corner of your work area when you seem to be struggling with a particular operation. Sometimes he looks like a paper clip; sometimes he twists into odd shapes; always he looks rather self-satisfied, like he knows something we don't (see Figure 2.4).

FIGURE 2.4
The Office Assistant is a paper clip with a lot of personality and perhaps just the procedures you need to get out of a confusing spot.

The purpose of the Office Assistant is to watch over your work and make suggestions when you seem to need it. You can put the Office Assistant away if he annoys you, by clicking the close button in the upper right corner of his window. When you want his help again, simply click the Office Assistant button (the tool on the far right end of the Standard toolbar).

Microsoft on the Web

You can get PowerPoint help surfing the World Wide Web. You'll find the *Microsoft on the Web* option in the Help menu. When you click the option, a submenu of Web sites appears (see Figure 2.5). Simply click the one you want and, if you have a modem and Internet access, the Connect dialog box appears so you can log on to the Internet. After you enter the necessary information and click Connect, you are taken to the Web page you selected.

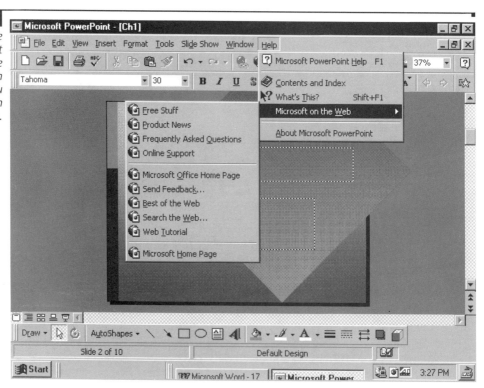

FIGURE 2.5
You can visit one of the Microsoft Web sites in the Microsoft on the Web submenu to get help with PowerPoint topics.

Creating a Simple Presentation

With PowerPoint's predesigned templates and the AutoContent Wizard, you have everything you need to assemble an on-the-fly presentation. You just need to plug in your own ideas and present. In this section, we'll take you on a quick tour of the steps involved in creating a simple presentation. Specifically, you'll learn how to do the following things:

- Work with the AutoContent Wizard
- Choose a template
- Add text
- Add a title
- Move text areas
- Resize text boxes
- Add art
- Resize art objects
- Start a new slide
- Start a slide show
- Save the presentation
- Print slides

Working with Wizards and Templates

We learn most things in our lives through imitation. If we see an office design that appeals to us, we try to design our office in a similar way. If we run across a particularly successful advertising gimmick, we might try to use the same approach in selling our product. Imitation can be a great teacher.

PowerPoint gives you two different ways of learning by imitation. The AutoContent Wizard interactively leads you through the process of creating a presentation by asking you a series of questions. Similarly, templates give you the bare bones of a presentation upon which you build using text and graphics. In both cases, you learn the process and basic design concepts while using the timesaving tools PowerPoint provides.

Using the AutoContent Wizard

The AutoContent Wizard will lead you through a series of questions to help you construct the basic content of your presentation. From your answers, PowerPoint will assemble an outline to which you can add your own text, graphics, multimedia objects—whatever.

First, choose the AutoContent Wizard in the PowerPoint opening screen, which appears when you start PowerPoint (see Figure 2.6).

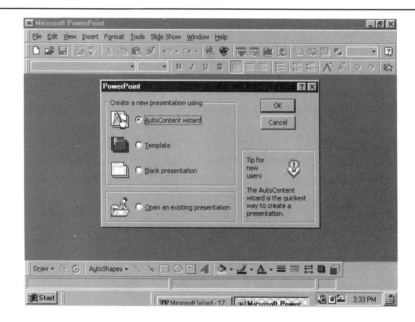

FIGURE 2.6

Start the AutoContent Wizard from the PowerPoint dialog box.

If you have been working in PowerPoint—that is, you're not just starting your work session—you can start a new presentation by opening the File menu and choosing New. The New Presentation dialog box, shown in Figure 2.7, appears.

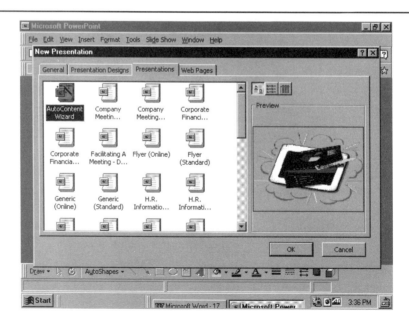

FIGURE 2.7

The New Presentation dialog box

When the Presentations tab of the New Presentation dialog box is displayed, the AutoContent Wizard always appears in the upper left corner of the window. To begin using the wizard, select it and click OK. The first screen of the Wizard appears, as shown in Figure 2.8.

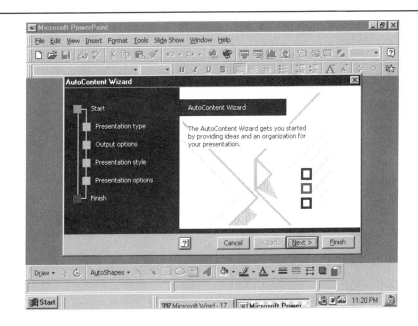

FIGURE 2.8

The opening screen of the AutoContent Wizard

Read the screens as they are presented, choose your response, and click the Next button to continue through the Wizard. First you need to choose the type of presentation you want to create. A number of different presentation types are listed, because the All button is selected by default. If you want to see what's available for a particular type of presentation, such as Corporate, click the button in the center of the dialog box. The list shows only those presentation types that correspond to the category you selected.

If you click the Carnegie Coach button in the bottom center portion of the dialog box, you'll get a list of various presentations on how to run a presentation meeting. These choices will help you produce a presentation that can be used to teach others how to hold meetings, prepare presentations, introduce speakers, and more.

Next you need to tell PowerPoint whether you are preparing the presentation for a meeting, if you need handouts, or whether you're publishing to the Internet or a kiosk. Make your choice and click Next. Now you choose the type of output you need and specify whether you'll print handouts. Again, click your choice and click Next. The next screen asks you for the presentation title, your name, and any other pertinent information. You may want to put your company name or department in this space.

The final screen tells you to click on Finish to complete the process. After you do so, PowerPoint puts all the information together and displays the presentation in Outline View (see Figure 2.9).

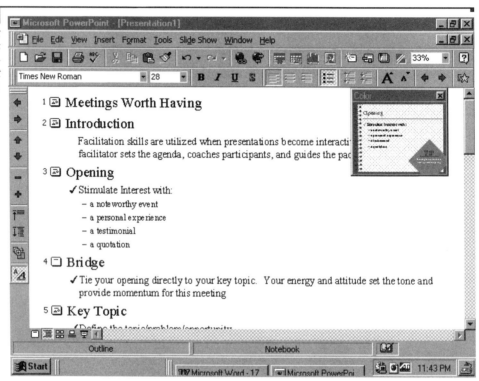

FIGURE 2.9
The AutoContent Wizard completes the basic presentation and displays it in Outline View.

Now you need to add your own text, graphics, and multimedia objects. You can add text quickly here in Outline View. You just highlight the text you want to replace and type the new text. For more information about entering, editing, and enhancing text, see Chapter 3.

CREATING A SIMPLE PRESENTATION

When you are ready to add graphics, charts, and multimedia objects, change to Slide View. To do that, click the Slide View button or choose View ➤ Slide. Figure 2.10 shows the presentation in Slide View.

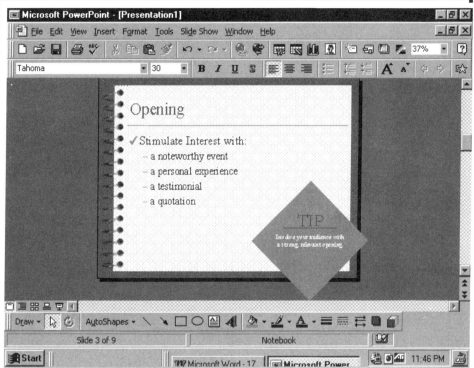

FIGURE 2.10

Display the AutoContent Wizard's creation in Slide View.

Using Templates

PowerPoint 97 includes a number of new templates on which you can base your own presentations. Some include basic design elements for the background and text that are already set for you. Others include both these settings and sample text for your presentation.

To choose a template, either select the Template option in the PowerPoint dialog box that appears when you first start the program, or click on the Presentations tab or the

Presentation Designs tab in the New Presentation dialog box. Figure 2.11 shows the Presentations tab with the Product Overview template selected. This is a template for a presentation designed to be given online, either on your company intranet or over the Internet. Notice that a preview of the template appears to the right of the icon area.

FIGURE 2.11

Choosing a pre-designed presentation template

Here we need to make a distinction between the Presentations and Presentation Designs templates:

- A Presentation is a sample presentation that includes text prompts suggesting the topics to cover in a specific order in your presentation. Figure 2.12 shows the Product Overview presentation displayed in Outline View, so you can see the text that has already been entered.
- A Presentation Design includes background color selections, text settings, formatting specifications, and background graphics, but no text. When you choose a Presentation Design and click on OK, PowerPoint prompts you to choose a page layout and then displays the first page you choose in Slide View, as shown in Figure 2.13.

CREATING A SIMPLE PRESENTATION

FIGURE 2.12

The Product Overview presentation template in Outline View

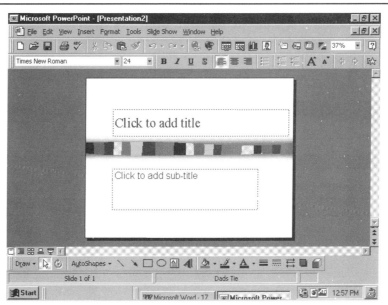

FIGURE 2.13

The first page of a presentation based on the Dad's Tie presentation design

MASTERING THE OPPORTUNITIES

If you're new to presentation graphics, starting out with either the AutoContent Wizard or a template is your best bet. The AutoContent Wizard will help you create the content of your presentation, depending on what message you are communicating. Templates—either in the form of Presentation Designs, which give you only the basic design of the presentation, or Presentations, which provide complete multipage presentations you can use and then add your own text and graphics—show you how the experts put together presentations. You'll be able to see how the different elements of the presentation work together most effectively while you learn the basics of the program.

Exploring the PowerPoint Menus

PowerPoint uses nine different menus to house the commands you'll work with throughout your PowerPoint experience. You can also select commands by clicking the icons in the toolbar, just below the PowerPoint menu bar. You have the option of adding different tools to the existing toolbar and creating your own custom toolbars. For more about creating your own toolbars, see the section "Understanding Toolbars" later in this chapter. But let's start with a basic understanding of the menus.

As you become more familiar with PowerPoint's features and commands, you'll discover where the commands you use most often are stored. Each menu includes a group of commands related to a specific function. Table 2.1 explains the menus in more detail.

TABLE 2.1: AN OVERVIEW OF POWERPOINT MENUS

Menu	Description
File	Provides commands for creating new files; opening, saving, and printing files; setting up pages; preparing a file for the road.
Edit	Enables you to copy, cut, and paste objects; undo operations; establish hyperlinks; delete slides; and find and replace words or phrases.
View	Allows you to select the different PowerPoint views. Choose Slides, Outline, Slide Sorter, Notes Pages, or Slide Show, or display the Masters for selected page types on which you can add repeating background elements. You can also control the display of on-screen items like the toolbars, rulers, and guides. You can also magnify the screen up to 400 percent.

Continued

TABLE 2.1: AN OVERVIEW OF POWERPOINT MENUS (CONTINUED)	
Menu	Description
Insert	Allows you to insert any of a number of elements into your slides and presentations. Specifically, you can insert a new slide, the date, time, or page number, slides from another file or outline, clip art, graphics, tables, graphs, or a sound clip or video piece. You can even insert an entire presentation into your presentation, if you like.
Format	Controls items like font, alignment, spacing, color, shadow, styles, and basic presentation characteristics such as layout, background and color. You can also change the presentation design and replace fonts from this menu.
Tools	Provides add-on items that help you create effective presentations, including a spelling checker, AutoCorrect, AutoClipArt, Style Checker, a choice of transitions, and special effects. With the new Meeting Minder feature, you can take notes during a presentation or set up for presentation conferencing. Write-Up allows you to prepare notes and slides for use with Microsoft Word. Additionally, with commands in the Tools menu you can customize the displayed toolbar and control editing and general display options.
Slide Show	The commands in the Slide Show menu are concerned with displaying the show. You can choose to start the slide show, rehearse the timing of the show, create and set up animations, choose transitions, create custom shows, and more.
Window	Controls the look of your screen. New Window displays a new presentation window for you to work in; Arrange All tiles the slides on the screen; Fit to Page displays windows one at a time with no overlapping, and Cascade displays windows in overlapping style. Additionally, this menu shows you the names of any open presentation files.
Help	Includes commands for getting you out of tight places in PowerPoint. You can look through the Help Contents & Index, use What's This? to find out about an object or item, and get understandable answers and references; or go online with the Microsoft on the Web option. This menu also includes Microsoft PowerPoint Help, which starts the Office Assistant (if it's not already running) and displays the What Would You Like to Do? window.

Understanding Toolbars

PowerPoint includes a number of toolbars that you can use to streamline your work. For example, when working with graphics, you may want to display the drawing toolbars (there are two) on the screen. When adding special effects to objects, you may want to display the Animation Effects toolbar.

A toolbar is a graphical representation of commands that exist in the PowerPoint menus. While you are working, it is often easier to click on a button than it is to find a particular command in one of PowerPoint's nine menus.

PowerPoint comes equipped with seven toolbars, each containing tools related to a specific function. Table 2.2 explains the different toolbars available in PowerPoint.

TABLE 2.2: UNDERSTANDING THE TOOLBARS

Toolbar	Description
Standard	The Standard toolbar includes tools for working with files and cutting, copying, pasting, and undoing operations.
Formatting	The Formatting toolbar contains the font, size, style, alignment, spacing, and bullet options.
Animation Effects	The Animation Effects toolbar includes several tools you can use to add motion and sound effects to objects in your presentation.
Common Tasks	The Common Tasks toolbar looks like a window that pops up over your slide; you can choose a new slide layout, add a new slide, or choose a new design.
Control Toolbox	The Control Toolbox is a set of controls from Microsoft Access that will enable you to create forms that readers can use for data entry.
Drawing	The Drawing toolbar contains commands for working with text used as a graphic element (i.e., logos, oversized first letters, etc.) and drawing shapes with various colors and fill patterns.
Picture	The Picture toolbar gives you a variety of options for importing and then editing images in PowerPoint.
Reviewing	The Reviewing toolbar is a palette of four tools you can use when you are reviewing a presentation.
Visual Basic	The Visual Basic toolbar includes tools that help you add programmability features to your presentation.
Web	The Web toolbar gives you standard browser buttons (like forward and back), the URL text box, and more.
WordArt	Displays a toolbar with the tool for creating WordArt and various tools for editing it.

You can display the toolbars available (and see which ones are enabled on your system) by choosing View and Toolbars. When you place the pointer on Toolbars, the drop-down menu shown in Figure 2.14 appears.

FIGURE 2.14
Displaying the available toolbars in the Toolbars cascading menu

If you like to use a specific set of tools, you can create a custom toolbar. To do this, display the Toolbars cascading menu, then click on the Customize option. The Customize dialog box appears. Click New. The New Toolbar dialog box appears, and you can enter the name for your new toolbar (see Figure 2.15). After you enter the name, click OK.

PowerPoint displays the new toolbar (named Multimedia in Figure 2.16) on top of the Customize dialog box. Click the Commands tab. In this tab, you will drag the commands you want to include in the new toolbar to the toolbar itself. As you add each tool, the toolbar grows. Figure 2.16 shows the Multimedia toolbar after a number of tools have been added.

FIGURE 2.15

Creating a custom toolbar

FIGURE 2.16

Creating a new custom toolbar

To close the Customize dialog box, click Close. If you want to close the toolbar you've created, just click on the Close box in the upper right corner of the box.

MASTERING TROUBLESHOOTING

Toolbars, Toolbars, Everywhere

PowerPoint includes many different toolbars you can use for various tasks as you assemble your presentations. But what if your screen is cluttered with the multitude of toolbars you display? Chances are that you use only a few tools from each toolbar for the majority of your tasks. You can create a general toolbar that holds just the tools you want to use, which reduces the toolbar clutter on your screen.

Create the new toolbar using the procedure described in this section. Then, if you want to *move* tools from one toolbar to another, display the toolbar you want to move the tools from and drag the tools to the new toolbar. Notice that the tools are removed from the original toolbar. If you want to *copy* the tools from the original toolbar to the new toolbar, press and hold Ctrl while you drag the tools from one toolbar to another. When you're finished, click OK.

Adding Text

Thus far in the chapter, you've learned how to start a PowerPoint presentation with both the AutoContent Wizard and a template. Figure 2.17 shows the first page of a presentation based on the Dad's Tie presentation design.

As you can see, a PowerPoint Presentation doesn't leave any guesswork for you. Prompts on the screen tell you where to type the title and subtitle, and the color is already chosen. All you have to do is follow the instructions and enter your own text. We'll do this in the next few sections.

Adding a Title

To enter a title on the title page, position the mouse anywhere on the title box and click on the mouse button to highlight the text box (see Figure 2.18).

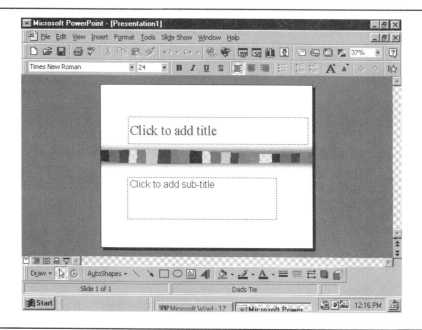

FIGURE 2.17
The first screen of the new PowerPoint presentation design

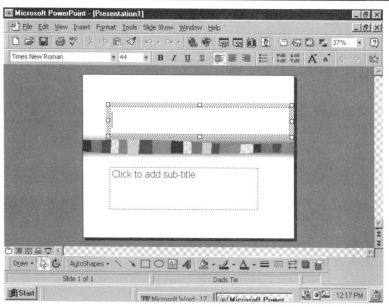

FIGURE 2.18
Displaying the text box for text entry

CREATING A SIMPLE PRESENTATION

Few things in life are as simple as this next step: Type whatever title you want, and PowerPoint formats the text in the font, style, color, and alignment of the template.

When you click outside the text box, the edges of the text box disappear (see Figure 2.19).

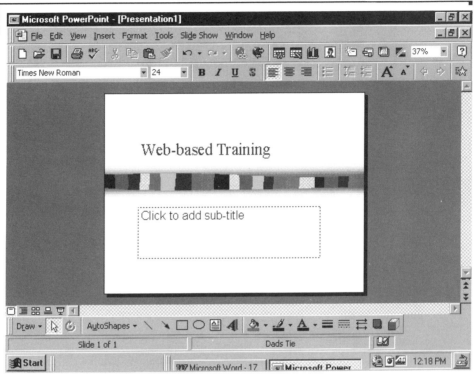

FIGURE 2.19
An entered title

After you add the title, you may decide that you want to change it. Simply position the mouse on the title and double-click. The text box will reappear and you can make your changes.

Adding a Subtitle

Adding a subtitle is just like adding a title, except that you click in the other text box and the text appears in a slightly different format, according to the template settings. Figure 2.20 shows the completed first slide.

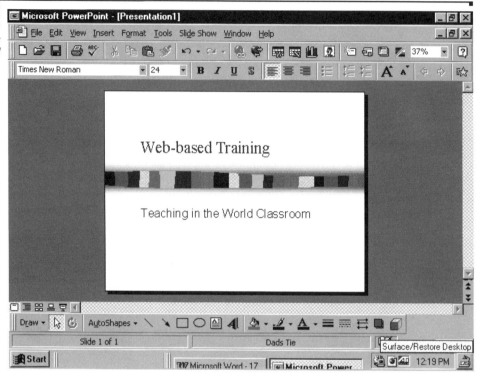

FIGURE 2.20
The first slide with the title and subtitle entered

Moving Text Areas

Relocating a box of text is easy. For example, suppose that you want to move the subtitle down. Just move the pointer to the edge of the text box. When the pointer changes to an arrow, press and hold the mouse button while dragging the box downward. When the text box is where you want it, release the mouse button.

Resizing Text Boxes

You might want to resize the text box so that it takes up less (or more) room on-screen. To do so, position the mouse pointer on the edge of the text box until you get a double-headed arrow, and then press the mouse button and drag the border, releasing the mouse button when the box is the size you want.

Starting a New Slide

Now that you've mastered the first slide, you're ready to tackle a few more. Let's add another slide so we've got room to work. You can add a slide one of three ways:

- Click on the New Slide button in the status bar
- Choose the Insert New Slide button from the toolbar at the top of the screen
- Choose Insert ➤ New Slide

Whichever you choose, the New Slide dialog box appears so you can choose the AutoLayout for the new slide (see Figure 2.21).

FIGURE 2.21

The New Slide dialog box

For example, select the layout in the bottom left corner of the dialog box and then click OK. A new slide with areas blocked out for title text, bullet text, and clip art appears, as shown in Figure 2.22. Notice that the status area tells you that you're looking at Slide 2.

FIGURE 2.22

The new slide

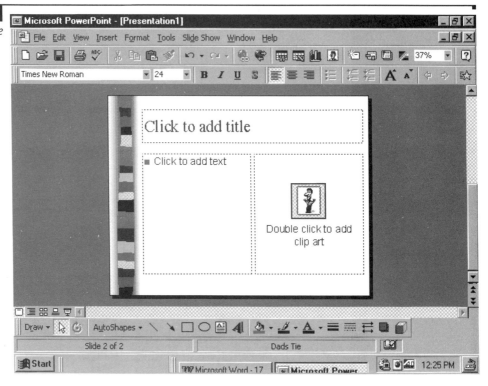

Before you add art to the slide, add the following text:

- In the title area, type **New Technology, New Tools**
- In the bullet text area, type each of the following items, pressing Enter after each phrase:

    The yardstick of yesterday

    Today's technological tools

    Focusing on the future: Fantasy or fact?

Adding Art

The slide we just added has a spot included for clip art. You can add clip art anywhere on a slide you want; however, the clip art boxes designed into your PowerPoint slide enable you to add clip art easily. Double-click on the *Double-click to Add Clip Art* box, and the Microsoft ClipArt Gallery appears, as shown in Figure 2.23. You can move through the categories to display the different pieces of clip art and then choose the art you want from the Pictures box. After you've selected the art you want, click on Insert, and PowerPoint adds the art to the slide.

FIGURE 2.23

The Microsoft ClipArt Gallery dialog box

Resizing Art Objects

Resizing an art object in PowerPoint is the same basic process as resizing a text box. Click on the object you want to select, position the mouse pointer on one of the handles, and press and hold the mouse button while dragging the mouse in the direction you want to resize the object. When the object is the size you want, release the mouse button.

You can add a variety of other art special effects to your presentations, including custom-drawn objects and shapes or color schemes, shading, and patterns. Now, in PowerPoint, you can also animate shapes and art on your slides. We'll talk more about custom artwork in Chapter 5, and about animating objects in Chapter 7.

Changing Views

Thus far, you've been working on the presentation in Slide View. By changing to different views, you can see how the content of your presentation—in terms of both text and slide design—is shaping up.

Display the presentation in Outline View by clicking the Outline button in the bottom left corner of the window. Figure 2.24 shows the presentation created up to this point in Outline View.

FIGURE 2.24
The two-slide presentation in Outline View

Slide Sorter View is also helpful when you have several different slides and want to be able to compare and/or reorder them. Change to Slide Sorter View by clicking the Page Sorter button, which also lies in the bottom left corner of the window. Figure 2.25 shows the presentation in Slide Sorter View.

FIGURE 2.25

The presentation in Slide Sorter View

Starting a Slide Show

Although we're several pages short of what might be considered a real slide show, try out the slide show feature of PowerPoint. You can start a slide show two different ways:

- By clicking on the Slide Show tool (the display-board icon beside the view buttons).
- By opening the View menu and choosing Slide Show.

When you choose the Slide Show command, the show begins. The slides appear one at a time, taking up the entire screen (see Figure 2.26). When you are ready to advance to the next slide, press Enter or click on the left mouse button. (To return to the previous view, press the Esc key.)

FIGURE 2.26

The Slide Show view

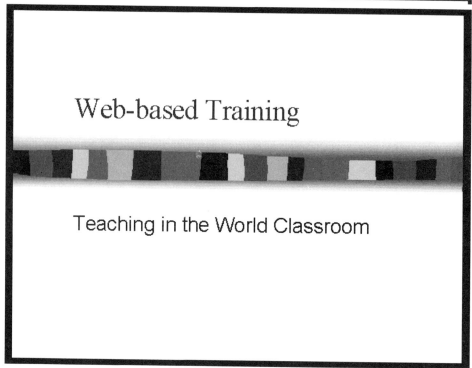

Saving Presentations

Periodically save the presentation you're working on. For best results, save regularly—don't wait until you're finished with the file. You never know when a badly timed thunderstorm or a trip over the power cord will interrupt power to your computer. Most people save their files after each major step in the creation process. In other words, you might pause to save the file the first time after you select the template and add the first slide of text; then again after adding subsequent pages; then again after adding art, charts, and so on.

The process of saving files in PowerPoint is the same as that of saving files in any other Windows application—just open the File menu and choose Save, navigate to the disk and folder where you want to store the file, enter the file name you want, and click on OK.

TIP

The next time you save the file by selecting the Save command you will not be asked to enter a file name; PowerPoint will use the name you specified in the initial save procedure. From this point on you can save the file by pressing Ctrl+S.

Printing the Presentation

PowerPoint makes it easy to print multiple copies of presentations, to print only selected pages, and to choose a number of different formats for printing (Slides, Notes, Handouts, or Outlines). You can also specify print quality, print to a file, omit the background color, resize to fit the page, and change the print order (see Figure 2.27).

FIGURE 2.27
The Print dialog box

If you're having trouble getting pages to print, check to make sure you've got your printer set up to work with PowerPoint. (To do this, open the File menu, choose the Print command, and click on the Printer button.)

What's Next?

In this chapter, we've covered a lot of ground. From a basic understanding of the startup procedure for PowerPoint, you explored selecting templates and Wizards and investigating each of the PowerPoint menus. Additionally, you learned the basic tasks for creating a presentation, getting help, accessing the PowerPoint forum on MSN, adding text and clip art, resizing objects, adding new slides, displaying a slide show, and printing the presentation. In the next chapter, you begin Part Two of the book and start investigating each of the different tools that will help you create powerful PowerPoint presentations.

PART II

The Right Tool for the Job

LEARN TO:

- *Enter, edit, and enhance text in your presentation*

- *Add, modify, and enhance charts*

- *Work with clip art*

- *Import graphics files*

- *Add sound to your presentations*

- *Add and edit video clips*

- *Set transitions, timing, and navigation controls for your presentation*

Chapter 3

Entering, Editing, and Enhancing Text

FEATURING

Text Rules

Before You Add Text...

Entering Text

Using the AutoContent Wizard

Editing Text

Formatting Text

Chapter 3

Entering, Editing, and Enhancing Text

The text of your presentation carries a lot of weight. Even though you'll be presenting, which means you'll have notes or a script to narrate from as you go through the slides, viewers are further clued in to your message and its meaning as they watch the story unfold on the slides. From the text you use—and the way you use it—your audience will understand:

- What's most important about your presentation
- What items you're covering
- Where they need to ask questions
- What response you hope to elicit

In this chapter, you'll learn to use text to its best advantage. We won't waste time proselytizing about the power of the printed word—you already understand that. The power you're working with here is a combination of platforms—multimedia—and the trick lies in knowing what to put on-screen and what to say. Where will text help and where will it detract from your presentation? You'll learn to make those types of judgments in this chapter.

Once you get the basic content of your presentation down, take a good long look at it. Proofread it carefully. Watch the punctuation. A good presentation can be blown out of the water by bad grammar or incorrect punctuation. This chapter will help you get a handle on the editing aspect of your presentation.

Finally, you need to think about the way your text looks. Your text's appearance—although perhaps set by a wizard or a template—conveys quite a bit about your message. You may want to change the typeface, size, color, or other elements. Later in this chapter, you'll find out how to make these and other enhancements to your text.

Text Rules

This section gives you a few pointers for preparing the text content of your presentation. If writing is old hat to you, feel free to skip this section and move on to "Using the AutoContent Wizard," later in this chapter.

Too Much Is Too Much

The temptation may be very great to pack too much text into your slides, especially if you are preparing slides that will also be printed as handouts (which means that they will go back to the office or home with audience members and you want them to be able to remember what each slide was about). Fight it. Including too much text on a slide is overwhelming for audience members—they will read the first seven words of any bullet point or paragraph and then move on to the next item. Keep your blurbs succinct.

For example, consider this bullet entry, taken from a sample presentation:

> *The new AsDec 400 uses the latest technology to bring a high level of commitment and quality to the marketplace.*

That sounds okay, but it's too long. By the time your audience gets to "bring" they've stopped reading. If you want to say that your company is far-and-away the best in a particular area, you could rearrange the text (more succinctly and more powerfully, too) using the bullet points shown in Figure 3.1.

The Clearer, the Better

Whenever possible, be as specific as you can with the information you're presenting. Granted, being specific without being verbose is a difficult line to walk, but you should be as clear as possible about what's being shown. For example, although a slide titled "Projections vs. Actual Sales Results" sounds professional, your audience may better understand the content of the slide (and the charts on it) if the title is, "How Did We Do This Month?"

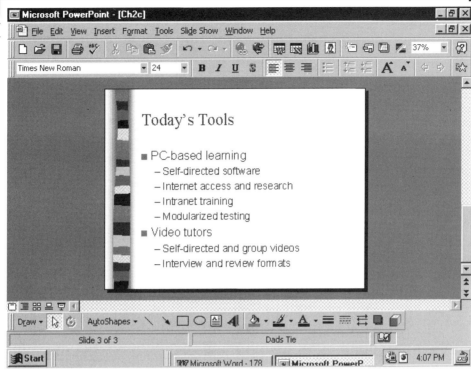

FIGURE 3.1
Using text sparingly but effectively

Tailor your presentation's tone to the audience you'll be speaking to. If conversational text won't fit their professional meeting, go with the flow and speak to them in the language they will understand.

Know Where You're Going

A presentation that wanders from topic to topic will seem disjointed and confusing to your audience. Make sure your text moves forward through a set series of topics—know where you want to go and then create the slides to get there. The sense of direction will help your audience better understand your presentation.

Use Text to Highlight, Not Narrate

Keep text to its essential, most powerful minimum: resist the temptation to write captions for your charts, add notes to slides where they aren't completely necessary, or use titles of more than one line. The narration of your presentation should be able to provide the bulk of the verbal communication. If you need to provide additional information, you can print handouts using Notes Pages view, which produces a reduced image of the slide plus any attached notes printed at the bottom of the page. Figure 3.2 shows an example of a page in Notes Pages view.

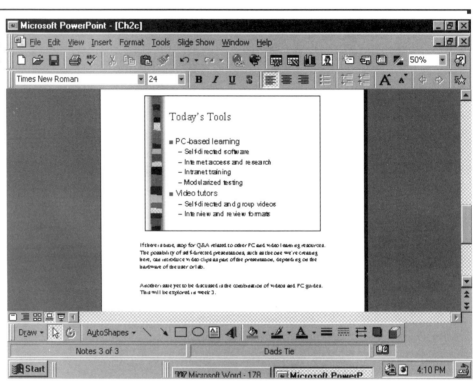

FIGURE 3.2
An example of additional text entered in Notes Pages view

Color and Contrast Are Important

Even though the color of the background and text may have been selected by the template you chose or the Wizard you used, you may need to make changes based on where you'll be presenting and how large your audience is. Make sure that you've got enough color contrast for your text to show up on-screen. Before you give the presentation, test the color combinations on coworkers to see whether they have any trouble reading the display under lighting similar to that in the place you'll be presenting. Generally, light text on a darker background is easiest to see, but you may need to test different color combinations to see what works best for your particular circumstance. If you're in doubt about what to use, try white or yellow text on a dark background. This combination is very legible in most presentation situations.

Think about Your Audience

Before you begin composing the text, think about your audience. Who are they? Are they engineers, sales people, managers? Are they support personnel, students, or prospective employees? The "who" will help you determine the tone of your presentation. Remember to speak the language your audience will readily understand.

Timing Is Everything

Consider carefully the amount of time you'll need in order to discuss everything you need to discuss about a particular slide. You can either use Manual timing and advance the slides by clicking the mouse button when you're ready to move on, or use Automatic timing to have PowerPoint advance the slides automatically after a preset period of time. Manual gives you more control, but Automatic helps you stay within a specified time frame.

For more about controlling the timing of slide display, see Chapter 8, "Finishing a Slide Show."

Before You Add Text...

Assuming that you've selected your presentation's template and are ready to start entering text, take a minute to write down the key points of your presentation. This will help you create a basic game plan from which to work.

Experienced presenters and writers often prefer the question-and-answer approach to outlining ideas. In this method, you brainstorm about the basic questions your presentation should answer and then answer each one.

For example, if you are creating a presentation to promote a new service your company is offering, you might come up with these ideas.

- What is the name of our service?
- What does it offer?
- Who does it appeal to?
- What benefits does it offer?
- How much does it cost?
- When does it start?
- How do I find out more?

Then, to flesh out the basic progression of the presentation, you'd answer each question in turn:

- AsDec On-Site Training
- Corporate, individual, and group training on the AsDec 400
- Corporations and small businesses who have recently purchased or upgraded to an AsDec 400
- Professional trainers; on-going technical support; clear, useful manuals
- $1200 per three-day seminar, unlimited participants
- Seminars are scheduled on a bimonthly basis
- Call 1-800-55-ASDEC or write AsDec Industries, One Redfern Way, Sausalito, CA 94015

You can now build a presentation based on the answers you provided to your own questions. This gives you a basic plan for the presentation and makes sure that it moves logically from slide to slide.

Entering Text

In the previous chapter, you learned how to enter text quickly in the process of creating your first presentation. This section slows things down a bit and shows you the various ways you can enter and work with text in your presentation.

Once you've sketched out your ideas for the presentation, you're ready to get it on-screen. You can enter text in either Slide view or Outline view. The following sections explain how to do just that.

Adding Text in Slide View

When you first start PowerPoint and choose a Page Layout to begin a worksession, the first slide of your presentation appears on the screen. The text entry sections are already blocked out on the screen. Whether you started your presentation by choosing a template or opting to start with a blank publication, prompts on your screen tell you where to enter text (see Figure 3.3).

FIGURE 3.3
Text sections on a title page

Whether you've chosen to work with a template or start a file from scratch, PowerPoint applies certain default text settings to the words you type. You can change the text's typeface, size, style, and color at any time during your PowerPoint work session. For more about changing the font and enhancing your text, see "Enhancing Text," later in this chapter.

What's a font? A font is a certain typeface in a particular size and style. For example, Times Roman 16-point italic is one font, and Times Roman 12-point bold is another.

To enter text, click on the text box you want to use. An entry box appears, as shown in Figure 3.4. Notice that the text cursor blinks in the center of the box. This happens because the alignment setting chosen by PowerPoint (another default) is centered. Type the title for the presentation in this top text box, assuming that you've displayed a Title page layout.

As you type, the letters appear in the text box. After you finish typing the title, click outside the text area. PowerPoint closes the text box and the text is displayed in the title area at the top of the slide.

To enter the second section of text, repeat the same steps: double-click on the text box, and type the text you want to appear. If your text takes up more than one line, PowerPoint automatically wraps the text to the next line for you. You don't need to press Enter; in fact, doing so will tell PowerPoint that you are adding another item in a list (such as a bulleted list) and the text will show up as two separate items in Outline view. Now PowerPoint will underscore words it doesn't recognize or thinks you have misspelled; you can right click on the word to see a list of possible spelling alternatives.

If PowerPoint wraps the line automatically for you and you don't like the way it breaks, you can resize the box by positioning the mouse pointer on the corner and dragging the corner to reshape the box.

FIGURE 3.4

The text entry box

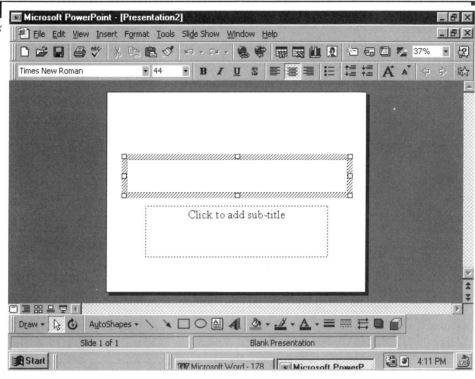

To add another item in the same text box, press Enter at the end of the first item and PowerPoint moves the cursor to the next line.

After you finish entering text, click outside the text box. Later, you can make any modifications you want by moving the text; changing the size of the text box; selecting a different font, size, or style; or even deleting the text at any time from Slide view.

Adding New Text Boxes

There will be times when you want to add more text than Slide view leaves room for. For example, suppose that on a particular slide, you want to add a line that shows the date the presentation was prepared.

Simply click the text box tool (it looks like a small document icon, and lies in the center of the drawing tools row, just below the work area) and move the cursor to the point on the slide where you want to add the box. Hold down the mouse button while dragging the mouse down and to the right, releasing it when the text box is the size you want. The cursor and a data-entry area appear, as shown in Figure 3.5. You can move the text box around just like the original text boxes—by dragging it.

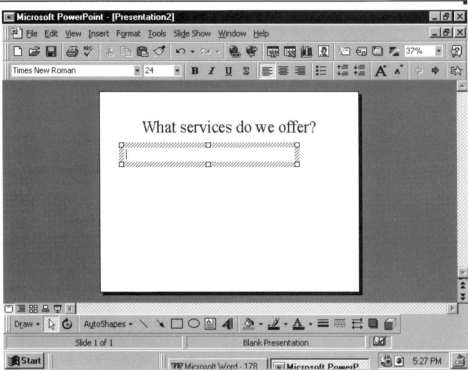

FIGURE 3.5

Creating a new text box

Adding Text in Outline View

Outline view gives you another perspective from which to view your text. This view shows you only the text in your presentation, organized to show the indention levels, in standard outline format.

To display the presentation in Outline view, click the Outline View button in the lower left corner of the screen or choose View ➤ Outline. You'll see any text you've entered in the presentation, as shown in Figure 3.6.

ENTERING TEXT

FIGURE 3.6

Text displayed in Outline view

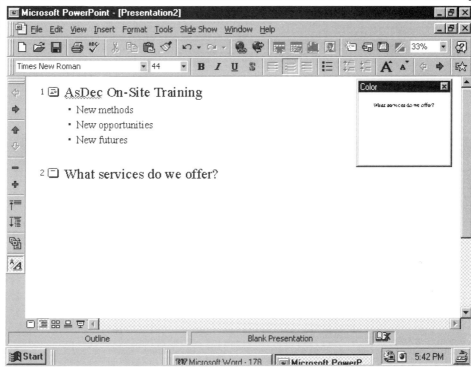

Outline Elements

The Outline screen looks quite a bit different from the Slide View screen. You see different tools along the left side of the window, and a different look in the work area itself. Table 3.1 explains each of the buttons in the Outline View toolbar.

Button	Name	Description
⇐	Promote (Indent less)	Moves selected text to the left
⇒	Demote (Indent more)	Moves selected text to the right one level
⇑	Move Up	Moves selected text up one page in the presentation

TABLE 3.1: OUTLINE BUTTONS

Continued

Button	Name	Description
	Move Down	Moves selected text down one page in the presentation
	Collapse Selection	Hides all sublevels of the currently selected slide
	Expand Selection	Displays all sublevels of the currently selected slide
	Show Titles	Shows only slide titles
	Show All	Displays all text in the presentation
	Summary Slide	Creates a summary slide based on the highlighted text
	Show Formatting	Works as a toggle to display text in the selected font and size; click again to disable formatting display and show text in uniform size and style

For more about working with the different tools in Outline view, see "Editing in Outline View," later in this chapter.

Adding, Indenting, and Outdenting Text on the Current Slide

To add text to the existing slide, use the arrow keys to move the cursor to the desired point. To begin a new line indented to the same point, simply press Enter, or press Tab to indent the line further. To "outdent" (that is, to move the insertion point to the left) the line, press Shift+Tab. Then type your text.

Creating a New Slide in the Outliner

To add a new slide, position the cursor in the slide after which you want to add the new one. Then move the pointer to the New Slide button in the status bar at the bottom of the screen and click the mouse button. Another number appears in the left column of the Outliner, indicating that you've started a new slide. The cursor is positioned so that you can add the title text for the slide (see Figure 3.7).

FIGURE 3.7

The added slide in Outliner view

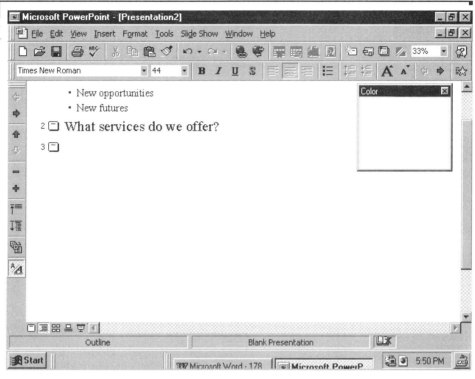

You can also add a new slide by pressing Enter after the preceding slide or by "outdenting"; that is, press Shift+Tab to move the line of text out to the left margin as a new slide entry.

Inserting Text from Microsoft Word

If you've previously created an outline in Microsoft Word and want to use it directly in your PowerPoint presentation, you can use PowerPoint's drag-and-drop feature to use the text as-is. Just minimize PowerPoint so that it appears only in the Taskbar; open the Windows Explorer, and locate the file containing the text you want to import.

Click on the file, and then, holding the mouse button down, drag the file to the PowerPoint tab in the Taskbar. After a moment, PowerPoint opens automatically, and you can drag the Word file's icon to the presentation. PowerPoint copies the information from the Word file directly into a new presentation file.

Working with Text Levels

Each of the text levels in PowerPoint is assigned a different text size so you can easily distinguish between them. Here's how it breaks down:

- The first level, shown in 44-point type, is the page title
- The second, displayed in 32-point type, is marked by a square bullet and indented two spaces
- The third, displayed in 28-point type, is marked by a dash and indented four spaces
- The fourth, shown in 24-point type, is marked by two greater-than symbols and indented six spaces
- The fifth, displayed in 20-point type, is a square bullet at eight spaces
- The sixth, also displayed in 20-point type, is a dash at ten spaces

The exact point size and appearance may vary depending on the template you use.

To indent text to a new level, you can either position the cursor at the beginning of the text and press Tab, or click the Demote button (the right-pointing arrow in the text settings row).

Figure 3.8 shows the different levels of indentation available in Outline view.

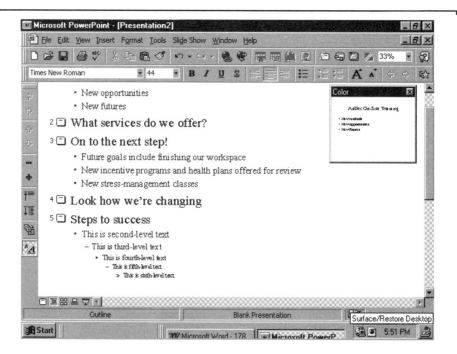

FIGURE 3.8
Outline view showing text indents

Using the AutoContent Wizard

Another way to enter text in your presentation is to let PowerPoint do it for you. You can use PowerPoint's AutoContent Wizard to make sure you've got a clear, targeted presentation that includes information people will be sure to understand.

When you select the AutoContent Wizard from the Presentations tab of the New Presentation dialog box (see Figure 3.9), you are presented with a series of four pop-up screens. Each screen asks you for information about the presentation you're about to create.

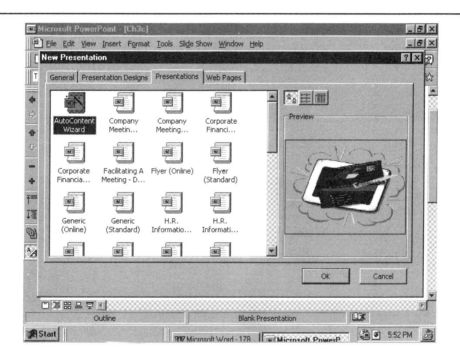

FIGURE 3.9
Choosing the AutoContent Wizard

Select the type of presentation you're going to give.	You are asked to choose the type of presentation you want—strategy, selling, training, reporting progress, communicating bad news, or general.
How will this presentation be used?	You select the way you will present information—presentations, informal meetings, handouts; also Internet, kiosk.

CHAPTER 3 • ENTERING, EDITING, AND ENHANCING TEXT

What type of output will you use? and Will you print handouts?	You can choose from black-and-white or color overheads, on-screen presentation, or 35mm slides. For handouts, select Yes or No.
Enter information for your title slide.	This pop-up window asks you for information you would include on the title slide of your presentation—things like the title, the topic, your name, and company name.

When you click on the Finish button, the AutoContent Wizard assembles a basic presentation for you, complete with slide titles and text ideas. Figure 3.10 shows the second page of the AutoContent presentation.

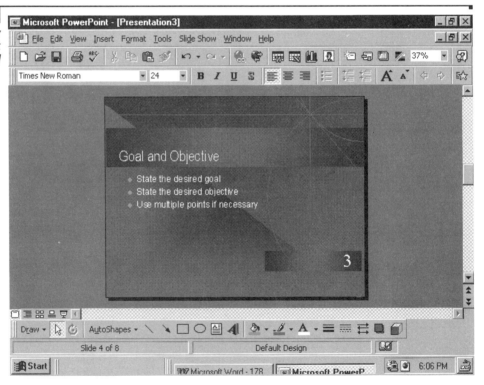

FIGURE 3.10

The text created by the AutoContent Wizard

Editing Text

Now that you've got some text to work with, you may be tempted to move things around a bit. Perhaps the text on page three would work better on page five. What if you want to change the indent levels of text you've already entered or move a paragraph from one side of a slide to another?

This section explores the various aspects of editing your text. Editing includes many things: changing individual letters, replacing words, moving sentences or fragments, resizing text blocks, and running the spelling checker. We'll talk about enhancing text in the next section, but here, you'll make sure that the text is as accurate as possible.

Any program that lets you work with text must offer two different kinds of editing tasks: keystroke editing, in which you can correct a misspelling or a bad line break by typing a key or two; and block editing, in which you mark a section of text as a block and move it, delete it, copy it, or paste it.

Simple Text Editing

Some typos don't even look like typos. How many times have you wondered how to spell the word "freind"? Is it I before E except after C, or what?

Luckily, the spelling checker can bail you out of spelling dead ends where nothing looks right. There may be times, however (like when you're trying to spell your new boss's name), when a spelling checker can't help. Then you are on your own, with only your own memory (or reference materials) and the backspace or Del key.

To edit text in a specific text block, your first step is to position the cursor at the point you want to edit the text. Click on the text box and the border appears, indicating that you've selected the box. Now position the cursor where you want to make your changes.

PowerPoint 97 now keeps an eye on your typing and highlights the text when it thinks you have entered a word incorrectly. Right-click the word to see suggestions for ways you may want to correct the spelling.

If you're having trouble seeing what you're doing, use the Zoom controls in the toolbar at the top of the screen to enlarge the display. Click the down-arrow beside 50% and choose from a larger percentage (100% is usually plenty). When you're finished with your up-close work, return to normal view.

When you're finished making the text changes, click outside the box.

Selecting Text for Editing

Some editing procedures require that you mark the text you want to edit as a block. A text block can be as small as a single character or as large as the entire presentation—PowerPoint recognizes whatever you highlight as the current block. For example, before you can copy text, you need to tell PowerPoint what block of text you want to work with. To do this, you position the cursor and then highlight the block.

If you want to highlight all the text in your presentation, click Edit ➤ Select All. You might want to do this, for example, to make a global change such as changing the font, style, or color of all text in your presentation.

Click the mouse button when the pointer is placed at the beginning of the text you want to mark, then press the mouse button and drag the mouse over the section you want to highlight. If you're using the keyboard to highlight the text you want, move the cursor to the beginning of the text, and then press on the right-arrow key while holding down the Shift key.

If you've marked a block and want to remove the highlight (deselect it) press Esc or move the pointer outside the text area and click the mouse button.

Cutting and Pasting Text

PowerPoint includes all the basic editing procedures you'll find in other programs—and they are in the same place, too (the Edit menu). The Copy, Cut, and Paste commands all enable you to work with blocks of text in your presentation. These commands use the Windows Clipboard as a temporary storage place for the information you're working with. For example, if you're copying a block of text, PowerPoint puts the copy on the clipboard. Then, when you paste the text somewhere else, PowerPoint copies the text from the clipboard to the cursor position.

PowerPoint gives you two different kinds of Paste commands: the regular Paste puts whatever is stored on the clipboard at the cursor location, and Paste Special preserves the formatting style for the clipboard contents you insert.

Drag-and-Drop Text

If you're working in Outline view, you can drag and drop text to move it from one place to another. This procedure allows you to bypass Copy and Paste from the Edit menu. Just highlight the text you want to move, position the pointer on the text, and drag the text to the new location. A bar cursor shows you where the text will be positioned as you drag the mouse. When the bar cursor is placed at the point you want the text to be inserted, release the mouse button.

Undoing Editing Changes

For those times when you press a key and think "I really wish I hadn't done that," PowerPoint includes the Undo feature. You can customize Undo to reverse up to 150 (!) of your most recent operations; the default is 20. To change the number of operations Undo will reverse, select Tools ➤ Options, and then select the Advanced tab. Change the setting in Maximum Number of Undos by clicking the up-arrow or down-arrow to increase or decrease the number.

PowerPoint 97 includes a multiple undo feature, which means you can undo your most recent operations up to any number of tasks you specify. Set the number of undos you want to allow by choosing Tools ➤ Options, selecting the Edit tab, and increasing the *Maximum number of undos* option.

Using the Spelling Checker to Catch Spelling Errors

Consider how many times you will have read the text of your presentation by the time you finish it, and you can see how easy it is to become blind to errors. By then, you've read the text so many times that typos begin to look right.

You can let PowerPoint read through the presentation for you to ensure that all your words are spelled correctly. The spelling checker will check every word in your presentation, including additional material such as speaker notes and chart labels.

PowerPoint's spelling checker looks for three different kinds of possible errors:

- Any word not recognized in PowerPoint's dictionary
- Any word that includes numbers
- Any word that includes strange capitalization

Start the Spelling Checker one of three ways:

- Choose Tools ➤ Spelling.
- Press F7.
- Click the Spelling tool (fifth from the left, showing the letters ABC and a small checkmark) in the toolbar.

When PowerPoint finds a word that's not in the dictionary, it displays a screen giving you a number of options. You can skip the word, correct it, add it to a personal dictionary, or choose a different word from a list of alternatives.

Using AutoCorrect

PowerPoint for Windows 95 includes a feature shared with other Microsoft products: AutoCorrect. If you are like most people, there are certain words you always misspell. You can "teach" AutoCorrect to watch for those words and correct them dynamically when you type them. Additionally, you can use AutoCorrect as a kind of shorthand interpreter—if you must type a long word or phrase repeatedly, you can teach Auto-Correct to find the phrase you type and substitute the long phrase for you. For example, you could type the letters *ref* and have AutoCorrect automatically substitute *Biographical Reference of American Sports Heroes*. AutoCorrect is available in the Tools menu.

Three options—Correct TWo INitial CApitals, Capitalize Names of Days, and Replace Text as You Type—are selected by default. You can disable each of those options by clicking the appropriate checkbox.

Enter the words you want to substitute in the Replace: and With: text boxes. Before doing so, use the down-arrow to scroll through the word list in the bottom of the dialog box to make sure the word isn't already entered.

Using the Style Checker to Catch Style Inconsistencies and Problems

Another tool included with PowerPoint 95 is the Style Checker. This automated utility goes through your presentation and checks its consistency, visual clarity, and style, taking the guesswork out of whether your presentation is ready to be presented. When you've finished entering the text of your presentation (and, for best results, use the Style Checker again after you finish entering all presentation elements, including graphics, charts, sound, and video), click Tools ➤ Style Checker. The Style Checker dialog box appears, as shown in Figure 3.11.

FIGURE 3.11

Starting the StyleChecker

The Style Checker allows you to check three different things: *Spelling*, *Visual Clarity*, and *Case and End Punctuation*.

Click on the Options button. The Style Checker Options dialog box appears, with the *Case and End Punctuation* tab showing (see Figure 3.12).

Case and End Punctuation enables you to choose the punctuation method of your text. You may want to add or remove periods for your text items or watch for incorrect punctuation characters that may inadvertently slip into your text. Make your selections and then click on the Visual Clarity tab (see Figure 3.13).

FIGURE 3.12

Setting up Case and End Punctuation in the Style Checker

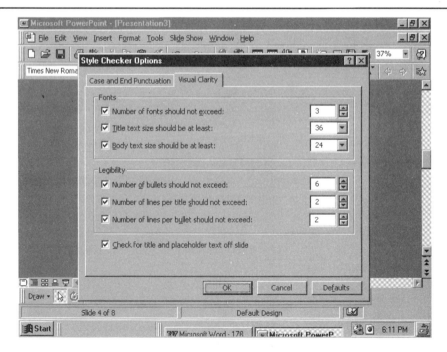

FIGURE 3.13

Making sure your presentation is visually clear

Visual Clarity refers to the way your text looks on the slide. The options in the Visual Clarity tab provide you with a number of choices regarding the number and sizes of different fonts; in addition, you can double-check the legibility of your text by making sure that you don't have too many bullets or lines on a slide.

When you're finished reviewing the options, click on OK to return to the Style Checker dialog box. Click on Start to begin the check.

If you make changes in the Style Checker Options but then want to revert to the original settings, click on the Defaults button.

If the Style Checker finds spelling errors, it displays the Spelling dialog box. You can choose the appropriate action and click OK to continue the check.

As the Style Checker looks for style problems, it displays the Style Checker dialog box. A message tells you which slide it is currently checking. When a problem is found, a description of the problem is displayed in the text box, as shown in Figure 3.14.

FIGURE 3.14
The Style Checker found a potential problem

You can Ignore or Change the problem. If you click on Ignore, the Style Checker moves on to check other slides. If you click on Change, the Style Checker automatically fixes the problem for you.

Editing in Outline View

Up to this point, most of the editing tasks we've been talking about apply to both the Slide view and Outline view. You can do simple editing—like using the backspace or Del keys to make minor modifications—in Outline view; you can mark a text block and cut, copy, paste, or clear it, just as you can in Slide view.

You learned earlier that instead of using Cut and Paste to move a text block, you can use the drag-and-drop feature in the Outliner to move highlighted text from one point to another. But there are additional editing features available to you in Outline view that you *can't* accomplish in Slide view. In fact, an entirely new set of tools appears along the left edge of the outline, enabling you to collapse and expand outlines, check titles, and take a look at formatting changes. Earlier in this chapter, Table 3.1 provided a basic description of the different Outline tools.

Collapsing the Outline

PowerPoint gives you a way to determine easily whether your headings are parallel and your outline is balanced. The trick is known as collapsing the outline, and it turns the outline shown on the left side of Figure 3.15 to the one shown on the right.

To fully collapse the outline, click on the Show Titles button (fourth from the bottom) from the row of Outline tools. All sublevels of information disappear. PowerPoint shows you which slides have additional information, however, by including a gray underline on those slides that contain hidden sublevels. Now you can compare the titles of your presentation to see whether they are parallel and present topics in the clearest possible manner.

To display all levels of the outline again, click on the Expand All button (third from the bottom) in the Outline tools row. The outline is displayed with all sublevels intact.

FIGURE 3.15

The outline before and after the collapse

MASTERING THE OPPORTUNITIES

Creating a Balanced Outline

A significant part of creating a good presentation lies in making sure your concepts are organized in an orderly way. In fact, as an English teacher or two along the way has probably told you, there's a very definite process to creating a solid outline. PowerPoint won't make you stick to any particular rules when you're creating your outline, but you can make a good presentation better by making sure your outline works.

In a balanced outline, every A has a B, every 1 has a 2, etc.—there are two of everything. Here's an example of a balanced outline (on the left, you see the basic outline structure; on the right, you see how it can be applied to the AsDec 400 sample presentation):

Level One	We're AsDec Industries
Sublevel B	Building a better future
Level Two	We're a "People Company," offering
Sublevel A	Training Services
Sublevel B	Ongoing Technical Support

Levels One and Two supply the basic ideas—in this case, the slide titles—and the sublevels underneath supply the supporting ideas—in this case, bullet entries.

Many people find it helpful to go through and write the main points of their outlines first, before adding detail in the sublevels. As you become more experienced at writing and revising your own outlines, you'll learn what works best for you.

Collapsing and Expanding a Slide

In some cases, you may want to collapse only a single slide, rather than the entire outline. You can do this by positioning the cursor in the slide you want to collapse and clicking on the Collapse Selection button (it resembles a minus sign). Only the collapsed slide's title will be displayed.

To expand a single slide, position the cursor in the title of the slide you want to expand and click on the Expand Selection button (it looks like a plus sign).

Moving Text Items in Outline View

One additional feature available in Outline view that you won't find in Slide view is the ability to move a single line of text up or down through the presentation. Suppose, for example, that you want to move the fifth bullet item up to the third position. You would position the cursor on the line you want to move and then click on the up-arrow (Move Up) button. The line exchanges places with the one above it. Click the Move Up button again, and the line is in the third position.

Similarly, you can move a line of text downward through the presentation by using the Move Down button. And you aren't limited to staying within the same slide; you can move text from slide to slide as necessary.

Creating a Summary Slide in Outline View

PowerPoint 97 gives you the option of adding a summary slide—a slide that includes key points, slide titles, or important phrases—and enables you to show your audience at a glance what you plan to cover in your presentation.

You can create a summary slide from either Outline or Slide Sorter view by clicking the Summary Slide button. First highlight (in Outline view) or select (in Slide Sorter view) the slides you want to include on the summary slide (see Figure 3.16). Then click the Summary Slide button. The summary slide is then created for you (see Figure 3.17).

FIGURE 3.16

Highlight the slides you want to summarize and click the Summary Slide button to create a summary slide.

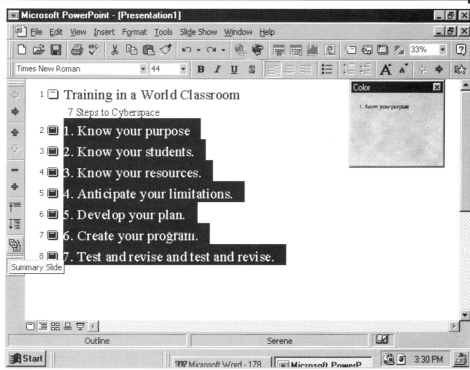

FIGURE 3.17

The summary slide is created automatically from the text you select.

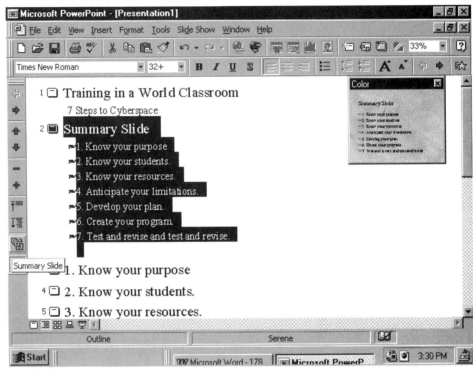

How will you use a summary slide? You might create a table of contents with hyperlinks that will take your audience—or individual users, if you're creating a self-directed presentation—to the slide covering the topic they select.

MASTERING THE OPPORTUNITIES

Hyperlinking the Easy Way

Hyperlinks are easy to add in PowerPoint. You simply highlight the text you want to use as a link and press Ctrl+K. The Insert Hyperlink dialog box appears, and you can click the Browse button beside the Named location in file box. The Hyperlink To Slide dialog box appears so you can select the page to which you want to establish the hyperlink. Click the page you want to link to and click OK. Click OK a second time to close the Insert Hyperlink dialog box and return to your presentation.

Editing in Slide Sorter View

Slide Sorter view, shown in Figure 3.18, doesn't look like a good place to edit text. After all, you can't see the text very well.

FIGURE 3.18
Displaying Slide Sorter view

But there is one major editing task you can perform in Slide Sorter view—a task that has a great deal to do with how your presentation will be received. While all your slides are displayed on one screen, you can visually scan through them and determine how the overall presentation is shaping up.

Don't remember how to get to Slide Sorter view? Go to the row of View buttons at the bottom of the screen (the row with four squares) and click on the third button from the left, or choose View ➤ Slide Sorter.

Earlier you learned that the overall structure and clarity of your outline is important—you need balance and parallelism to help viewers know where you're going. Similarly, you need to make sure that the sequence of your slides makes sense.

By displaying your developing presentation in Slide Sorter view, you can keep an eye on the overall progression of your slides. Do they move logically from one to another? Are you missing a step? Should you vary the style of the slides you're creating? Slide after slide of bulleted text may present your idea, but it may also put your audience to sleep.

PowerPoint 97 allows you to add speaker notes in Slide Sorter view. Simply click the slide you want to add notes to, open the View menu, and choose Speaker Notes. A popup box appears so you can type the text you want to save. Click Close when you're through and the Speaker Notes dialog box closes.

If you decide to rearrange the slides, it's a simple job in Slide Sorter. Just click on the slide you want to move and drag it to its new location. The other slides move to accommodate the change.

Remember to save your changes. After—and often before—every major change, take the few seconds to save the file. If you're preparing to make a sweeping change, like changing the color scheme, throwing out several slides, or selecting a set of off-the-wall fonts, back up the file first. Then, if you aren't happy with the new look, you can always go back to the original.

Expanding Slides

Now in PowerPoint 97 you can divide a crowded slide into slides with less text. The feature takes each top-level bullet item and makes it the title of an individual slide. Subpoints on the slides then become subpoints—one level up—on the new slides.

For example, take a look at the slide in Figure 3.19. This slide can be divided into three different slides to make it more manageable. Start by highlighting the text of the slide; then choose Tools ➤ Expand Slide. PowerPoint divides the slide into slides, using the top-level bullet point as the slide title (see Figure 3.20).

FIGURE 3.19

You can easily expand a single slide into shorter slides using the Expand Slide command.

FIGURE 3.20

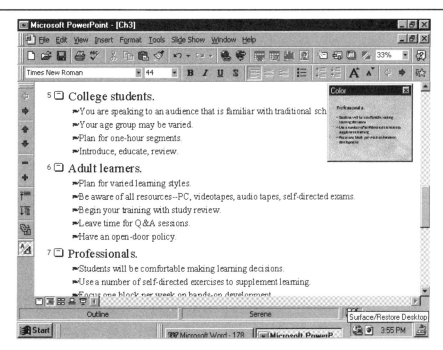

The slide is divided into three slides, separated by the top-level bullet points.

Formatting Text

What a presentation says—in words—is only part of its impact. How a presentation *looks* makes as loud a statement as the text itself. The way your text is positioned on a slide contributes to whether or not a viewer actually reads it. If the text is too small, in a font that's hard to read, or scrunched against other text, your audience may simply give up.

Once you get the text into your presentation, you may want to rearrange it and try it in different formats to see what's most effective. The way you go about making format changes depends on how far-reaching you want the changes to be. You can do simple changes yourself, like changing indents, moving tabs, and modifying line spacing. Or, you can go all the way back to square one by letting PowerPoint apply a design template for you. This section describes the different ways in which you can change the format of your presentation:

- Applying a new design template to the entire presentation
- Choosing a new page layout for the current slide
- Using the ruler, tabs, indents, and alignment options to change the way elements are positioned on the slide

Applying a New Design

The simplest and quickest way to change the look of your presentation uses the Apply Design command in the Format menu.

When you choose this command, the Apply Design dialog box appears. Choose one of the different templates (these are the same templates displayed in the New Presentation dialog box when you first choose a presentation design) and then click on Apply. The new design is automatically applied to all slides in your presentation.

Changing Format with a New Layout

One of the easiest ways to change the format is to select a different layout for the current slide. Suppose you're working on a standard bullet slide in Current Slide view. You can choose a different layout—but keep the same text—by clicking on the Slide

Layout button in the Standard toolbar. That opens the Slide Layout dialog box, shown in Figure 3.21.

FIGURE 3.21

The Slide Layout box

Click on the picture of the layout you want. Depending on the style you choose, you may have some additional work to do, however. For example, the new layout you choose may require that you add a chart or a table. When you click on Reapply, the new layout is applied to the current slide.

If you changed the layout and don't like it, choose Edit ➤ Undo. Your old layout reappears, good as new.

Displaying the Ruler

Many hands-on formatting issues—such as setting indents and tabs—involve using the ruler. If your ruler is not already displayed, choose View ➤ Ruler to show the rulers along the top and left sides of the PowerPoint work area. Two rulers appear; one along the top of the slide area and one along the left edge (see Figure 3.22).

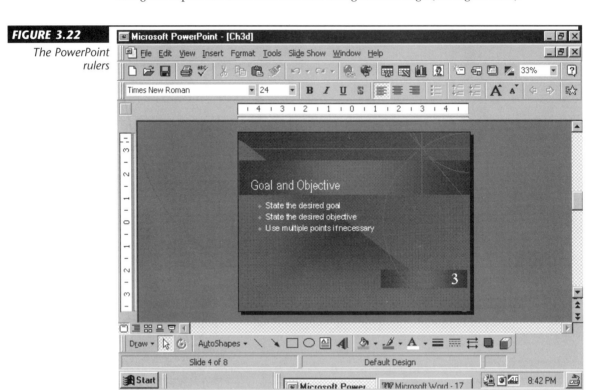

FIGURE 3.22

The PowerPoint rulers

Notice that, unlike a typical ruler, the PowerPoint rulers show 0 (zero) as their center point. This enables you to measure from the vertical and horizontal center of the slide, which helps you position elements accurately.

When the ruler is displayed and you highlight text or click in a text box, the ruler changes (see Figure 3.23). Now the ruler reflects the width and height of the selected text box; the ruler is no longer vertically and horizontally centered to 0. Additionally, the white area narrows to show only the width and depth of the current text box.

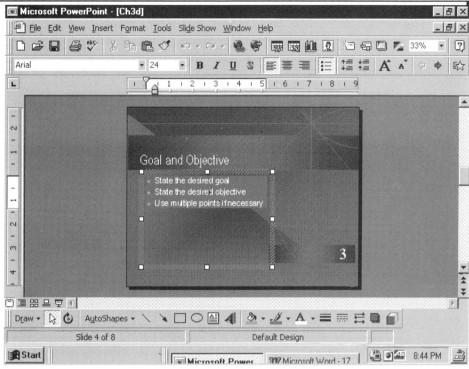

FIGURE 3.23
Changes in the ruler and what they mean

In the small square in the upper left corner of the PowerPoint work area, you see a tab symbol. At the left end of the top ruler, you see two markers—one pointing up and one pointing down. These are your indent markers.

Changing Indents

One of the first tasks you might perform using the ruler involves changing the indentation of specific text. There are several types of indents you could apply to presentation text:

- all lines of text indented evenly
- only the first line of text indented
- all lines except the first indented (used for bulleted and numbered lists)

To change the indent of a block of text, first select the block you want to change, then move the pointer to the indent marker you want to move. The top marker on the ruler controls the first-line indent, the bottom marker controls the indent of subsequent lines. Drag the marker to the new position on the ruler.

To move both markers but maintain their relative distance from each other (for example, suppose that you've created a hanging indent for a bullet and want to move all the text—just the way it is—to the right), click on the small rectangle beneath the bottom indent marker. Both markers move together, preserving the space between them.

Working with Tabs

The primary function of a tab is to help you align text in your documents as painlessly as possible. The tab is a small marker that tells the text, "Stop here." PowerPoint gives you the option of choosing four different tab stops: left, right, center, and decimal tabs. (The first three types are pretty common; a decimal tab lines up the numeric values you enter according to the decimal point. It enables you to easily format columns of numbers in your presentations.)

Setting Tabs

You'll need the ruler and a selected text box to add tabs. After that, the steps are simple:

1. Choose the type of tab you want by clicking in the tab selection box until the tab type appears. Table 3.2 shows how the different tab icons appear.

2. Move the pointer to the ruler bar and click on the point at which you want to add the tab.

TABLE 3.2: POWERPOINT TAB TYPES

Button	Tab Type	Description
L	Left tab	Left-aligns text at the tab
⌐	Right tab	Right-aligns text at the tab
⊥	Center tab	Centers text at the tab
⊥	Decimal tab	Aligns text on decimal point

Moving and Deleting Tabs

You can easily move or remove tabs you no longer need. First, you can simply slide them to a new location. Just move the pointer to the tab you want to move, press and hold the mouse button, and drag the tab to a new location.

Not good enough? Delete the tab by dragging it off the right end of the ruler. The tab just disappears, with no additional fanfare. Please note that Undo won't restore the tab.

Aligning Text

Another big part of formatting includes the position of the text on the slide. Depending on what other elements you include on the slide—such as a chart or other art items, or a table—you may want to experiment with different alignments. With PowerPoint, you can align your text in the following ways:

- Left aligned: the text is aligned with the left margin and is ragged along the right.
- Right aligned: the text is aligned with the right margin and is ragged along the left.
- Centered: the text is centered and ragged along both margins.
- Justified: the text is aligned with both the left and right margins.

How do you know which alignment to use? Table 3.3 provides ideas of when you might use the different alignment options.

TABLE 3.3: ALIGNMENT IDEAS

Alignment	Use For
Left	Bullet text
	Single paragraphs
	Chart legends
	Paragraph-style bullets
Right	Figure captions
	Data labels
	Special text effects
	Aligning against a chart or graphic item
Center	Titles
	Subtitles
	Chart titles
Justified	Two-column bullet slides
	Text along a chart or graphic item
	Text notes on a chart

If you are choosing either left or centered alignment, you can do so by simply clicking in the text box you want to change and then clicking on the appropriate button in the toolbar (see Figure 3.24). The text automatically changes to reflect your selection.

FIGURE 3.24
Choosing a different alignment

You can also change the alignment of text by opening the Format menu and choosing Alignment. A small pop-up box of different alignment choices appears.

Working with Line and Paragraph Spacing

PowerPoint takes care of the spacing of your text automatically. Type the text, and PowerPoint puts it where it needs to go. Sometimes, however, you may want to change the spacing PowerPoint has set for you. You might want to fit one more line of text on a slide, for example, or add space between lines.

You can modify the spacing between lines in your text box by choosing Format ➤ Line Spacing. The dialog box shown in Figure 3.25 appears.

FIGURE 3.25
Choosing the Line Spacing for your presentation

In the Line Spacing area, you can choose the number of lines you want separating text lines. You can select either Lines or Points as the spacing measurement. To change the value, click either the up-arrow or down-arrow to increase or decrease the number.

A *point* is a standard typographical measurement, used in desktop publishing and presentation projects. 72 points roughly equal one inch. This means that if you set your title to 72-point Helvetica font, the letters will be one inch tall.

You can change the spacing increment point by point or in .01-inch increments. This gives you precise control over the way your lines are spaced. Use the Preview button to see how the change will look before you click OK to accept it.

Selecting Paragraph Spacing

Also in the Line Spacing dialog box are the Before Paragraph and After Paragraph settings, which, respectively, control the amount of space before and after the current paragraph.

The only trick to using the Before and After Paragraph settings is that you must highlight the text you want to work with before you choose the Line Spacing command to display the dialog box, so PowerPoint knows which text to adjust. If you're not sure how your changes will affect the text, use the Preview button to get a glimpse before you return to the slide.

Enhancing Text

Now that you know how to enter, edit, and format the text in your presentation, you need to know how to change its font, size, style, and color. PowerPoint also makes it easy for you to add your own unique bullets to the presentation. This section introduces each of these text enhancements.

Changing Text Font and Size

Unless you have time to study typography and graphics design, you're going to rely on your own instincts when it comes to choosing fonts for your presentation slides. In most cases, you won't have to do much choosing: PowerPoint chooses the typefaces, text styles, colors, and sizes for you when you use a Presentation or Presentation Design as the basis for your file.

The text font you choose for your presentation is an important choice. The text should reflect whatever tone you are projecting. Is it a serious presentation? Stick with conventional-looking text. Is it a brainstorming session? Go for a font that gives you a little more creative freedom.

When you're working with fonts, fight the temptation to overdo it—remember that *legibility* is your first goal.

To change the font, either:

- Click on the down-arrow beside the font box in the text settings row (see Figure 3.26).
- Choose Format ➤ Font. The Font dialog box appears, as shown in Figure 3.27.

FIGURE 3.26

Displaying font options

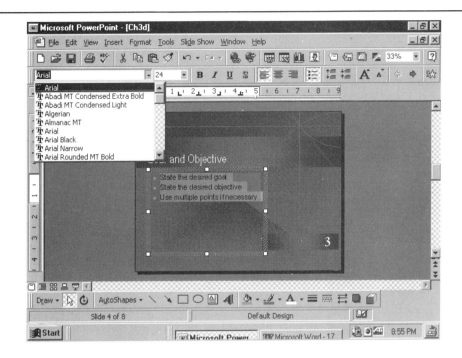

FIGURE 3.27

The Font dialog box

To choose a new font, select your font choice in the drop-down list. The text you selected appears in the new font.

If you use one font in your presentation and then find something you like better, you can search for and replace the first font with another. Use the Replace Fonts command in the Tools menu. Enter the name of the font to replace and the name of the font to replace it with. When you click on OK, PowerPoint makes the change.

Changing the size of text is also a simple process. First highlight the text you want to change, then do one of the following:

- Click the down-arrow beside the size box in the Formatting toolbar.
- Click the Increase Font Size button in the Formatting toolbar.
- Click the Decrease Font Size button in the Formatting toolbar.
- Open the Format menu and choose Font; then select the size from the appropriate box.

Of these options, the easiest is to highlight the text and click on the down-arrow beside the size box in the text settings row (see Figure 3.28).

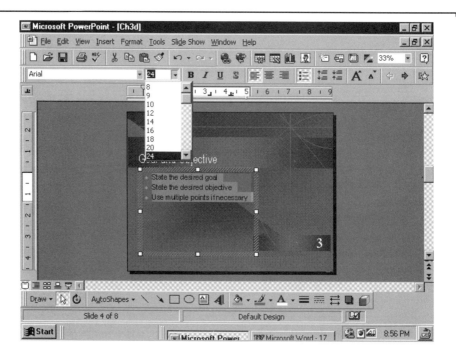

FIGURE 3.28

Selecting a new text size

To bump the size up one notch, you can click on the Increase Font Size button (on the right side of the Formatting toolbar). PowerPoint increases the font to the next available size. To shrink the font a little, click on Decrease Font Size. PowerPoint reduces the highlighted text one font size.

Some fonts work better in larger sizes. For example, some of the specialty fonts, such as Mistral and Gradl, are barely readable until you enlarge them. Experiment with font sizes until you get what you want. And remember to consider the slide from your audience's perspective: will everyone be able to read the words from several feet away?

Setting the Style

The style of text allows you to call attention to individual words or phrases. For example, you might want to boldface a new product name or italicize the name of a report you're quoting. PowerPoint offers Regular, Bold, Italic, and Bold Italic text styles. After you highlight the text you want to change, you can choose a new style by clicking one or more of the buttons in the Formatting toolbar (see Figure 3.29). If you prefer, you can choose the style by selecting Fonts from the Format menu and clicking on the style you want in the Font dialog box.

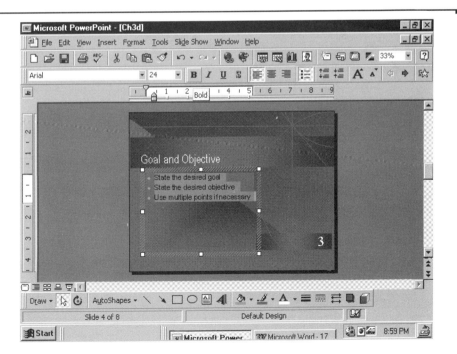

FIGURE 3.29

The style and effect buttons in the Formatting toolbar

To select more than one item in the text settings row, just click the buttons you want. For example, if you want to make a word bold and italic, just highlight the word, click on B and then click on I.

Selecting Text Effects

Text effects are slightly different than text styles. Styles affect the text's appearance: regular, bold, or italic. Effects, on the other hand, include underlining, shadowing, embossing, superscript, and subscript.

You can select these effects in the Font dialog box, available by choosing Format ➤ Font. You can also choose two of the five effects (Underline and Shadow) from the Formatting toolbar.

Changing Text Color

If you started your presentation using the Pick a Look Wizard or a template, the colors of your background and text are already selected for you. The product designers at Microsoft put together effective color palettes that you can use as is or modify to suit your tastes.

To change the color of text on a particular slide, highlight the text, then click the Text Color button in the Drawing tools row at the bottom of the screen. (You can also use the Font dialog box to set the color.) When you click the tool, a small color pop-up box appears, as shown in Figure 3.30.

FIGURE 3.30

The color pop-up box

Click on Other Color to see a larger palette of choices. For more information on mixing and matching color schemes, see Chapter 9, "The Dynamics of Color."

To change the text color for all similar slides in your presentation, change the slide's master, rather than the individual slides. For example, to change the color of all bullet text, choose View ➤ Master ➤ Slide Master to highlight the appropriate text level, and choose a different color.

Now PowerPoint 97 shares a common palette with other Office 97 applications. When you choose a color of blue in Word, you can be sure it's the same color blue when you copy the text to PowerPoint. This helps you create a consistent look among all your business applications.

Picking Up and Applying Styles

If you have used a particular set of text effects that you like, you can copy the settings (font, style, effect, color, alignment, and spacing) and apply them to another block of text. This little trick, which involves the use of the Format Painter, may make your text-enhancement duties easier.

Start by highlighting the text that already has the style you want to use. Then move the pointer up to the Format Painter tool in the Standard toolbar. Click the tool. PowerPoint copies the style information to the Clipboard.

Next, highlight the text that is to receive the style. When you release the mouse button, the text settings are applied to the new text selection.

If you want to apply a format to several pieces of text, double-click the Format Painter tool when you select it.

Using Bullets

Even a small change like the type of bullet you use can change the look of your presentation. PowerPoint gives you an incredible choice of bullets to use in your presentation.

Before you start the process of selecting a different bullet character, highlight the bullet lines you want to change. If you want to change only one line, position the cursor in that line. Choose Format ➤ Bullet, and the Bullet dialog box appears, as shown in Figure 3.31.

FIGURE 3.31

The Bullet dialog box

You can select a different set of bullets by clicking on the Bullets From: down-arrow and choosing the font you want to work with. To choose a different bullet type, make sure the Use a Bullet checkbox is checked; then select the color, size, and the individual bullet character you want. When you click on the bullet, the bullet enlarges so you can get a better look at it (see Figure 3.32).

When you click on OK, PowerPoint applies the bullet to all highlighted bullet points.

FIGURE 3.32

Getting a closer look at a bullet

What's New?

In this chapter, you learned how to enter, edit, format, and enhance the text in your presentation. You now know how to plan the basic text in your presentation, create an outline, use the Spelling and Style Checkers, work with the AutoCorrect feature, and perform a number of formatting and text-enhancement operations.

For the best results, take a few minutes and review your presentation after you've entered the basic text. Try printing the presentation in Outline view so you can show it to a few coworkers and get their input on the content you've got thus far. Making sure your text is the way you want it gives you a good basis for building the rest of your PowerPoint presentation. We'll start with the next step—creating and enhancing charts—in the next chapter.

Chapter 4

Creating and Enhancing Graphs

FEATURING

A Few Graph Ideas

Using Excel Graphs in Your Presentation

Creating a Graph

Importing Chart Data

Editing Graphs

Enhancing Graphs

Creating and Enhancing Graphs

The text of your presentation is important, but it doesn't provide much in the way of visual instruction. You couldn't look at a printed page and know at a glance, for example, that sales in a particular area have increased dramatically or that your department has almost reached its productivity goal. A chart can call attention to that information immediately, letting you skip over the read-and-figure-it-out stage and see immediately what point the presenter is trying to make.

A Few Graph Ideas

How do you know what will work as a graph? Here are a few possibilities:

- **Comparisons.** Graphs can help you illustrate relationships between data. For example, you can illustrate how the price reduction of an item increases or decreases sales, or show the hierarchy in your organization.

- **Processes.** If you've got several slides full of bullets, think about whether one could be converted to a graph. The change will break up the monotony of bullet lists and convey information in a new and interesting form.

- **Trends.** When you need to show data trends, graphs can help you compare the progress of two data sets, whether those items are sales regions, products, or salaries.

Certain types of graphs are better than others for showing certain kinds of information. For example, if you want to compare two or more items, you can use bar charts, bar-line charts, and area charts to help readers visually identify the differences between the contrasted data series.

Is This PowerPoint or Microsoft Graph?

The graph capability of PowerPoint is not PowerPoint's own—it is actually Microsoft Graph 97, an embedded graph utility you can use to create graph objects in your presentation. You won't notice any difference when you move between PowerPoint and Microsoft Graph—you'll simply use the Graph datasheet to enter the data for the graph and then use various Graph options to choose the graph type, set options, change the format, and enhance the graphs you create.

Using Excel Graphs in Your PowerPoint Presentations

If you, as an Office aficionado, have already created Excel graphs, you may not need to worry about creating any PowerPoint ones. Instead, you'll paste the Excel charts directly onto the slide. Microsoft Graph is also used to create Excel's charts, although Excel actually leads you through the process of creating the chart by using the ChartWizard.

Excel's ChartWizard is much like PowerPoint's AutoContent Wizard, in that it leads you through the process of creating the item by asking you a series of questions.

To use an already-created Excel graph in your PowerPoint presentation, you have several choices. You can copy the graph from Excel to PowerPoint, use Edit ➤ Paste Special to paste the graph on the slide while maintaining the link to Excel, or tile both the Excel and PowerPoint windows side-by-side and drag-and-drop the graph from Excel to PowerPoint.

The process of linking an object—a graph is considered an object—enables you to make sure the object is updated whenever the original file changes. This means that whenever you change the data in your Excel spreadsheet, the changes will automatically be reflected in your PowerPoint file.

An Overview of Graph Types

When you're creating two-dimensonal or three-dimensional graphs from scratch with PowerPoint, you've got a number of different graph types to choose from, including these:

- *Area graphs* show one or more data trends over time
- *Bar graphs* show how data series "stack up" against each other
- *Column graphs* are similar to a bar graph, except that the bars are stacked on top of each other instead of side-by-side
- *Doughnut graphs* plot more than one data series as parts of a whole
- *Line graphs* compare data series over time
- *Pie graphs* show how individual data items relate to the whole
- *Radar graphs* compare data series
- *XY (scatter) graphs* plot data points according to x and y axes
- *Bubble charts* compare three sets of data
- *New 2-D and 3-D charts* offer cylinder, pyramid, and cone shapes

Each type of graph includes a number of subtypes. In addition, each of these graph types is available in 3-D (which means that the Line graph category becomes 3-D Line graph).

Once you choose a basic chart type, you select individual options to create the kind of graph you want. You might start with a bar chart, for example, and then select options that enable you to create a *stacked* bar chart—with data ranges stacked one on top of another.

Creating a Graph

First, you need a slide with a graph area. If your current slide doesn't have a graph area blocked out, click the New Slide button to display the New Slide dialog box (see Figure 4.1) and choose a slide with a graph area built in. When you've selected the file you want (click in the scroll bar to see more choices), click OK. The new slide appears on the screen with the graph area blocked out (see Figure 4.2).

CHAPTER 4 • CREATING AND ENHANCING GRAPHS

FIGURE 4.1
The New Slide dialog box

FIGURE 4.2
The new slide with the graph area marked

Starting the Graph

When you double-click the graph area, PowerPoint churns away for a moment before displaying first a graph and then a datasheet. The datasheet already includes data, put there to provide an example of how PowerPoint's graphing capability works (see Figure 4.3). The idea is that you'll replace PowerPoint's data with your own, and choose the graph that best suits your needs.

FIGURE 4.3

PowerPoint puts data in the datasheet for you.

Working with the Datasheet

The datasheet contains the data PowerPoint uses to build your graph. You enter the labels for the data you want to graph across the top and left rows of the datasheet. Each row represents a single data series and shows what type of symbol—in this case, a 3-D bar—represents the data in the series.

Before you can enter anything of your own, you need to get PowerPoint's fake data off the datasheet. Use Edit ➤ Clear ➤ All to remove all information on the datasheet so you can start with a blank slate.

Entering Data Labels

Your first step is to replace the labels in the datasheet with your labels. The datasheet looks a little like an Excel spreadsheet, organized in a row and column fashion. The intersection of each column and row is called a *cell*.

Each row is a single data series, and each column shows the data values compared in each data series. For example, if you are comparing the sales of two products, the labels Product A and Product B might be listed in the label area of rows 1 and 2, and the column labels might list the months (see Figure 4.4).

FIGURE 4.4

An example of row and column labels

Entering Data

To enter new information in the datasheet, click in the cell where you want the data to go and type. The new data replaces the old. To move to another cell, use the arrow keys or move the mouse pointer to the new cell and click.

Editing the Datasheet

Once you enter the data for the graph, it's likely that you'll want to make some changes. To modify the data you entered, just click in the cell and retype the data. You can also copy, cut, or undo data, using the commands in the Edit menu.

Deleting Datasheet Rows and Columns

To delete entire columns or rows on the datasheet, click the label area for the row or column to highlight it as shown in Figure 4.5. Press Del, and it's gone.

FIGURE 4.5

Removing entire columns and rows in the datasheet

Resizing Datasheet Columns   When the data you need to enter is too wide for the cells in the datasheet, you can widen the column to accommodate the data. Position the cursor on the dividing line between two column labels so that the cursor changes to a double-arrow. Drag the mouse in the direction you want to widen the column, releasing the mouse button when the column is the width you want. To have Power-Point automatically adjust the column width to the text, double-click the dividing line. The column width will close to the widest data entry in the column.

Closing the Datasheet

After you've entered your own data labels and data, you are ready to close the datasheet and begin experimenting with graph types. Close the datasheet in one of three ways:

- Double-click the control-menu box in the upper left corner of the datasheet,
- Click the View Datasheet tool, or
- Select View ➤ Datasheet

At some point, you may want to redisplay that datasheet to make additional changes. Click the View Datasheet button or choose View ➤ Datasheet to display the datasheet again.

Choosing the Graph Type

Now that you've entered the data you're going to work with, the next step is to choose the type of chart you want. You can select a chart type in one of two different ways:

- Click on the Chart Type button in the Toolbar to display the drop-down chart box (see Figure 4.6).
- *Or* choose Chart ➤ Chart Type.

If you don't see a Chart Type command in your Chart menu, you haven't selected the graph.

FIGURE 4.6:
Choosing the type of graph you want to add to the slide

 MASTERING THE OPPORTUNITIES

The Four Most Effective Graphs

When you are displaying information visually, you want to show data in the clearest form possible. For that reason, if you have only a short amount of time to spend on each graph you create, be sure to choose a graph type that will be recognized by your audience and will suit the type of data you are presenting.

One of the most common types of graphs is the ***bar graph***. A bar graph is used to depict a particular data series. For example, suppose you are tracking the sales of four different regions. Each region would be represented by a bar on the graph. By looking at the height of the bars, audience members could easily tell which region had the highest sales, which had the lowest, etc. PowerPoint enables you to create both 2-D and 3-D bar

Continued

> **MASTERING THE OPPORTUNITIES CONTINUED**
>
> graphs for different looks. You can enhance the appearance of bar graphs in other ways, too: for example, you can add a grid or labels and titles, or create a stacked bar graph where the data series are stacked one atop another.
>
> A ***pie graph*** is another popular graph, used to show how portions of a data series relate to the whole. Suppose, for example, that you're doing a cost analysis of a recent project you've completed. What portion of your investment went to research and development? What portion went to production? How much was spent on marketing and distribution? By plugging these numbers into the datasheet and then creating a pie graph based on the data, you can show what percentage of the total expenditure was allotted to each of these categories. Each of the categories is a data series, each getting one slice of the pie. Like bar graphs, you can enhance the appearance of a pie graph in many ways: you can make either 2-D or 3-D pies, create multiple pies, make pie slices explode out from the body of the pie, and add or change labels and titles.
>
> ***Line graphs*** are popular for showing the progression of data over a specific period of time. You might be watching the development of a particular industry trend (How does the number of computers sold with CD-ROMs in 1994 compare to the number sold during each quarter of 1995?), tracking the expenses of a department (How much did Marketing spend on Federal Express charges over a 12 month period? How does that relate to the number of projects published?), or comparing projected and actual sales over a fiscal year. Again, line graphs can be flexible in appearance: you can choose 2-D or 3-D lines, change colors, add or remove gridlines, modify the legend, and more.
>
> Another type of graph used to show a data progression is an ***area graph***. An area graph allows you to compare two or more data series over time, representing the totals with a colored area assigned to the data series. For example, if you are comparing how well two products sold over a quarter, you could show the different data series cumulatively in an area chart. One colored area represents the first product; the other colored area represents the second. At a glance, viewers can see the total amount sold of both products and tell which product fared the best in the marketplace.

If you choose the chart by selecting the one you want from the list, PowerPoint automatically changes the chart in the selected box. If you select a chart with the Chart Type command, the Chart Type dialog box appears (see Figure 4.7).

FIGURE 4.7
The Chart Type dialog box

The first set of options in the Chart Type dialog box allows you to specify the type of chart you want. The second set enables you to choose the chart subtype. When you make your choice of chart type, the subtypes you can select appear in the display area on the left side of the dialog box. Click the type you want and then click OK to return to the slide.

Choosing Custom Options PowerPoint 97 also gives you the option of creating custom charts. Click the Custom Types tab in the Chart Type dialog box to see additional choices (see Figure 4.8). Click the type of chart in the column on the left side of the dialog box; subtypes appear on the right. You can now click the chart that best fits the type of data you're presenting. Click OK when you're through.

FIGURE 4.8
You can choose additional chart types by selecting the Custom Types tab.

Setting Chart Options Once you've selected the chart type, you can modify chart options. Open the Chart menu and choose Chart Options. The dialog box shown in Figure 4.9 appears.

The dialog box includes as many as six different tabs, depending on the type of chart you've selected. Pie charts, for instance, will offer only three of the following tabs, most of the others will show all six: Titles, Axes, Gridlines, Legend, Data Labels, and Data Table. The Titles tab gives you the space to enter chart titles and axis labels; the Axes tab lets you choose the measurement and type of the axes; the Gridlines tab controls where the gridlines are placed; the Legend tab enables you to choose the placement of the legend; the Data Labels tab lets you make selections about the data labels; and the Data Table tab helps you choose options for any data tables you display. In every tab, make your selections; when you are finished, click OK to close the dialog box.

Importing Chart Data

Microsoft Office is built on the enter-it-once, use-it-many-times concept. You can write an outline in Word, for example, and use it as the basis for a PowerPoint presentation.

FIGURE 4.9

The Chart Options dialog box gives you up to six different tabs of choices.

You can use a selected range from your Excel worksheet as the basis for your PowerPoint graph.

You're not limited to importing from Microsoft products; PowerPoint lets you work with data from other applications as well. This section explores a few of the kinds of data you can use to create PowerPoint graphs.

What Data Can You Import?

In addition to Microsoft Excel files, PowerPoint directly supports several different text files and Lotus 1-2-3 files. If your spreadsheet file names end with any of these extensions, your data can be imported into PowerPoint:

- XL* (Microsoft Excel)
- PRN, TXT, CSV (Standard text format)
- WK* (Lotus 1-2-3)

(In the preceding list, the asterisk character (*) is a wildcard, meaning that any character can be substituted for the asterisk. An acceptable Lotus 1-2-3 extension, for example, is WK1.)

If you use a spreadsheet program other than Excel or 1-2-3, you may still be able to use your data files with PowerPoint. Save the spreadsheet file in Excel or 1-2-3 format and then choose Edit ➤ Import Data to bring the information into PowerPoint. The instructions in your spreadsheet program should tell you how to save files in those formats.

If you're drawing data from a Windows application—perhaps Microsoft Works or another Windows program with spreadsheet capability—you should be able to copy data into the PowerPoint datasheet using Edit ➤ Copy in the other application and Edit ➤ Paste in PowerPoint.

Importing Files

To import data as the basis for your graph, you must first display and clear the datasheet. Select the area to clear, choose Edit ➤ Clear All to erase the information in the datasheet, and then enter any labels necessary to describe the data you're importing.

Position the cursor in the upper left corner of the datasheet work area and choose Edit ➤ Import File. The Import File dialog box appears, as shown in Figure 4.10.

As a Windows user, you should be able to navigate this dialog box without any difficulty; it works much like File Open. Begin by navigating to the folder containing the file you want; then select it and click OK.

After you click OK, PowerPoint searches for the specified file, places the data in the datasheet, and updates the graph.

Editing Graphs

You may not know exactly what you want in a graph until you see it drawn on the screen. Then your ideas on how to improve it ("What if I added a title? Would those bars stand out better if they were a different color?") can help you fine-tune the basic graph into something ready for presentation.

EDITING GRAPHS | **131**

FIGURE 4.10
The Import File dialog box

Basic Procedures: Cutting, Copying, Pasting, and Resizing Graphs

Working with a graph frame is like working with any frame in PowerPoint—you can easily resize, cut, copy, or paste graphs just like you would any other item. To perform these basic editing procedures, click on the graph to select it. The graph frame appears, with handles around its outer edge.

To resize a graph:	Click a handle and drag the graph to resize it horizontally or vertically.
To cut a graph:	Make sure the graph is selected; then press Del or choose Edit ➤ Clear.
To copy a graph:	Select the graph; then choose Edit ➤ Copy.
To paste a graph:	Move to the slide on which you want to paste the graph and choose Edit ➤ Paste.

When resizing a graph, you can keep its original proportions by dragging the graph corner at a 45 degree angle inward or outward.

Modifying Graph Elements

When you double-click the graph to select it, several changes happen on the screen. First, the frame outline takes on a different look—instead of a thin outline with white handles, the outline becomes a thick white outline with black handles.

The toolbar also changes. Now a number of new tools appear, all having to do with importing, creating, displaying, and modifying graphs (see Figure 4.11). Table 4.1 shows the different tools in the graph toolbar.

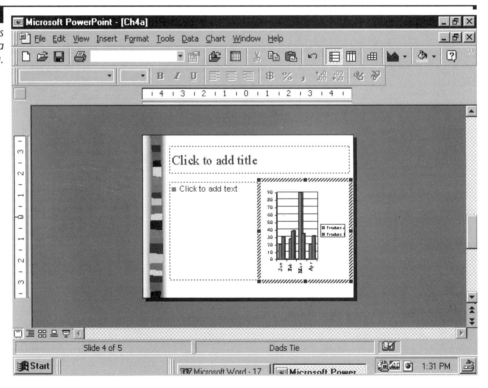

FIGURE 4.11

The screen changes when you select a graph for editing.

EDITING GRAPHS 133

TABLE 4.1: TOOLS IN THE GRAPH TOOLBAR

Tool	Name	Description
Series "Jan"	Chart Objects	Enables you to choose a chart element to modify
	Format	Displays the Format dialog box so you can change the way the selected element is displayed
	Import File	Imports an existing file from another application
	View Datasheet	Displays and hides datasheet
	Cut	Removes the selected item and places it on the clipboard
	Copy	Copies the selected item to the Clipboard
	Paste	Pastes Clipboard contents to selected area
	Undo	Reverses last action
	By Row	Associates data row-wise
	By Column	Associates data column-wise
	Data Table	Turns the selected chart into a data table
	Chart Type	Allows you to choose the chart type you want
	Fill Color	Displays a color palette
	Office Assistant	Displays the Assistant so you can get help on the selected topic

PART II

The Right Tool for the Job

If you plan on doing up-close work—like changing data values, adding labels, or changing markers and gridlines—you may want to Zoom the display so you can see what's going on. Click the Zoom down arrow to display the list of possible percentages; choose the display you want. You need to do this *before* you double-click the graph to display the graph toolbar and put the graph in editing mode.

Changing the Data Arrangement

There's a method to PowerPoint's madness when it comes to the way data is displayed in your graph. When you enter data in the datasheet, PowerPoint graphs the information first by row, then by column. This means that if you're working with the datasheet in Figure 4.12, PowerPoint will show how Product A and Product B (rows) did over the first four months of the year (columns). The resulting chart is shown in an enlarged view in Figure 4.13.

FIGURE 4.12

PowerPoint graphs the information in the datasheet first by row, then by column.

EDITING GRAPHS | **135**

FIGURE 4.13

The graph created from the default values in the datasheet

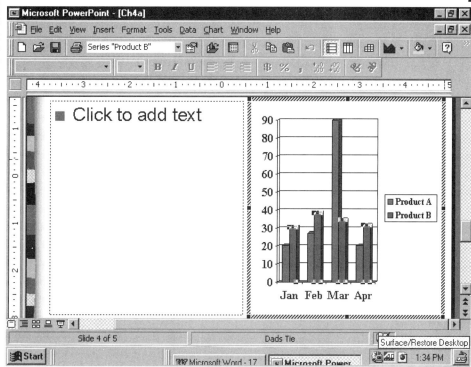

You can change the way PowerPoint displays the data—that is, you can put the row data where the column data is and the column data where the row data is—to display your graph another way. That way, instead of showing how Products A and B did over four months, you show how the months look for each of those products.

For example, you can change the way the data is arranged (this is also called the association of the data) by clicking the By Column button in the toolbar. When you click By Column, PowerPoint graphs Product A and Product B separately, with each bar in the graph associated with a particular month (see Figure 4.14).

If you're having trouble portraying your data just the way you want it, try switching the association of the data. If the By Row button is clicked, try using By Column, or vice versa. Sometimes data arranged differently makes more sense.

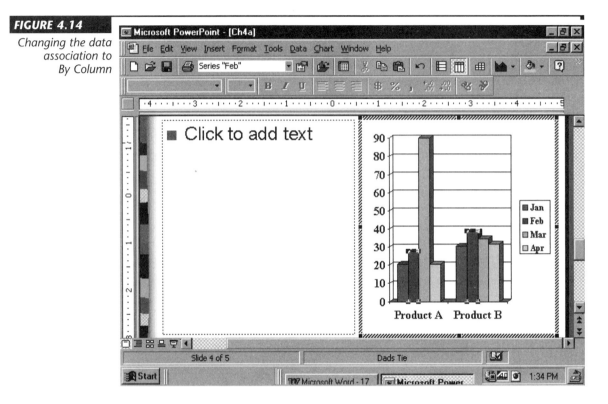

FIGURE 4.14
Changing the data association to By Column

Creating a Data Table

Now you can easily turn a chart into a data table with the simple click of a button. When the chart is displayed on the screen, click the Data Table button, in the Chart tools row. The chart is redrawn as a data table (see Figure 4.15). If you want to change the data table back into a chart, click the Data Table button again.

Changing the X and Y Axes

You may want to change the way the axes of your graph are displayed. For example, you might want to change their color or thickness, or you may want to change the tick marks and the way they appear.

FIGURE 4.15

A data table displays the best of both worlds: graphical and numeric data.

> The Y axis extends vertically; the X axis is horizontal. Tick marks are the small lines that mark off increments on the axes.

To modify the axes on your graph, double-click on the axis you want to change. Figure 4.16 shows the Format Axis dialog box that appears when you do this.

Like other Windows 95 dialog boxes, this one is divided into tabs. First and foremost in the Format Axis dialog box are aesthetic concerns. What color do you want the axis to be? How do you want the tick marks to appear? A sample line at the bottom of the Patterns screen shows you your selections.

FIGURE 4.16
The Format Axis dialog box

Other tabs behind Patterns include Scale, which allows you to set the increment values between tickmarks; Font, which controls the font of the axis labels; Number, which controls the numeric format of values displayed; and Alignment, which allows you to choose the basic layout of text.

You can modify these settings at any time during your work with PowerPoint. Simply make your selections and click OK to return to the graph.

Enhancing Graphs

Your graph is done. You've added and edited its data and arranged it to your liking. The only problem? It's boring. What might you do to spruce up a chart? Add some color, maybe. Tack on a text note. Add a title or data labels. Maybe change a font or style. To round out our discussion of graphs, we'll talk about how you can enhance their appearance.

Changeable Chart Elements

You can select and change any of the following elements by double-clicking on them:

- Individual data series
- The plot area
- The X and Y axes
- The legend
- The gridlines

In most cases, you can also change chart element settings by using a menu command or a tool. Use whichever method is most convenient for you.

Working with Graph Text

You can change some of the text—the axis labels—by double-clicking on the axis you want to change and choosing Font from the displayed screen. There are other types of text you might want to consider working with and/or adding. This section explains how you can add a graph title and data labels and shows how to make basic graph text changes.

Adding a Title

This graph needs a title. Make sure the graph is selected and then choose Chart ➤ Chart Options. The dialog box shown in Figure 4.17 appears.

If the Titles tab isn't already displayed, click it now. Type the text you want to use as the chart title and then click OK. A text box is added to the chart area where the title will go. Type the text for the title and click outside the Title box.

The best titles say it quickly and clearly. Make sure the graph title reflects in as few words as possible the basic concept of your graph. "December Sales Results" is much easier to understand than "Net Sales Based on December's Total Receipts."

FIGURE 4.17

The Chart Options dialog box

Rotating Chart Text

PowerPoint 97 now makes it possible for you to rotate chart titles, axis titles, or data labels. You might want to use this feature when you want the y-axis title to span the length of the axis, for example. To rotate chart text, begin by selecting the text item you want to change. Then open the Format menu and choose the command that corresponds to the item you want to rotate. (For example, to rotate the axis title you have selected, click Axis Title.) The Format Axis Title dialog box appears; click the Alignment tab. This tab gives you the option of choosing the alignment for the text (see Figure 4.18). Either enter the percentage of the angle you want in the Degrees box, or drag the small red diamond up or down on the arc to angle the text. When you're finished, click OK.

FIGURE 4.18

You can rotate chart text by typing a value or by dragging the marker.

Adding Data Labels

Depending on the type of data you are displaying, you may find it helpful to show the data values or labels on or beside the bars, lines, or columns themselves. To add data values or labels, choose Chart ➤ Chart Options; then click the Data Labels tab (see Figure 4.19).

You can add either values or labels. If you add values, the numeric values appear beside the data series items. If you add labels, the names of the data series appear beside the graph elements. Some items in your dialog box may appear dimmed, depending on the type of graph you're working with.

After you make your selection, click OK.

Once you add the data labels to the graph, things may look too crowded. You can drag one of the graph frame handles outward to enlarge the graph and make more room for all the elements inside.

FIGURE 4.19

The Data Labels tab of the Chart Options dialog box

Changing Font, Size, and Style

The look of your text says a lot about your presentation. You may want to try using a different look—especially if you're worried about whether your data labels or graph titles will be legible to the people in the fourth row.

To change the font of something you've added, like a title or text note, click inside the text box and then open the Format menu in the menu bar. The first command there should reflect the item you've selected. For example, if you've selected a chart title, the command is Selected Chart Title. If you've selected a legend, the command is Selected Legend. Click the command. The Format dialog box—either Format Legend or Format Title, depending on what you selected (see Figure 4.20)—will appear.

If you've been working with text in your PowerPoint slides, these options won't surprise you. In the Font screen, you choose the font, style, size, color, background, and effects of the text you've selected. The Sample box in the bottom of the screen shows you how your choices look. In the Alignment tab, you choose the alignment of text.

ENHANCING GRAPHS | 143

FIGURE 4.20

The Format Chart Title dialog box

If the x-axis labels on your graph bunch up and are difficult to read, you have three options: enlarge the graph, reduce the size of the label text, or change the orientation of the text so that the labels run vertically up the side of the data items instead of horizontally below the graph.

Adding Gridlines

Gridlines can add a sense of proportion to the graphs in your presentation. If you've got a series of bar charts but no gridlines, it may be difficult for someone in the fourteenth row to tell how one data series compares to another. Gridlines help make it obvious which data series outreaches the other—even when it's a close call.

PowerPoint allows you to add two different kinds of gridlines: horizontal and vertical. The gridlines are tied to the major tick marks in the axes, so if you want to change the spacing of the gridlines, you'll need to make modifications on the X or Y axis of your graph. Figure 4.21 shows how the chart looks with both vertical and horizontal gridlines.

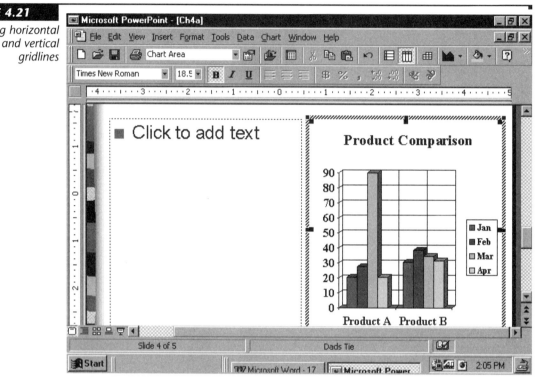

FIGURE 4.21

Adding horizontal and vertical gridlines

To change the gridlines settings, open the Chart menu and Chart Options; then click the Gridlines tab. The Gridlines dialog box appears, as shown in Figure 4.22. If you want to attach the gridlines to the minor gridlines—which means you'll have more of them in your graph—click Minor Gridlines. You might want to do this, for example, if you are graphing data series with data points close together; the minor gridlines will help you read the placement of the data. When you've finished making changes, click OK.

FIGURE 4.22
The Gridlines dialog box

Remember that the actual tick marks and increments are part of the axis settings. To change the spacing between gridlines, double-click on the axis you want to change.

Hiding and Displaying the Legend

The legend of your graph is like the key to a map; it shows viewers, at a glance, which data series is represented by which bar, color, line, or pie slice. By default, PowerPoint adds a legend to your graph. In some instances, you may want to remove the graph legend from the display, if only temporarily. This could give you more room for other items or save you from cluttering your slide unnecessarily when the data speaks for itself.

To hide the graph legend, display the Chart Options dialog box and click the Legend tab. Next click the Show Legend checkbox to remove the X. When you click OK to close the dialog box, the legend is gone. To redisplay the legend, open the Chart Options dialog box again and click the Show Legend checkbox.

Adding a Text Box

Another tool in the graphics toolbar allows you to add text to your graph. You might do this to call attention to a certain feature or add a note to the presentation slide.

To add a text box, click the Text Box tool and use the mouse to draw the box in the graph editing area. The cursor is positioned in the upper left corner of the new text box, ready to accept your text. Type the text for the note and click outside the box.

Once you add the text, you can change it easily: highlight the text and choose Format ➤ Font. Then make the necessary changes to font, style, color, size, and effect settings. Click OK when you're finished.

Specifying Color

Earlier you learned to choose the color of individual data items. Now you can use the Color tool to choose the background color of specific areas of your chart. For example, you might change the background color of the text note you just added.

Select the text box and then click the down-arrow beside the Fill Color tool. A pop-up palette of colors appears below the toolbar (see Figure 4.23).

Click the color you want. Instantly, the palette disappears and the color is applied to the selected element—in this case, the text box.

For more about which colors work best under which conditions, see Chapter 9, "The Dynamics of Color."

PowerPoint 97 gives you some additional choices for the way you fill the bars of your charts. Now, in addition to choosing the color for chart elements, you can add a custom touch by using pictures, textures, or gradient fill patterns for the chart items.

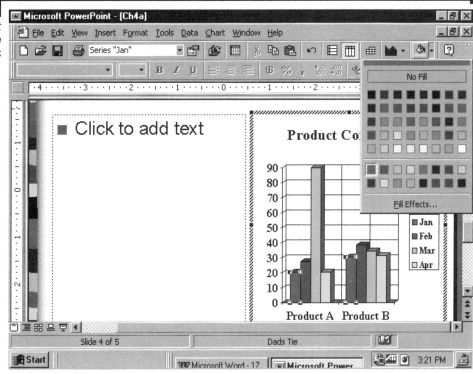

FIGURE 4.23
Selecting a different color for graph elements

Changing Patterns

Like color, pattern also affects the background of elements in your chart. After you select the item you want to change, you can choose from a variety of patterns by clicking the Fill Effects option in the color palette. This displays a dialog box that enables you to make more choices about the textures and patterns used in the chart. To see the available patterns, click the Pattern tab (see Figure 4.24). When you make your selection, the palette closes and the new setting is applied to the selected element.

FIGURE 4.24
Choosing a different pattern

Animating Charts

Trying to think of new ways to keep your audience interested? How about having charts grow right before their eyes? Now, with PowerPoint 97, you can animate charts so they change and grow as your audience watches.

To animate a chart, begin with the chart displayed on your screen. Make sure the regular toolbars—the Standard and Formatting toolbars—are displayed; you don't want the Graph toolbar displayed. Click the chart one time so the handles appear. Then open the Slide Show menu and choose Custom Animation. The Custom Animation dialog box appears, as shown in Figure 4.25.

Notice that the Chart Effects tab is selected. To choose what you want animated, click the Introduce Chart Elements down-arrow and select the option for the way you want the elements introduced: all at once, by Series, by Category, by Element in Series, or by Element in Category. Next, you can control the way the items appear and whether they are accompanied by a sound effect by choosing the options in the Entry animation and sound option boxes. Finally, if you want the element to be dimmed after it appears, you can set the After Animation option. Try out the effects you've selected by clicking Preview. When you are finished, click OK.

FIGURE 4.25
Animate a chart in the Custom Animation dialog box.

Chapter Summary

This chapter rounds out the discussion of graphs in your PowerPoint presentation. In this chapter, you've learned to create, edit, and enhance the appearance of your graphs. You found out how to choose a graph type, edit data values, add titles, labels, and legends, and make a variety of other changes. In the next chapter, you'll learn to add custom drawings to your PowerPoint slides.

Chapter 5

Picture This! Custom and Clip Art

FEATURING

Checking Out PowerPoint's Clip Art

Importing Art

Drawing Art

Modifying Art

Animating Art Objects

Picture This! Custom and Clip Art

As a society, and as a generation, we like pictures. Sure we can read text, but we expect photos, too. And graphs. And drawings, logos, and special design elements to keep our interest.

Not too many years ago, text was about as exciting as it got. When you made that presentation to the board about the new hummer motors for the pocket fans, you slapped a few acetate sheets full of bullet points on the projector and read off your lines of text. The board approved or denied your ideas based on whether you held their attention long enough to get your point across.

Today, the presentations you create can definitely hold attention. Your slides can wake up with some of PowerPoint's clip art—if you're not sure what will look right where, you can even let PowerPoint suggest what art you should use. Use art files created in another program, scanned images, or commercial clip art in your PowerPoint presentations. You can even create your own art on screen using PowerPoint's Drawing tools.

This chapter introduces you to your artistic possibilities and helps you make a graphic statement in your PowerPoint presentation.

Checking Out PowerPoint's Clip Art

PowerPoint strives to make things as simple as possible, so adding art to a slide can be as easy as point-and-click. This section explores working with clip art and the options open to you.

Letting AutoClipArt Make the Choice

If design isn't your strong point, you may not feel comfortable deciding what kind of art you want to use to illustrate the text in your presentation. For that reason, PowerPoint 95 includes AutoClipArt, an automated feature that suggests what art to use where. The program searches for key words in the presentation's text by which it has indexed pieces of clip art. Each piece of art in the Clip Art Gallery is assigned a few descriptive words, such as *Focus*, *Quality*, and *Goal*, by the program developers. You can also add your own index words, as you'll see in the section, "Organizing Clip Art," later in this chapter. Finally, PowerPoint 97 adds additional keywords, so now AutoClipArt gives you even more art choices related to your presentation text.

To use AutoClipArt, display the slide to which you want to add clip art, then choose Tools ➤ AutoClipArt. You'll see the AutoClipArt dialog box shown in Figure 5.1.

FIGURE 5.1

Auto ClipArt selects art based on key words in your presentation.

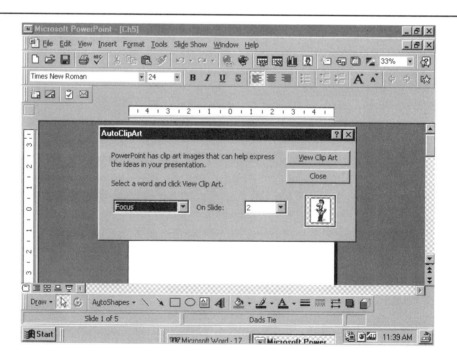

As you can see in Figure 5.1, PowerPoint found the word *Focus*. (You can choose other words PowerPoint recognizes from the drop-down list beside the word.) Click the View Clip Art button to view all clip art associated with the word *Focus*. A popup dialog box tells you that you can find more clip art on the CD-ROM packaged with PowerPoint. Click OK to close the dialog box. Then the ClipArt Gallery dialog box appears, showing you the pieces of clip art linked to that word (see Figure 5.2). Notice that the words used to index the clip art appear in the Description line at the bottom of the Gallery window.

FIGURE 5.2
The clip art associated with the selected word appears in the Gallery when you click on View Clip Art.

To choose the art you want, click the clip art and then click Insert. The art is then added to your slide.

Adding New Clip Art Slides

The AutoClipArt feature is helpful when you need art suggestions in a flash and aren't interested in experimenting with the many other clip art offerings PowerPoint includes. In some cases, however, you may want to scout around in the ClipArt Gallery to choose just the art you want.

When you want to add clip art to a slide, start with the *Double-click to add clip art* box. If necessary, create one by clicking the New Slide button and choosing one of the slides with clip art already mapped out for you (see Figure 5.3). Choose the slide you want and click OK.

FIGURE 5.3

The New Slide dialog box includes two slides with clip art blocked out.

When the new slide appears, double-click the clip art area. The Microsoft Clip Gallery 3.0 appears, as shown in Figure 5.4.

FIGURE 5.4

The Microsoft Clip Gallery 3.0 stores and organizes all the clip art that comes with PowerPoint.

> You can also choose Insert ➤ Picture ➤ Clip Art to display the Clip Gallery so you can add clip art to a slide.

If you see the clip art you want, click it in the Pictures window, or click the down arrow at the end of the scroll bar in the Pictures window to see additional pictures. If you know the category of the art you want, click it in the Categories window. For example, to see art that has something to do with music, click the Music category. The Pictures window changes to show you the clip art that falls into that category (see Figure 5.5).

FIGURE 5.5

Choosing a different clip art category

FIGURE 5.6

The Clip Gallery is added to the slide.

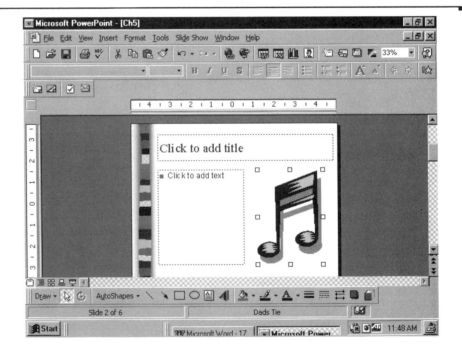

Finding Specific Clip Art

If a specific piece of art is eluding you, click the Find button in the Clip Gallery to display the Find Clip dialog box shown in Figure 5.7. In the Keywords box, enter a phrase that describes the clip art, or leave it set to All Keywords (the default). In the Filename Containing box, type any characters you know that appear in the clip art's filename, and in Clip Type, choose the file format in which the clip art is saved (BMP, TIF, etc.). When you've entered your search criteria, click Find Now. The Clip Gallery shows the results of the search in the Clip Art tab of the Gallery. On the left side of the window, in the Categories list, [Results of Last Find] is the selected category. Click Close to exit the Clip Gallery.

FIGURE 5.7
Searching for a specific piece of clip art

Organizing Clip Art

You can create a full library of clip art from all kinds of different sources: mail-order catalogs, other programs, magazine CD-ROMs, and online communications services.

(We'll discuss *how* you accumulate these masses of clip art in the "Importing Clip Art" section later in this chapter.) If you get into the clip-art accumulation habit, you'll need a way of organizing the files you gather. Luckily, you can display and organize all those files right there in the ClipArt Gallery by using the Edit Categories button.

To organize your clip art files, display the Gallery window (choose Insert ➤ Picture ➤ Clip Art) and then click the Edit Categories button. The Edit Category List dialog box appears, as shown in Figure 5.8.

FIGURE 5.8

Keeping your clip art files straight in the Edit Category List box

Consider your categories carefully before you delete one in the ClipArt Gallery—once you delete the category, it and all the clip art it represents will be unavailable for display.

In this dialog box, you can create new categories for clip art, or delete or rename ones you already have. If you want to create a new category, click the New Category button and type the name of the new category; then click OK. To delete a category, simply click the one in the list you want to delete and then click Delete Category. Rename a category by clicking the one you want to rename, clicking Rename Category, typing the new category name, and clicking OK. Exit the dialog box by clicking Close when you are finished.

The Clip Properties dialog box appears when you click the Clip Properties button in the Clip Gallery. This dialog box enables you to enter a description for the selected art and choose or create a category for the art (see Figure 5.9).

FIGURE 5.9
Changing the properties of selected clip art

The Keywords line of Clip Properties contains the keywords for which AutoClipArt searches when it looks for a piece of clip art for your presentation. You might have a piece of clip art showing a sunset, for example, and enter the words *sunset, vacation,* and *get-away* in the Keywords line. Then, whenever your presentation includes one of those three words and you use AutoClipArt, that piece of sunset clip art will always be among your choices of art automatically selected.

Importing Art

You'll be able to get clip art from all kinds of places. Other programs—Microsoft's and otherwise—include clip art libraries for use in word processing, desktop publishing, and multimedia applications. You can purchase clip art collections from third-party manufacturers, and you can download countless clip art files from the Internet. The PowerPoint CD-ROM includes additional clip art, as does PowerPoint Central, a source for graphics, sounds, templates, and more.

Another source for clip art is a direct link to the Internet via the Microsoft Clip Gallery 3.0. In the lower right corner of the dialog box, you see a button with an icon of the world. This is the *Connect to the Web for additional clips* button. If your PC is Internet-ready, you can click the button to connect to the Internet and download clips. Figure 5.10 shows the Microsoft Web site you connect to when you click this button in the Clip Gallery dialog box.

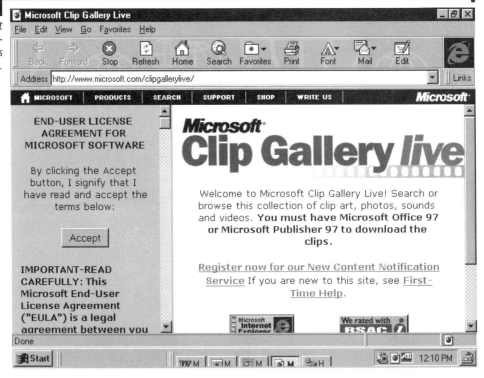

FIGURE 5.10

Clicking "Connect to the Web for additional clips" takes you to this Web site.

Another way to bring that creative flash to your presentations is to use art objects created in other programs, whether they're snazzy pop-art renderings that you created in another program or funky graphics from CompuServe or another online service. You can import your art files using the Picture command in the Insert menu.

NOTE

Notice that now we're talking about art *objects*, as opposed to clip art. When you add clip art to PowerPoint, use the Import Clips button in the Clip Gallery dialog box. When you insert art objects into your PowerPoint slides, you import the art file with Insert ➤ Picture.

PowerPoint is flexible when it comes to art-file tolerance. PowerPoint will accept art files in any of the formats shown in Table 5.1.

TABLE 5.1: IMPORTING ART FILES

Extension	Full Name	Possible Programs
BMP	Windows bitmap	Most popular paint programs, including Windows Paintbrush, PC Paint, Paintshow, and Painter
DIB	Windows bitmap	Windows paint applications, like Windows Paintbrush
EPS	Encapsulated Postscript	Any object-oriented program; PowerPoint, Adobe Illustrator, Freehand, Micrografx Designer
GIF	Graphics Interchange Format	An image format used extensively on the Internet; originally created by CompuServe
JPEG	Joint Photographics Expert Group	A form of graphics file used on the Internet that compresses images into a smaller file without significant loss of quality
PCT	Macintosh PICT	Macintosh paint programs like Superpaint, MacPaint, and Painter
WMF	Windows Metafiles	Windows Draw packages such as Micrografx Designer

If your graphics program won't save files in a PowerPoint accepted format, don't despair. There are several graphics file conversion utilities available that will change an art file from one format to another so you can use it in different applications.

GIFConverter and Paint Shop Pro for Windows are two popular examples of graphics file conversion utilities. Other file conversion utilities are available as shareware on the major online services. The MULTIMEDIA and GRAPHICS forums on CompuServe are good places to look for graphics utilities, for example.

To import an art file into your presentation, choose Insert ➤ Picture ➤ From File to open the Insert Picture dialog box (see Figure 5.11). If you want to use clip art from another directory or drive, click the Look in: down arrow and choose the folder you want to see from the list. Choose the file type from the Files of Type box. When you've selected the file you want, click OK.

FIGURE 5.11
The Insert Picture dialog box

If the art you import doesn't look right, you may be able to clean it up using a few simple editing techniques. See the section "Modifying Art" for more on changing the art on your slides.

Drawing Art

There's a blank spot in the middle of the first page of your presentation. The boss is looking over your shoulder. "Can't you just draw something in there real fast?" she asks. "Like our new logo or something?" Your pulse quickens. "It doesn't have to be anything perfect," she says.

Oh, good. *Now* you feel better. Thirty minutes until the corporate meeting and she wants you to draw the company logo. Get a piece of company letterhead to use as a reference and roll up your shirtsleeves. Lucky for you, PowerPoint's drawing tools are easy to use and make working with the objects you draw an easy task. This section gives you the basics of drawing with PowerPoint—enough to get that logo done, hopefully, in thirty minutes or less.

The Difference between Drawing and Painting

In the world of computer art, you'll find two different camps: drawing programs and painting programs. They may sound alike, but they're not:

- A *drawing program* creates illustrations by putting together a series of shapes, lines, and curves. The *objects*, as they are called, are then grouped together into an object you can move, resize, copy, paste—whatever—without distorting it or losing any of the quality. This type of art is known as *object-oriented* graphics.

- A *painting program* creates illustrations by "painting" individual dots on the screen in the colors you select. These items are not shapes, they are just patterns of dots. That means that you *cannot* select them to resize or manipulate them. When you edit a paint graphic, you do so by changing the color of the individual dots in the picture. Painted graphics cannot be resized—especially enlarged—without a loss of quality. This type of art is often called *bit-mapped*, or *raster*, graphics.

If you are working with scanned photos in your presentations, you may want to touch them up with a paint program before you import them into PowerPoint. Scanned photos are saved as raster graphics, and in order to get the best possible quality and highest contrast, they may need some tweaking before you use them in your PowerPoint presentations. Popular paint programs with great bitmap editing capabilities include Adobe Photoshop and Fractal Design Painter.

PowerPoint is a drawing (not painting) program. You use the various drawing tools to create shapes and lines and then combine, or group, them to make the complete object. You can change the color, pattern, rotation, and a variety of other object settings once you've grouped components into the object. If you later want to change the drawing, you can ungroup the object into its original pieces to make the modifications you want.

Even though PowerPoint only has draw capabilities, you can import raster graphics files into PowerPoint for use in your slides. Common extensions for raster graphics files are PCX, TIF, BMP, JPEG, and GIF.

Planning the Art You Want

Taking a few minutes to think about what you want to accomplish with the art you create is a good investment of your creative time. Here are a few questions that may help you plan your illustrations:

- What is the tone of the art you're creating? It might be a technical illustration, a light-hearted cartoon, a businesslike graphic, or a dramatic logo.
- Will the art you create be used only on one slide, or on every slide of your publication? If you want the art to appear on every slide, put the art on the Slide Master.
- Does the art need to be an exact size? If so, make sure you use the ruler when drawing or resizing.
- Is the art a file you've downloaded from an online service or borrowed from a clip art collection? Be sure you check out any licensing regulations that apply. Some art is available for all to use, but there may be some regulations about using the clip art for profit. An information file (.INF or .TXT) or the collection's Help information will inform you of any restrictions on uses of the art.
- Do you want to create your own art from scratch or modify existing clip art?

You can use the Edit ➤ Cut and Edit ➤ Paste commands to move art from the slide where you created it to its final location.

Displaying the Drawing Tools

Before you can begin drawing your own objects, you've got to display the drawing tools PowerPoint has available and create a workspace. First, start with a blank slide. Click the New Slide button and select the blank slide from the lower right corner of the New Slide dialog box. The blank slide appears in Slide View; notice the drawing tools along the bottom of the window (see Figure 5.12).

FIGURE 5.12

The drawing tools in Slide View appear on the bottom of the screen.

If you don't know what a certain tool in the Drawing Toolbar does, just put the pointer on it and the name of the tool appears. This is the ToolTips feature, an instant help flashcard that tells you what you're looking at before you have time to ask.

Figure 5.13 shows a sample ToolTip when the pointer is positioned on the Rectangle tool.

FIGURE 5.13

When you position the pointer on a tool, a ToolTip is displayed, telling you the name of that tool.

Even with the information in the ToolTip, you may be left wondering how you'll use the various drawing tools. Table 5.2 lists all the drawing tools in Slide view and briefly describes each. PowerPoint 97 now includes a Bezier curve tool that enables you to make accurate arcs on your presentation slides.

TABLE 5.2: DRAWING TOOLS

Tool	Name	Description
Draw ▼	Draw menu	Displays a pop-up menu of drawing options
▷	Select Objects	Chooses objects on the screen
↻	Free Rotate Tool	Rotates the selected object
AutoShapes ▼	AutoShapes menu	Displays a palette of shapes from which you can choose

TABLE 5.2: DRAWING TOOLS (CONTINUED)

Tool	Name	Description
	Line Tool	Creates lines
	Arrow Tool	Adds arrowheads to the line, arc, or polygon you select
	Rectangle Tool	Creates rectangles
	Oval Tool	Draws circles and ovals
	Text Box Tool	Creates text objects
	Insert WordArt Tool	Allows you to draw a WordArt box
	Fill Color	Fills the selected object with the color and pattern selected
	Line Color	Applies the selected line options to the current object
	Font Color	Enables you to choose the color for selected text
	Line Style	Allows you to choose the style of the line used in the selected object
	Dash Style	Creates a dashed or dotted line for the current object
	Arrow Style	Enables you to choose the type of arrowheads you want
	Shadow	Adds (or removes) the default shadow to (from) a selected object
	3-D	Makes the selected item three-dimensional

Using Drawing Tools

Most basic drawing tools—Line, Rectangle, Oval, and Arrow—require the same steps to get objects on the screen:

1. Click the tool you want.
2. Move the pointer to the work area.
3. Hold down the mouse button while dragging the mouse in the direction you desire. This "draws" the object.
4. Release the mouse button when you are finished.

The Shift key is of special interest when you're using the basic drawing tools. If you are using the Oval tool, for example, pressing Shift while you draw gives you a perfectly round circle. If you press Shift while you use the Line tool, you get a perfectly straight line. In short, if you want a precise and symmetrical object, press Shift while drawing.

MASTERING THE OPPORTUNITIES

The Beginner's Guide to Electronic Drawing

If you're not formally trained in computer graphics, it may feel a little odd to use a mouse for drawing. If this is your first time working with drawing on-screen, take a few minutes to consider these rules of thumb:

Have a reference—For best results, sketch out what you want to draw, or work from a model, such as a photo or diagram. Having something to refer to helps you unlock any potential creative blocks you may run up against when you start drawing. (Remember that if you're using someone else's image as a reference, you may need to think about licensing permissions or credits.)

Know your tools—Before you start drawing, explore the tools you've got available in PowerPoint. Display the drawing toolbars and spend a few minutes playing around with the tools to see how they work. Check out the colors and line styles and look for the patterns and textures. (More about this later in this chapter.) In short, learn what choices you've got ***before*** you begin making choices—this can help you turn an ordinary drawing into something that really gets attention.

> **MASTERING THE OPPORTUNITIES CONTINUED**
>
> ***Don't draw unnecessarily***—If you've got something on file that will work for your purposes, or you've got a saved art file that will do with just a little tweaking, go for the shortcut and save yourself some work. Do the leisurely on-screen doodling at home, not in a time-sensitive, pressured situation like the workplace. Think about any options you have for acquiring the art before you try to create it yourself.
>
> ***Create an art library***—Once you begin creating your own art, be sure to store it in a library of art you can use again and again. You can add your art to the ClipArt Gallery (you found out how earlier in this chapter), or you can simply save the art to disk and file it away someplace safe. It's often helpful to print a copy of the art and label it with the file name so you can easily find it again later.
>
> ***Changing is (usually) easier than starting again***—Especially at first, drawing on screen can be difficult; there's a definite learning curve involved in using the tools and options as expediently and accurately as possible. Even though you may be tempted to wipe out all you've done and start again when frustration strikes, remember that it's usually easier to modify what you've drawn than it is to start from scratch. Resize boxes and lines, relayer objects, change colors—but try to work with what you've done before you scrap it all and start over. It might save you minutes—or hours—recreating the basics of a drawing you could have recycled.

If you don't like what you just drew, press Del while the handles are still displayed to delete the object.

Using AutoShapes

Object-oriented drawing is the process of putting objects—lines and shapes—together to create an image. That means that many of the items you create with PowerPoint's drawing tools will be composed of shapes. To help you draw shapes quickly and accurately, PowerPoint includes AutoShapes. AutoShapes are predrawn shapes you can apply to your own drawings. When you click the AutoShapes button in the Drawing toolbar, a popup menu of AutoShapes palettes appears (see Figure 5.14).

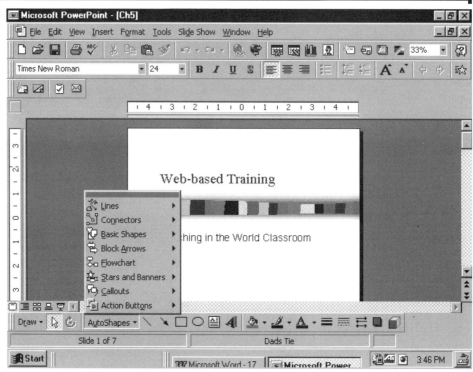

FIGURE 5.14

Displaying the AutoShapes menu

Choosing AutoShape Groups

PowerPoint 97 includes new AutoShape groups. Now you can choose from stars and banners, callouts, block arrows, connectors, flowchart elements, and action buttons. To see the individual shapes within each AutoShape group, click the AutoShape button, and position the pointer on the group you want to see. A palette of choices appears so you can make your choice.

You can "tear off" the AutoShapes palette and move it anywhere on screen. Click on the palette's title bar and drag it to the new screen location.

Drawing one of the shapes from the AutoShapes palette is just like drawing a shape in the Drawing palette: click the tool you want, move the pointer to the work area, and click and drag the mouse to draw the shape. When the shape is the size and proportion you want, release the mouse button. Figure 5.15 shows a star drawn with an AutoShapes tool.

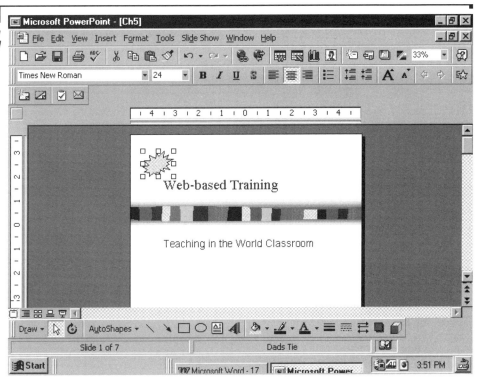

FIGURE 5.15
Adding a shape with an AutoShape tool

Setting AutoShape Options

Another new feature of PowerPoint 97 that impacts the AutoShapes is the ability to change 2-D into 3-D objects. You can also control the way lighting reflects on the image—showing where the point of light hits the object. You also have the option of adding shadows with different perspectives to AutoShape drawings.

To display the AutoShape options, select the AutoShape you want to modify, open the Format menu and choose AutoShape. The Format AutoShape dialog box appears, as shown in Figure 5.16.

FIGURE 5.16

Setting AutoShape options in the Format AutoShape dialog box

In the Format AutoShape dialog box, you can change the colors and lines, size, and position of the object. Here you find options for making the object semi-transparent or opaque. You can also create a shape that precisely matches the measurements you need or occupies a specific area of a slide. When you're finished making selections, click OK to close the dialog box and return to your presentation.

Once you draw a shape in PowerPoint, you can enter text inside it by clicking the text tool and then clicking the shape and typing the text. You can even rotate the object using the Free Rotate Tool, and the text stays put inside the shape—that is, the text is essentially glued to the shape and moves however the shape moves.

If you want to add artwork to a graph you've created, you display graphics mode by double-clicking the graph. This displays the graph in graphics editing mode and you can easily access the drawing tools.

Modifying Art

You now know the basic ways of getting art into your presentation: draw from PowerPoint's ClipArt Gallery, import it from another source, or create it yourself using the drawing tools. No matter how you bring the art to your PowerPoint slides, you have the option of changing the art to fit the image you've got in your mind.

One of the great things about multimedia is that no presentation is done until you say so. Just because you use a piece of PowerPoint's clip art doesn't mean you have to use it as-is. You can use PowerPoint's drawing tools and color and pattern palettes to change the look of the art until you get just the right effect.

You might want to group or ungroup objects, rotate or flip objects, change an object's line thickness, color, or pattern, or change the way objects are layered on the screen. This section gives you a quick overview of art editing techniques.

Basic Art Editing

The basics of resizing, copying, pasting, and cutting objects in PowerPoint are the same no matter what the content of the object. You resize an art object the same way you resize a text object—just click it and then drag its corner. (If you've added text to the object, as described earlier, the text is resized with the object.) Clip art is copied and pasted just like graphs are—just use Edit ➤ Copy and Edit ➤ Paste or drag-and-drop the item from slide to slide.

The fastest way to bring up the editing commands is to click the right mouse button while the pointer is positioned on the object. When you do that, the small popup menu shown in Figure 5.17 appears.

FIGURE 5.17
Display art editing options with a right mouse click.

The editing menu contains the usual commands—Cut, Copy, and Paste. You also see a few new commands. Custom Animation enables you to animate the object you just drew. This gives you the freedom to perform some snazzy onscreen calisthenics and really grab your viewer's attention. Other options enable you to further customize the art object you have selected. When you are finished with the popup menu, click outside the area or press Esc to close the menu.

Editing an Image with Format Picture

A new feature with PowerPoint 97 enables you to edit your images within the program. You can use the Format Picture dialog box to change a variety of things about the piece of art you've selected. Start by clicking the image and then open the Format menu and choose Picture. The Format Picture dialog box then appears, as Figure 5.18 shows.

BASIC ART EDITING | 177

FIGURE 5.18

You can edit graphics by using the Format Picture dialog box.

The Format Picture dialog box includes five tabs:

- **Colors and Lines,** which enables you to choose the line color, style, and arrows for the art;
- **Size,** so you can determine the size of the image;
- **Position,** which enables you to control cropping and brightness;
- **Picture,** which gives you control over cropping and color adjustments;
- **Text box,** which is disabled for graphic images.

Make your selections and changes and click OK to return to the slide.

For more about using Animation Effects, see "Animating Your Art Objects," later in this chapter.

Grouping and Ungrouping Objects

Once you learn to edit the individual shapes in your drawing, you may want to put them together to create a bigger effect. Because of the way object-oriented drawings go together—piece by piece—it would be difficult to move and/or resize several shapes at once without some means of lumping all the pieces together (grouping).

Even the clip art you use is comprised of a bunch of small shapes and lines. For example, consider the clip art in Figure 5.19. As you can see, the world graphic has been "ungrouped"—that is, separated into its individual circles, rectangles, lines, and so on. It would be a nightmare to try to move each of these pieces individually.

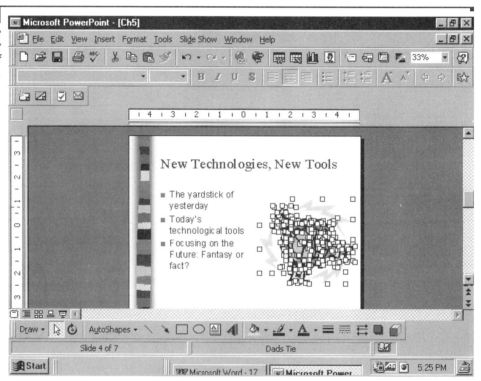

FIGURE 5.19

Ungrouping a piece of clip art may result in dozens of small objects.

When you group objects, you combine them into one. This allows PowerPoint to treat the whole group as a single object so that when you cut, copy, paste, move, or resize the object, it is treated as one piece of art instead of a bunch of separate objects electronically glued together.

GROUPING AND UNGROUPING OBJECTS   179

WARNING

When you try to ungroup some clip art, you may get a warning telling you that the art is an imported object and not a group. This means that in order to ungroup the object and reduce it to its individual elements, the file must be converted to a PowerPoint object, meaning that any OLE links will be broken. If it's not important for you to maintain a link with the creating application (meaning that the object is not likely to change), click OK. Otherwise, click Cancel.

To group a number of objects into one object, select the Select Objects tool and drag a rectangle around the objects. Then choose Draw ➤ Group from the Drawing toolbar. The objects are grouped into one and their individual handles replaced by four group handles, one at each corner of the newly grouped object (see Figure 5.20).

FIGURE 5.20

Grouping many objects into one enables you to move, resize, and copy items easily.

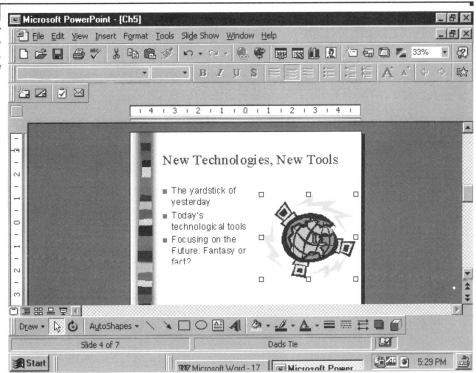

Layering Art Objects

Another concept along the lines of the group/ungroup thing involves the use of layering. We've already established that PowerPoint's method of art—object-oriented drawing—enables you to produce drawings by combining shapes, lines, and curves. In order to get the right look, you need to be able to put some items in front of other items.

You can change layer arrangement of your objects in four different ways. Each operation starts with you displaying the Draw menu in the Drawing toolbar and choosing the Order option. Then select one of the following, depending on what you want to do with the selected item:

- **Bring to Front** moves the selected object in front of all objects.
- **Send to Back** sends the selected object behind all objects.
- **Bring Forward** moves the object one layer forward.
- **Send Backward** moves the object one layer backward.

Changing Object Layering

Before you can choose any of these commands or tools, you need to select the object you want to use. In Figure 5.21, one of the shapes has been moved to the front of the others using the Bring to Front command.

Before you use the Bring to Front command, ungroup the objects you're working with. Otherwise, Bring to Front will not be available.

Moving an object to the back of other objects is also easy. Just select the object and choose Draw ➤ Order ➤ Send to Back. If you're following along, you'll notice a small problem—sending the object to the back sends it too far back—so you need to click the Bring Forward tool to move the shape up one layer.

To move an object all the way to the front or back of a stack of objects, use Bring to Front or Send to Back. To move an object forward or backward one layer at a time, use Bring Forward or Send Backward.

FIGURE 5.21
Moving an object to the front of other objects

Changing Object Color and Fill Effects

Because so much of PowerPoint is done for you, the first time you draw a shape you may wind up with a color you didn't expect. You can change any object's color easily, however, by first selecting the object and then clicking the Fill Color tool (in the Drawing toolbar). When you click this tool, the popup box in Figure 5.22 appears.

Click one of the colors in the color scheme laid out for you at the top of the box, and the object is then displayed in the new color.

Other commands in the Fill Color popup menu include No Fill, Automatic, More Fill Colors, or Fill Effects, all of which allow you to choose additional options for the color of the object. No Fill removes all coloring inside the object, Automatic colors the object in whatever color is chosen as the default, More Fill Colors gives you a rainbow of options from which to choose, and Fill Effects enables you to choose a fill color that shows shading in a horizontal, vertical, or diagonal format. When you click Fill Effects, the Fill Effects dialog box appears, as shown in Figure 5.23.

FIGURE 5.22
Choosing a new color

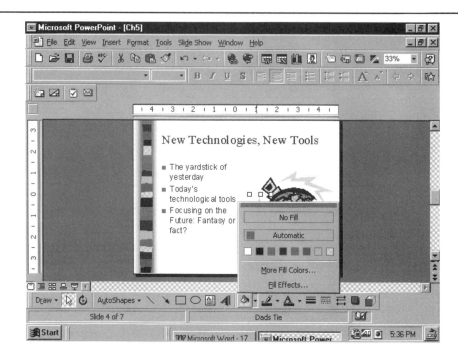

FIGURE 5.23
You can control the shading of a fill color by choosing the shade style and color balance.

LAYERING ART OBJECTS | **183**

TIP

If you try out the Fill Effects feature—and you should (it's cool)—be sure to click the Preview button to preview the art object before you click OK and return to the slide.

If you choose Pattern in the Fill Effects dialog box, the Pattern fill dialog box shown in Figure 5.24 appears. Here you can choose a different pattern for the inside of the object.

FIGURE 5.24

Choosing a basic pattern for the object's fill area

The Texture choice in the Fill Effects dialog box displays a large selection of textures (see Figure 5.25). You can select from woodgrain or marbled textures to create just the right effect for your graphics, backgrounds, or special text.

FIGURE 5.25

Special textures are now available for art objects.

If you want to add textures from another source for special effects, click the Other button in the Textured Fill dialog box to display the Add Texture dialog box. Now you can choose the drive and folder from which you want to add the texture.

Now, in PowerPoint 97, you can use a picture in an object you are recoloring. Display the Fill Effects dialog box and click the Picture tab. Click Select Picture and choose the picture file from the dialog box that appears. Click OK to add the picture to the object.

If you choose Automatic in the Fill Color popup menu, PowerPoint makes the object the same color as the currently selected Fill Color.

Finally, the More Fill Colors option lets you mix a color not displayed on the palette at the top of the popup menu. When you choose More Fill Colors, the Colors dialog box appears, as shown in Figure 5.26. You can choose the color you want or click Custom to create one of your own. For more about working with colors in PowerPoint, see Chapter 9, "The Dynamics of Color."

FIGURE 5.26
Choosing a different color for the selected object

Changing Line Color and Style

The internal color and pattern of an object is not all you have to worry about. You might want to change the line color and style as well. To do this, select the object and either choose Format ➤ Colors and Lines or position the mouse pointer on the object and click the right mouse button, then choose Colors and Lines. Either way, the Colors and Lines tab of the Format AutoShape dialog box appears, as Figure 5.27 shows. (*Note*: If you selected an object that is *not* an AutoShape, the Format Objects dialog box will be displayed on your screen.)

FIGURE 5.27

The Colors and Lines tab enables you to select different fill and line color style settings.

Although you made your color choices in the Fill Color popup menu, you can also change the fill color in Colors and Lines. You can also make four different choices about the way the selected line appears, specifying:

- The color of the line
- The thickness and style of the line
- Whether the line is a dashed, dotted, or continuous line
- Whether the line has an arrowhead

Click the down arrow of the option you want to select and make your choice from the displayed list. The lines in the selected objects are changed.

PowerPoint 97 gives you the option of choosing a variety of arrowhead styles when you use the Arrow tool in the Drawing toolbar. You can change the width, heighth, and color of arrowheads used in the images you create.

Animating Art Objects

One of the neatest features of the newest version of PowerPoint is the ability to animate objects. What is animation? The ability to move your objects—text, graphics, charts, logos—across, up, or down the slide. You can have text screeching into place, birds flying over the title, charts levitating from their places on slides, and hundreds of other effects you dream up yourself.

Start by selecting the object you want to animate; then click the right mouse button. When the popup menu appears, click Custom Animation. At first, all the options are dimmed, but click the down arrow in the Entry Animation and Sound area and select any option other than No Effect. The dialog box then looks like the one displayed in Figure 5.28.

FIGURE 5.28
Using Custom Animation to animate art objects

In the Effects area, click the first down arrow to display the available animation choices (see Figure 5.29). As you can see, you've got a wide range of choices. Click the one you want to select it.

FIGURE 5.29

You can select the animation effect you want from the displayed list.

To add a sound to the animation, click the Sound down arrow to see your choices (see Figure 5.30). PowerPoint comes equipped with several special sound effects, and you can also get a number of other sounds from a variety of third-party sources. (For more about adding sound effects and sound objects to your presentations, see Chapter 6, "Adding Sound.")

You can make choices about the way in which text in animated on the slide. Do you want text items to fly in, one by one, or do you want all text to appear as a block? Your choices are in these areas.

To see how the animation effects work, click the Preview button. Then, when you're ready, click OK to return to the slide.

You can add more animation effects by displaying the Animation Effects toolbar and working with those tools. Display the toolbar by clicking Animation Effects in the Formatting toolbar at the top of the screen. To find out more about animating your slide objects, see Chapter 8, "Producing a Slide Show."

FIGURE 5.30
PowerPoint includes a number of sounds you can assign to the animation.

Chapter Summary

This chapter has introduced you to a number of artistic considerations, including possible sources of artwork and the most essential editing procedures.

The next chapter introduces you to the idea of adding sound to your PowerPoint presentations—putting the multi in multimedia and allowing you to capture and hold your audience's attention.

Chapter 6

Adding Sound

FEATURING

Sound Basics

The Multimedia-Ready PC

Using PowerPoint's Sound Effects

Adding Sound to Animations

Inserting Sound Objects

Recording Your Own Sound

Reviewing Different Sound Choices

Some Sound Advice for Presenting

Adding Sound

Have you ever watched television with the sound turned off? People gesture, move, make faces—and most of it escapes you. You may be able to tell roughly what the plot line is, but you'll lose the intricacies of the story without hearing what's going on. Similarly, a football game loses some of its excitement without the roar of the crowd, the speeding car seems slower without the squealing tires, and the poignant moment loses some of its poignancy without the lilting music in the background.

Music or sound effects in your presentations can make a big difference in the way your audience perceives what you're showing them. Just a few years ago, our simple presentations didn't incorporate sound—our own voices were the only sound we worried about. Multimedia has changed all that. Now you can add sound in the form of music or special effects to reinforce points, hold your audience's interest, add a spark of humor, or provide a smooth, sophisticated opening.

This chapter explores what adding sound to your presentations can mean in PowerPoint. After a brief exploration of sound basics, you'll learn to add PowerPoint sound effects to your slides, use sound files from other sources, and even record your own sounds for use in a presentation.

Many of the special sound effects you use in your presentation will be tied to other things; for example, you'll play a sound when you advance a slide, build bullet text, or use a special text effect. Fly From Left is just one example of the special effects discussed in Chapter 8, "Putting It All Together: Producing the Slide Show."

 MASTERING THE OPPORTUNITIES

What a Difference a Sound Makes

Sound can add a whole new dimension to your presentation. Here's how:

Support animations—When you have text "Fly From Left" to the center of the screen, you can make it screech to a halt with a sound effect.

Link sounds to actions—Assign a special click or other unusual sound effect (a bell ringing, a buzzer sounding, the click of a typewriter key being pressed, etc.) to play when you click the mouse on a particular button.

Provide instructions—You're designing a self-running presentation that customers can display at the upcoming trade show. You know that many of the potential customers may not be familiar or comfortable with computers, so you want to make the presentation as easy to use as possible. You can record and attach an instruction to a particular slide, such as "Click here to start our product demonstration!" so customers know exactly what to do when the slide appears.

Set the atmosphere—You want to open your presentation with a segment of a theme song affiliated with your company.

Add humor—You want to use an audio clip of Porky Pig's "Th-th-th-th-at's-all, folks!" at the end of your presentation. You even get to watch cartoons all afternoon so you can tape Porky signing off.

Sound Basics

If you are trying your hand at a multimedia presentation for the first time, sound may be a new issue for you to deal with. We'll start out this basic introduction with an introduction to some of the common terms and acronyms you'll find linked up to sound discussions.

A Sound Glossary

Sound file   A sound file is the analog or digital recording of music or a sound effect.

Sound object   When you add a sound element to a selected slide, PowerPoint treats the sound as an object on the slide. You can have the sound play automatically or you can manually control the sound by clicking the object. See the section "Adding Sounds from Other Sources" to learn more about inserting and working with sound objects.

Sound card   A sound card is a special interface card that plugs into your computer to make it capable of high-quality sound reproduction. Having a sound card means you can play audio CDs, add full-score symphonic background to your presentations, or play cool sound effects for the games you play when work is done. Without a sound card, your sophisticated sound effects will be tinny noise.

PC speaker   All PCs come equipped with a PC speaker. The PC speaker is a small, bare-minimum device that broadcasts the beeps, squeaks, and dings affiliated with basic system functions. The PC speaker cannot produce the sound quality you need for a multimedia presentation, however. You'll need a sound card, which offers more sophisticated sound capability, for that.

Waveform file   A waveform file (*.WAV) is an analog recording of a sound—like something you might record on a cassette recorder or your answering machine. Sounds are actually waves in the air—the deeper the sound, the longer the wave. When you speak into a microphone to record a voice-over note or introduction, you are creating a waveform file. You can play waveform files with a basic PC speaker, although they won't sound very good.

MIDI file   MIDI (Musical Instrument Digital Interface) is a digital format for saving audio files. A MIDI file (*.MID) is not a representation of the sound waves (like a waveform file) but rather digital instructions of how to re-create the sounds. Think of a MIDI file as the sheet music your sound card uses to play a sound. MIDI files can be played only on a computer with a sound card and speakers.

Sampling   Sampling is the process of recording a sound as a computer file. For your presentations, you might want to sample sounds like footsteps, doors opening or closing, a car accelerating, a crowd cheering, or a number of other special effects. Or you might not—sampling is not for the faint-hearted, and bulletin boards and online services, as well as many vendors, can provide you with a wealth of sound effects and music clips. Exhaust these resources before trying to sample sounds yourself.

Sound Recorder   The Sound Recorder (choose Start ➤ Programs ➤ Accessories ➤ Multimedia ➤ Sound Recorder) is a special Windows applet that enables you to record sounds for use in multimedia projects (see Figure 6.1). Only use the Sound Recorder to record simple, short sounds—the sounds are saved in WAV format and waveform files can be huge. For more about working with the Sound Recorder to add sound effects to your presentation, see "Recording Your Own Sounds," later in this chapter.

Media Player   Media Player (choose Start ➤ Programs ➤ Accessories ➤ Multimedia ➤ Multimedia Player) is another Windows applet that enables you to coordinate multimedia features, including sound, animation, and video (see Figure 6.2). You can play WAV and MID files, or a music CD, using Media Player.

Voice-Over Narration   Now, in PowerPoint 97, you can record your own narration for your presentations. Simply choose Slide Show ➤ Record Narration and make your recording.

FIGURE 6.1

With the Sound Recorder, you can easily record voice-over notes and sound effects

FIGURE 6.2
The Windows Media Player enables you to play and work with multimedia objects

WAV and MID Sound Files: Which Do You Need?

As you learned in the last section, WAV files are waveform files that save the sound you record in a format similar to the one in which the sounds exist: as sound waves.

WAV files give you good-quality sound, but because they store so much information, WAV files grow to be enormous very quickly. A five-second sound clip—that's a full second shorter than the Microsoft Sound that plays when you start Windows 95—takes up over 50KB. The longer your recording, the higher the storage considerations. Depending on the amount of RAM in your computer, you may find yourself maxing out with WAV files very quickly.

NOTE

A one-minute song-and-video clip—often saved in an AVI format (more about this in Chapter 7)—can take up as much as 10MB of space on your hard drive, or even more.

WAV recordings are high-quality, but their huge size makes them impractical for sounds longer than a second or two. MIDI files are tightly compressed, so they take up less room than WAV files. Although the compression reduces the quality of the recording, MIDI files are the only practical way to store longer sound clips.

MIDI files are great for storing musical scores—especially when you have a long piece of music, scoring you want to run in the background, or music that interacts with other action on the screen. But for sounds that must be clear, like a short voice-over on an important slide of your presentation, a WAV file will give you better quality.

MIDI and WAV files are available from a number of sources—as shareware, freeware, and purchased products. If you're using sound files from a third-party source, be sure to find out about usage limitations and restrictions. Some original music pieces may be protected as intellectual property, permitting you to use the music only as part of a demonstration or for your personal use—they cannot be included in anything you charge revenues for. This includes a presentation you give as part of a training service or a product you create and sell to clients to present to their company.

The Multimedia-Ready PC

Many computers sold today are multimedia equipped. Chances are, the computer you're using—or the system you will use to give the presentation—is equipped with a sound card and enough memory to adequately support your multimedia presentation.

Here's what the experts say you need in a computer for bare-bones multimedia success:

- A 486 or higher computer
- 16 megabytes of memory
- A 250-megabyte hard disk
- A sound card (8-bit or 16-bit; 16-bit is better)
- A CD-ROM drive
- Internal or external speakers
- A microphone, if you plan to do your own recording

NOTE

What's the bit in 8-bit? The terms *8-bit* and *16-bit* reflect the size of the path between the sound card and the motherboard it's plugged into. The wider the path, the more data can travel to the motherboard at one time and the higher the sound quality. 16-bit sound does not automatically sound twice as good as 8-bit sound, however—many other factors can come into play.

The following short sections review what you need to get sound out of your PC for presentation purposes.

What You Need for Sound

Even in your basic, no-frills PC (that is, not multimedia-ready), the PC speaker does the job of playing WAV files. This means you can get bells, whistles, and other special effects no matter what kind of equipment you've got.

Although a PC speaker can play WAV files, they won't sound very good. For presentations, you'll need a sound card that can do more than grunt and beep. You need a system that can keep up with anything from an opening gong to Beethoven's Fifth Symphony. (The following grouping of sound cards is based on reviews in industry magazines.)

If you want to:	You'll need this:	A few examples:
Play simple sound effects	A basic sound card	Media Vision ThunderBoard (8-bit, from Media Vision) Media Vision Pro (16-bit, from Media Vision)
Play high-quality audio and music	A good-quality (preferably 16-bit) sound card	Sound Blaster Pro (Creative Labs) MultiSound card (Turtle Beach Systems) Microsoft Windows Sound System (Microsoft) Cambridge SoundWorks (Creative Labs)
Record and edit sound files	Software that allows you to record and edit waveform files	Wave for Windows Sound Forge Altec Lansing's ACS52 Sound Blaster SWE64 Gold
Take a presentation—with sound—on the road	A special sound card for portable computers	DSP Portable Sound Plus (DSP Solutions) Media Vision Audio Port (Media Vision)

NOTE

No matter how good your sound card is, you're not going to hear the quality without a good set of speakers. Depending on what you want and need for presentation sound, there are a number of good speakers available. Basically any stereo speakers that you can plug into a sound card can be adapted for multimedia output, but some speakers—such as Altec Lansing's ACS52 ($128), Altec's ACS53 ($180), and Labtec's LCS-3210 ($170)—stand out for solid sound.

Does all this sound hardware and software make you wonder what's coming next? Voice recognition is here—the latest and greatest PC models are all being sold with attached extending microphones. It won't be long until you're speaking into your portable mike from the center aisle of the presentation room, telling Power-Point "Advance to the next slide, please." How did you prepare this presentation? Via straight dictation, with your sound card being your computer's ears and the voice recognition software deciphering and entering your words into the Power-Point Outliner.

Today the age of voice-directed applications is nearer than ever. Programs such as Simply Speaking from IBM enable you to command your PC by dictating. In just a few steps, you can dictate the file, export it to Word, and then pull it into PowerPoint. The process may be a little cumbersome today, but we can be sure the process will be streamlined—almost effortless—in the future.

Upgrading for Sound

Okay, so you're convinced that sound would give your presentations that extra something they need to really make your work stand out. You're sure you'll get departmental funding with a little more glitz and glamour. You know your training will go better if you can add sound to the teaching tools—charts and text—you already use.

If you are the one responsible for upgrading the system for sound, don't despair—the process is easier than ever, now that Windows 95 has added plug and play technology. *However*, let your company's technical support person install the card, unless you've been trained to know your way around a PC.

TIP

Don't pop the cover off your PC unless you know what you're doing. You could be voiding a warranty if you take matters into your own hands without the proper permissions. When in doubt, ask.

Once the sound card itself is installed, the rest is up to Windows. The new plug-and-play technology will find supported cards (most popular cards). If Windows doesn't recognize your sound card, make sure that the card is installed properly. If it is, then use the disk included with the card to install the necessary drivers on your system.

To see what sound card Windows sees for your system, click Start; then choose Settings ➤ Control Panel ➤ Multimedia. The Multimedia Properties dialog box appears, as shown in Figure 6.3.

FIGURE 6.3

Look in the Audio tab of the Multimedia Properties dialog box to see which sound card you've got installed

The sound card Windows has located on your system is displayed in the Preferred device box. As you can see, the device on this system is a SoundBlaster card.

Windows' plug-and-play system should find your sound card automatically and display it in the Preferred device box without fail. If you don't see your sound card in the Preferred device box, click the down arrow to see whether it is in the displayed list. If it's not, contact your technical support person to make sure the hardware has been installed correctly.

Other considerations in the Multimedia Properties dialog box affect the volume and quality of the recordings you play in your presentations. You can select MIDI devices, play CD music files, and set up other multimedia drivers with the various tabs in this dialog box.

Now that you know the basics of sound and the elementary considerations of sound files, software, and hardware, you're ready to see how to best use sound in your PowerPoint presentations.

Using PowerPoint's Sound Effects

One of the easiest ways to add sound to your slides is to assign a sound to the slide's transition. That is, you select a sound (called a transitional sound effect) to play when the slide advances to the next slide or when it first appears. You can either use the preset sound effects included with PowerPoint or add sound effects from another source—perhaps a multimedia collection disk or CD-ROM with sound and video files.

PowerPoint 97 now enables you to record the presenter's voice to deliver a presentation in a continuous slide show, which means you don't even need to be there to give your own presentations! Just record your voice and let it speak for itself while the presentation runs. For more about recording narrations, see the section "Record Your Own Sound," later in this chapter.

Choosing Transitional Sound Effects

To add a transitional sound effect, display the slide to which you want to add the transition and then choose Slide Show ➤ Slide Transition to open the Slide Transition dialog box. Click the down arrow in the Sound box to display the available special sound effects (see Figure 6.4).

The Slide Transition dialog box gives you the option of repeating—or looping—the sound until the next sound is chosen for another slide. Or, to turn off a previously selected sound, you can click the down arrow in the Sound box and choose [Stop Previous Sound].

Adding Sound from Other Sources

If you have sounds on disk or CD that you're eager to try out, insert the disk in the drive and display the slide to which you'd like to add the sound. Choose Slide Show ➤ Slide Transition to open the Slide Transition dialog box.

USING POWERPOINT'S SOUND EFFECTS

FIGURE 6.4

The Slide Transition dialog box provides a place where you can add transitional sound effects to your slides.

Click the Sound down arrow and move the highlight to the last item in the list, Other Sound. The Add Sound dialog box appears. Look through the folders in the displayed list—if you're using a multimedia collection (perhaps using the PowerPoint CD-ROM), you'll see all kinds of folders related to different aspects of multimedia (Mpeg, Tiff, Bmpsmall, etc.). It should be obvious which folder is the one related to sound from its name (it may be named something like "Sound")—if not, look for the small sound icon. Figure 6.5 shows the sound files stored in the Office 97 folder. Notice the small sound icons beside each file name.

Select the file you want by clicking it and clicking OK. PowerPoint adds the name of the file to the Sound box and immediately begins playing the sound so you can decide whether that's the one you want. If you want a different sound, click the Sound down arrow again and choose a different file. Click OK when you've got the one you want.

FIGURE 6.5

Open the folder that contains the sound files you want to use

Sound files are computer files like any other. You can copy or delete them from your system just as you would clip art files. Just be sure to know what, if any, licensing restrictions apply to your situation.

You can add sound effects from a variety of sources. Many third-party products are available in the form of sound libraries—on both CD-ROM and disk—that can give you literally thousands of sound effects for use in your presentations. Check out PowerPoint Central for additional sound clips and be sure to search on the Internet for the latest sound files and soundtracks.

Adding Sound to Animations

In some cases, you'll want to play a sound that is connected to the appearance of a certain element on the screen. For example, you might want to play the sound of a typewriter as the title of your presentation is "typed" on the screen. Or you may attach the sound of brakes screeching to a bullet item zooming in from the side, or a bell ringing when a logo appears.

You apply sounds to objects by first clicking the object you want to assign the sounds to; then choosing Slide Show ➤ Custom Animation. When the Custom Animation dialog box appears, click the Effects tab; then choose an effect in the *Entry animation and sound* drop-down to activate the other drop-down lists. In the Sound drop-down, choose an effect for the item. Next, click the box currently displaying [No Sound]. A list of sounds available for use with the selected object appears, as shown in Figure 6.6. Click on the sound to choose it, then click OK.

FIGURE 6.6

You can assign a sound to a specific object in the Custom Animation dialog box

PowerPoint 97 includes, in the ValuPack folder on the CD-ROM, a set of music tracks, appropriately named "Music Tracks," which you can use along with animations or as background music for your presentations. You simply choose the style, length, and tempo you want and Music Tracks does the job for you.

Inserting Sound Objects

Another method of adding sound to your PowerPoint presentations involves working with sound objects. A *sound object* is different from a sound effect in that when you insert an object, a sound file is placed on the current slide.

> Sound files can add dramatically to the size of your presentation, so if you're running tight on RAM or storage space, don't overload your system with a huge symphonic background piece when a simple 15-second intro will do.

To insert a sound file as an object on your PowerPoint slide, display the slide on which you want to begin the sound file, and then choose Insert ➤ Movies and Sound (see Figure 6.7). A submenu of sound choices appears, from which you can choose whether to add a sound from a file, CD, or the Clip Gallery, or to record a sound. To insert a prerecorded sound file, select Sound from File. The Insert Sound dialog box then appears.

Use the Look in box to navigate to the disk and/or folder where the sound files are stored. When the files are displayed in the file area, choose the file you want to use and click OK. PowerPoint adds the file as a small sound object icon in the center of the slide, as you can see in the magnified view shown in Figure 6.8.

> You can drag the sound object to an inconspicuous place on the slide—no need to leave it right there in the middle of things.

Recording Your Own Sound

For some presentations, you may want to do your own recording. In fact, with PowerPoint 97, you can record an entire script to play along with your presentation.

FIGURE 6.7

When you choose Movies and Sounds, a submenu of sound choices appears.

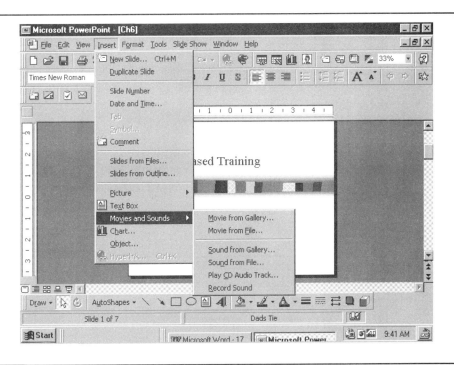

FIGURE 6.8

PowerPoint positions the sound object on the slide

The basic process of recording sound is easy. You can use either the Record Narration feature in PowerPoint 97 or use the Windows 95 Sound Recorder, an application included specifically for recording audio files.

The first step is to plug a microphone into the sound input jack (you may find it as part of the sound card in the back of your computer or along the right or left sides of the system unit).

Recording Narration

If you are interested in recording a script or voice-over for your presentation, you can easily do that with PowerPoint 97. For best results, start with a script that includes everything you plan to say. Small hesitations and stumbles in a voice-over become huge pauses and awkward phrasing and will distract your viewers.

You may want to use the Outliner to print the text in your presentation; then you can simply read that aloud as you record your narration.

To start recording your narration choose Slide Show ➤ Record Narration. The Record Narration dialog box appears, as Figure 6.9 shows. You see how much disk space you have available to store the narration, what the quality will be, and so on. To change the options, click Settings. The Sound Settings dialog box appears, so that you can change the quality, file format, or other configurations (see Figure 6.10). Make any necessary changes and click OK to close the dialog box. Then click OK again to begin recording the narration.

After you complete the presentation, a message box tells you that the narrations have been saved with each slide and asks you whether you want to save the slide timings also. If you click Yes, the timing with which you advanced each slide is saved in addition to the narration you recorded. If you click No, only the narration is saved.

When you run your presentation by clicking the Slide Show icon in the lower left corner of the work area or by opening the Slide Show menu and choosing View Show, you will hear the narration you have recorded.

You can change the recording and playback volumes by modifying the settings in the Multimedia group of the Control Panel. Choose Start ➤ Settings ➤ Control Panel ➤ Multimedia and click the Audio tab. Increase the volume as needed, and click OK and then the Close box to return to the presentation.

RECORDING YOUR OWN SOUND | 209

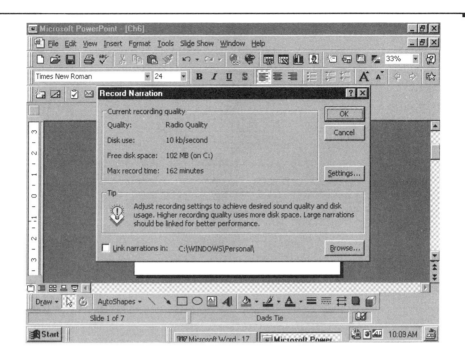

FIGURE 6.9

The Record Narration dialog box

FIGURE 6.10

The Sound Selection dialog box enables you to make choices about your recording.

Using Sound Recorder

If you want to use the Sound Recorder to record your sound, follow the process in this section. First, start Sound Recorder by clicking the Start menu and choosing Programs ➤ Accessories ➤ Multimedia ➤ Sound Recorder. Figure 6.11 shows the Sound Recorder, with the cursor positioned on the Record button.

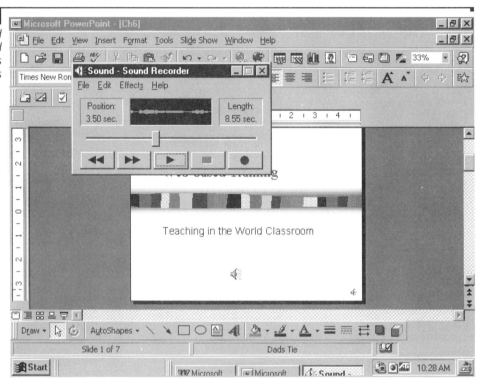

FIGURE 6.11

Using the Sound Recorder to record your own sounds is a simple process

Now simply click the Record button and speak into the microphone (or sing, or yowl, or whatever it is you're planning to do). When you're finished recording, click the Stop button (to the left of the Record button).

You can do all sorts of things with the Sound Recorder—mix the sound with another file; insert it in another file; increase or decrease the volume and speed; add an echo; even play it backwards. For more about working with the Sound Records, see the Sybex book *Sound & Music Workshop* (1996), by Richard Grace.

After you're finished recording, be sure to use File ➤ Save As to save the file. You can then import the sound into your PowerPoint presentation, attach it to an animated object, or play it at a slide transition.

You can record sounds from sources other than your own voice, such as a television show, radio interview, or some other preprocessed source. Just be sure to get the necessary permissions if you're using someone else's material.

Reviewing Different Sound Choices

We've talked about several different ways to add sound to your PowerPoint presentations. Here's a quick review of how you can incorporate sounds into your presentations:

- To play a sound object placed on a slide, click the object. You use Insert ➤ Movies and Sounds to add a sound object to a specific slide.
- If you want a sound to play automatically when slides change, use Slide Show ➤ Slide Transition to attach the sound to the slide transition.
- Use Slide Show ➤ Custom Animation to attach a sound to a specific element on your slide, such as the build text of a bullet list, a title, or an animated logo.
- To add custom voice-over notes or simple recorded sound effects, use the Windows Sound Recorder and a microphone to create your own sounds.

Some Sound Advice for Presenting

Here are a few things to keep in mind as you add sound to your presentation:

- **Don't overdo it.** With any cool feature comes the temptation to use it for everything. Fight the pull to assign bells and whistles to every event in your presentation. At most, you'll probably want an opening and concluding music piece with selected sound effects in between. If your presentation requires background music all the way through, don't overlay other sound effects. Remember that it's the full mix of the media—text, visuals, and sound—that makes the full statement of your presentation.

- **Make sure there's a reason for the sound.** Another potential pitfall in working with the creative aspects of multimedia is the craving to use something where it's really not needed. If you're doing a presentation to show the new technical specifications of a new minicomputer to a room of busy engineers, you don't need a swirling musical introduction to capture their attention. They just want to get the information and get back to work.

- **Tailor the sound to the presentation.** Think through the logic of the sound before you use it. If you have a special effect of a title being handwritten across the screen, for example, you wouldn't want to use the Typewriter sound effect. You wouldn't want to introduce a dry professional presentation with music stamping out a conga beat.

- **Consider your presentation equipment.** Before you spend a lot of time compiling, testing, and assigning sound to your presentation, think about what you'll be presenting on. If you won't have strong speakers that can project volume and quality good enough for the audience you're presenting to, don't invest your time in music production.

Chapter Review

This chapter has introduced one of the newer media aspects of multimedia: sound. If you've never worked with sound before, you may be surprised at how easy it is to add simple sound effects and even more complicated musical scores to your presentations. A little sound adds a whole new dimension to the text and visuals on your presentation screen; so, if you've got the computer power, the time, and the desire—make those presentations sing!

Chapter 7

Ready, Set, Video!

FEATURING

Getting Started

Adding Movies to PowerPoint Slides

Resizing and Moving Movie Objects

Editing Movies

Chapter 7

Ready, Set, Video!

In any good presentation, all elements contribute to the final product. The text provides the information, the fonts create a certain mood, the graphics catch and hold the viewers' attention, and sound effects add liveliness that printed handouts can't offer. But video—especially good-quality, entertaining, and interesting video—does much more than any of these elements can do.

Video *moves*.

It's not just that our media-crazed culture demands sound, color, and movement in order to hold its interest. It's not just that we've become desensitized to stimulation and need more and more to feel that we're getting what we came for. It's that video has something to offer that no other media has: simulated experience. Through the eyes of the video camera, you're on the French Riviera, you're the one repairing that 737, or you're in the center of that fire at 9th and Central. The movie plays and you play right along with it.

Getting Started

In a business setting, video is fast becoming an irreplaceable tool. A few years ago, in order to have video of a training course, a corporate meeting, or the installation of an assembly line, you'd have to hire a professional video company to come in and do the video for you. Then you'd need to be able to show the video—time and time again—on your trusty VCR in order to get the video seen by all who needed it. Quite an expense—both in time and money. If you need lots of high-quality video, you'll still need the video production company, but if you want to catch clips of people working, showing off different products or demonstrating procedures, you can capture the video yourself. Then import the video into a presentation that can then be circulated on disk, accessible over a network, or set up on an open-access computer where employees can run through a self-directed demo whenever they like.

The availability of PC hardware and software to support the use of digital video has made it easier for people to use video both in their presentations and in other business settings. Even if you don't own a video camera yourself, you can benefit from those who have created extensive video libraries with clips you can use in your own projects.

Why Use Video Clips in Your Presentations?

A well-placed video clip in your presentation can make the difference between keeping your clients' interest and losing it. Motion, sound, color—what more do you need to get a message across? Following are a few ideas of how you might incorporate video in your PowerPoint presentation:

- Your corporate meeting begins with a video of the CEO, welcoming all attendees and announcing the corporate theme for the upcoming year.
- You put together a collection of your department's top news stories with clips from your nightly news show interspersed with still photos and text from actual articles.
- Your presentation introducing a new method of teaching includes a video showing preschool children working with your materials.
- Your presentation to promote the computerization of your company's assembly line shows a video of how it's done now and an animation (which is simply a movie made of drawings) of how it *could* be done in the future.

- Your presentation of vacation resorts includes a running movie of a boat sailing on a sun-swept lake while displaying a continuing slide show of different time-share condominiums.

What You Need to Use Video

If you are planning on simply working with movie files, you need a standard multimedia computer. The more RAM, the better—8MB is good, but 16MB or more is better. You'll also need adequate speakers for presentation, and plenty of hard disk space—video files aren't small.

If you are planning on capturing and working with the video yourself, you need a video capture board installed in your computer and a video editing package that enables you to capture the video in a digital format that can be used by your computer. And, depending on the quality, complexity, and timing of the video you want to capture, you need lots and lots of storage space! A full discussion of video capture is beyond the scope of this book, but recent editions of Mark Minasi's *The Complete PC Upgrade and Maintenance Guide* (Sybex) discuss the mechanics of video capture and purchasing issues.

What does a video capture board do? It takes the signal from your television, camcorder, or VCR—known as an analog signal—and turns it into a digital signal that the computer can understand.

Once you get the basic hardware and software in place, the Media Player applet that comes with Windows 95 enables you to choose specific clips, colorize, and edit the movie sequences you use. For more information on editing movies with the Media Player, see the section, "Advanced Editing: Using Media Player," later in this chapter.

Where Do You Get Video?

Video clips for use in standard business presentations are available on a number of CD-ROMs from a variety of sources. One popular source is a company called Jasmine, which often includes clip samples on disk packaged with its multimedia collections. Many other companies, such as Kodak, offer extensive clip art and movie libraries with videos and animations ranging from funny to professional. To find these companies, check out recent computer publications such as *Multimedia Online*, *CD-ROM Today*, and *Multimedia World* and keep an eye on the ads.

Today's computer magazines, such as *CD-ROM Today*, are often packaged with a disk that sometimes includes special multimedia selections you can use in your own work. Additionally, many books on multimedia include CD-ROMs or disks with sample files you can use in your presentations.

The multimedia and computer software forums of various online services offer yet another resource for video clips, but be sure to check any files you download for potential viruses. Also, check out any licensing restrictions or shareware fees—use of the video in any product offered for sale may be restricted.

MASTERING THE OPPORTUNITIES

Checking Out PowerPoint Central

When you are first considering adding video to your presentations, you may not know where to look for sample video clips. Luckily, PowerPoint takes care of that problem for you. By including PowerPoint Central in PowerPoint 97, Microsoft includes access to a wide range of multimedia clips—art, sound, video, templates, and more.

PowerPoint Central is a feature that is built into PowerPoint 97 but is updated on a regular basis from Microsoft's Web site. When you first choose the PowerPoint Central command from the Tools menu, you may see a popup dialog box asking whether you'd like to update the files. Click Yes. This logs you on to the Microsoft Web site and downloads the latest files for PowerPoint Central.

When the PowerPoint Central window is displayed, you can choose the types of files you want. Click the *FREE sounds, clipart, textures, photographs, and video* option to get to the video files. Follow the on-screen prompts to get video either from your CD-ROM or from the Microsoft Web site.

Understanding Video Formats

Video files are available in a number of formats. The most common format is AVI, a format introduced when Video for Windows arrived on the scene. The AVI format (AVI stands for Audio Video Interleaved) interleaves audio and video data together in the same file, one after the other. Apple QuickTime for Windows is another format that mixes audio and video together.

Because video files are often so large, data compression is important. Data compression stores the data in a file that takes up less room than the uncompressed file. JPEG (Joint Photographic Experts Group) and MPEG (Motion Picture Experts Group) are two compression techniques often used with video files. JPEG removes some of the video data in order to compress the file but does it so that the change is transparent—or almost transparent—to the eye. MPEG is a higher standard of compression than JPEG, requiring an add-in board and software that is able to read and write the MPEG format. MPEG can actually "predict" what will happen next in the video and make choices about what colors or patterns should remain on the screen; it is much better quality than JPEG and now the highest standard for video. Although it requires additional hardware that used to be extremely expensive, high-end multimedia systems today are being touted as MPEG-ready.

MASTERING TROUBLESHOOTING

What Makes Good Video Good?

Whether you've got the right video for your particular presentation depends on many different factors. The first decision you've got to make is, "What kind of movie best represents what I'm trying to say here?" If you're trying to get your potential customers dreaming about their next vacation, you would want a colorful, inspiring video that makes clients think, "Boy, I'd like to be there."

Once you decide what kind of video you'd like, you need to either videotape it yourself or find it in a video file collection. Then the issue becomes one of quality. Here are a few questions you should ask about the movie you use in your presentation:

Are the images sharp? The first criterion should be the crispness of the video image. Remember that the larger the movie object, the poorer the resolution will be. For a good-quality video, display the movie in a box about the size of one quarter of the slide space. Anything larger than that size may distort the image or make it choppy. Speaking of which…

Is the movement smooth or choppy? This may be more of a memory consideration than a video consideration, but the size of the movie file will influence how easily it is handled in your computer's RAM. If the video is jerky, try a different clip. Video with hiccups that distract your audience is worse than no video at all.

Do the colors complement the presentation's color scheme? You may spend a great deal of time finding just the right movie to fit your presentation, and then insert it onto a slide and discover that it clashes terribly with the background colors of your slides. You can fix this with PowerPoint's Recolor Picture command, available when you right-click the movie object. You can exchange one color for another (for a total of up to 64 colors), thus making sure that you get just the right mix of colors for your presentation.

> **MASTERING TROUBLESHOOTING CONTINUED**
>
> ***Is the sound clear?*** Sound can make or break a movie in your presentation. If the sound is distorted, crackling, or muffled, your audience is going to be straining to make out what's being said and miss what's being shown. Before you select a movie file, make sure the sound holds up its end, too. (Note: Not all movie files include sound as part of the format. AVI, a popular format introduced with Video for Windows, incorporates both sound and video in the same file.)
>
> ***Does a certain segment of the video work best in this presentation?*** Just because a movie segment you select is 40 seconds long doesn't mean you have to use the entire 40 seconds. You can use the Media Player to select just the segment you want.

Adding Movies to PowerPoint Slides

So you've got the movie clip you want to use and know the slide on which you want to use it. To put the movie in the presentation, you'll start by displaying the slide in which you want the movie to begin playing.

Now you have a choice to make: do you want to display the movie as a poster or an icon? A movie poster displays the first frame of the movie on the slide. A movie icon shows up as an icon that you click to play (similar to the sound icons we discussed in the last chapter).

PowerPoint 97 enhances the AVI movie capability. Now you can play AVI movies—that's sound and video together—and get better, smoother playback and truer colors, as well.

Making Movie Posters

The easiest way to add a movie to your PowerPoint presentation is to choose Insert ➤ Movies and Sounds. A popup menu appears, as Figure 7.1 shows, enabling you to choose whether you want to select a movie from the Clip Gallery or from a file. When you click Movie from File, the Insert Movie dialog box appears, as shown in Figure 7.2; choose the movie file you want and click OK.

After a moment, the file appears in a small (approximately 2.5×2 inches) window on the screen. There's the movie—now you can move, resize, edit, open, and even recolor it.

ADDING MOVIES TO POWERPOINT SLIDES | 221

FIGURE 7.1:
Preparing to insert a movie file

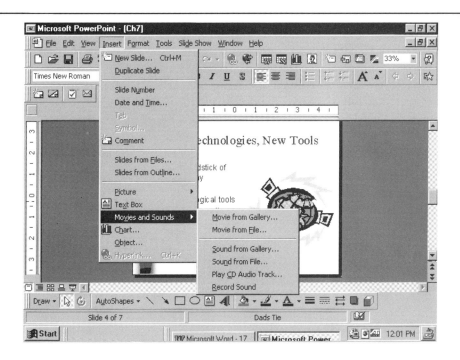

FIGURE 7.2:
Choosing a movie file to use in your presentation

Adding a Movie Icon

Instead of including a movie clip with the first frame of the movie showing, you may want to include the movie as an icon so you can activate it manually during your presentation. You might do this, for example, with a video clip that shows a segment of a training program. Suppose that you know you will give your presentation several times—once to managers, once to line workers, and once to shareholders. You might want to show the training video to the line workers and the managers, but not the shareholders. In this case, using an icon lets you control whether the movie plays, saving you presentation time by allowing you to customize the presentation for your audience's needs.

Including a movie as an icon uses a different process than making it a poster. Again, display the slide on which you want to place the movie object, but choose Insert ➤ Object. The Insert Object dialog opens, so you can find the movie file for which you want to create the icon. Click *Create from File* (see Figure 7.3). Next, click Browse to display the Browse dialog box in which you can search for the movie file you want, or type the path. When you locate the file in the file list area, click the file you want and then the Link checkbox.

FIGURE 7.3:

Selecting the movie file you want to include as an icon

NOTE

When you add a movie to a slide, the movie is linked rather than embedded. A linked file maintains its link to the original file, so if the movie in the original file is edited, the changes are reflected in the PowerPoint file. If the file was embedded, the movie would actually be stored in with the PowerPoint file. Because of the size of most video files, embedding is impractical and taxing on your computer's resources.

To finish, click the Display As Icon checkbox. An icon appears beneath the checkbox, showing a default icon that will be used on your presentation slide. To select a different icon, click the Change Icon button to see additional choices and click the one you want. Figure 7.4 shows both the default movie icon and your choices in the Change Icon dialog box. To change the caption displayed beneath the icon, click in the Caption box and type a new caption.

FIGURE 7.4:
Customizing the icon appearance of a movie object

After you click OK in the Insert Object dialog box, PowerPoint redisplays the current slide and shows the movie icon you selected in the Insert Object dialog box. You can now drag the icon to a convenient point on the screen.

If you need to take your presentation on the road or store it on disk, use the Pack And Go Wizard to gather up all the pieces (video files, sound files, presentation file, etc.) of your presentation into one neat bundle. The file is automatically named PNGSETUP.EXE. The exact size of your file will depend on the components of the presentation (an 8-page basic presentation that included the Viewer took 55K), but the Wizard will prompt you for multiple disks if necessary. You'll find the Pack And Go Wizard in the File menu.

Resizing and Moving Movie Objects

If you've decided to add the movie as a poster, you may want to change the size of the movie as it appears on the slide. Resize it as you would any PowerPoint object: drag a corner or side of the object and enlarge or reduce the object as necessary. When the object is the size you want it, release the mouse button. If you change the proportions of the movie poster, the video is reproportioned to use the allotted space.

Moving the object from one place to another is also old hat by now—just position the mouse pointer on the object, press and hold the mouse button, and drag the movie to the new location. When the movie poster is positioned where you want it, let go of the mouse button.

Playing Movies

Once you find the clip you want and get it positioned on your slide, you'll be anxious to check it out in your presentation. This section shows you how to test the movie clip you've added and make choices about when you want the movie to play.

Testing the Movie Clip

If you're like most people, you're anxious to see how that movie looks the moment you position it on the slide. You don't want to wait for the presentation to find out that the clip really doesn't fit your topic.

You can play the movie without running the presentation by positioning the mouse pointer on the movie object and double-clicking.

Choosing When You Want the Movie to Play

The movie's now in the slide; the only remaining task is to define when it plays during the presentation. You can display a menu of movie options by right-clicking on the movie object (see Figure 7.5). To control when the movie plays, select Custom Animation. When you select this option, the Custom Animation dialog box appears. In this dialog box, you can determine how you want the movie object to "act" when the current slide is displayed in the presentation. Do you want the movie to play automatically, or sit dormant until clicked?

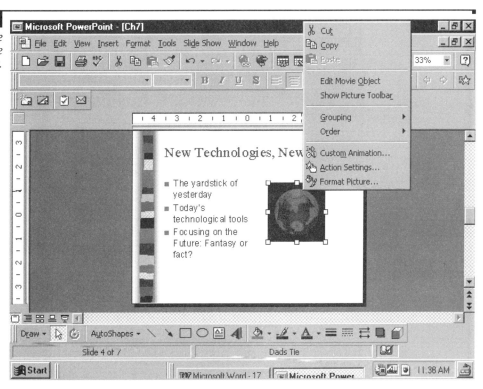

FIGURE 7.5:
Right-click the movie object to see movie options.

NOTE

When you right-click a movie object, the names and number of options in the menu displayed will depend on the type of movie file it is.

Figure 7.6 shows the Custom Animation dialog box. The Play Settings tab is displayed. Click the option *Play using animation order* to have the movie begin automatically; if you leave the option blank, you will need to click the movie object during the presentation to cause it to begin playing. When you click the option, the *While playing* choices also become available (see Figure 7.7).

FIGURE 7.6:

The Custom Animation dialog box

FIGURE 7.7:

In the Custom Animation dialog box, you choose whether you want the clip to play automatically when the slide is displayed in the presentation.

You can choose whether you want to pause the slide show while the movie plays or continue running the slide show during the movie. You can also click *More options* to see additional movie and sound choices (see Figure 7.8). If you want the movie to continue repeating until you stop the presentation, click *Loop until stopped*. If you want the movie to play only once and then rewind itself, click *Rewind movie when done playing*. Click OK to return to the Custom Animation dialog box; click OK to display the presentation.

FIGURE 7.8:
You can select additional movie and sound options in the Play Options dialog box.

Editing Movies

The commands for editing your selected movie file are also tucked away in the pop-up menu that appears when you right-click the movie object.

Simple Editing

The first three commands—Cut, Copy, and Paste—are standard editing commands. You can cut and paste a movie from one slide or presentation to another, or even cut and paste a movie from your PowerPoint presentation into your Word document (or vice versa).

Advanced Editing: Using Media Player

When you position the pointer on the movie object and click the right mouse button, the pop-up menu appears. Choose the Edit Video Clip Object command, and the display of your presentation window changes (see Figure 7.9). What you're looking at is actually the Windows 95 Media Player, which enables you to:

- edit video
- select clips of video you want to use in your presentation
- move through a video clip forward and backward
- control the volume for AVI clips
- determine whether you want a border around the clip
- choose whether you want the control bar displayed at the bottom of the clip
- make copies of video clips you select

Time is just one of the ways you can display the different aspects of your video. You can also choose to display the movie by frames or by track. The only difference is the method of selection—some people find it easier to cut a piece from 370 to 385 than they would cutting 00:00:24 to 00:00:34. To change the sequence scale, click the Scale menu and choose the sequence style you want to see.

Media Player includes different menus than the ones you're accustomed to in PowerPoint. Table 7.1 gives you a quick rundown of Media Player features; Table 7.2 introduces you to the tools in the Media Player toolbar.

FIGURE 7.9:

When you edit a video clip, it is displayed in the Windows 95 Media Player.

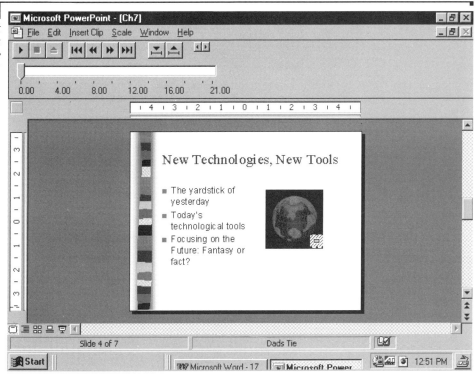

TABLE 7.1: MEDIA PLAYER MENUS	
Menu	**Contains Commands For**
File	Opening, saving, packing, and sending movie clips
Edit	Copying movies, setting movie options (such as displaying the control bar, setting Auto Rewind and Auto Repeat, and options for the display and playing of the object in the current presentation)
Insert Clip	Adding a new video clip, reviewing file properties, or controlling volume
Scale	Choosing the measurement by which the file is sequenced—time, frames, or tracks
Window	Choosing the file you want to work with and specifying the arrangement of windows on the screen
Help	Accessing Media Player help

TABLE 7.2: TOOLS IN THE MEDIA PLAYER TOOLBAR

Tool	Description
Play	Begins playing the movie from the selected mark
Stop	Stops the movie being played
Eject	Closes Media Player and abandons changes
Previous Mark	Rewinds the movie to the preceding marked place
Rewind	Rewinds the movie to the beginning of the clip
Fast Forward	Fast forwards the movie to the marked spot
Next Mark	Forwards the movie ahead to the next marked place
Start Selection	Marks the beginning of a selected sequence of the movie
End Selection	Marks the end of a selected movie sequence
Scroll Backward	Moves backward through the movie a frame at a time
Scroll Forward	Moves forward through the movie a frame at a time

Setting Video Options

Some things that look impressive on-screen are actually very easy to do. For example, you can add a great deal to a continually running presentation with an Auto Repeat feature, which will run your video over and over again until you tell it to stop. Or, if the presentation is a user-controlled demo, you could turn on the Auto Rewind option so the user can repeat the video. Both of these features, and others, are set in the Options dialog box (see Figure 7.10), accessible by choosing Edit ➤ Options. To turn on Auto Rewind and/or Auto Repeat, simply click the corresponding checkboxes that you see here.

Auto Rewind and Auto Repeat aren't your only options, however. To remove (temporarily or permanently) the control bar that appears beneath the movie, click Control Bar On Playback. (Removing the checkmark hides the control bar; adding the checkmark displays it.)

You can also enter a new caption to be displayed beneath the movie until the movie begins. For example, you could type an instruction ("Click here to start!"), your company name, or the name and title of a person interviewed in the movie sequence.

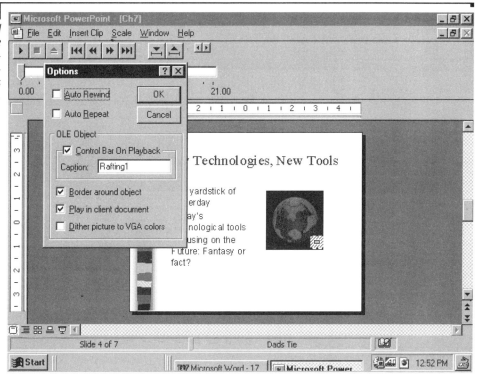

FIGURE 7.10:
You can control the way the movie plays and the controls that are available in the Options dialog box.

Getting the Clip You Want

Whether you are using video created just for your presentation or a movie from a collection of video clippings, you will probably need to trim the clip to just the images you want in your presentation. Many popular multimedia CD-ROMs include a number of video files, and some of those are a compilation of short movies from which you can cut the pieces of video you want.

Entering Timing Coordinates

It's easy to clip just the part you want out of a larger movie by displaying the movie as a poster on the slide of your choice, then clicking the right mouse button on the object. When the Media Player appears, choose Edit ➤ Selection to open the Selection dialog box shown in Figure 7.11. Now you can type the timing coordinates of the segment you want (if you know them), by clicking in the appropriate box and typing the timing value. If you don't know the exact coordinates of the video clip you want, you can easily select the clip yourself using the process described in the next section.

FIGURE 7.11:

The Set Selection dialog box enables you to choose the section of video you want for your presentation.

Does your Set Selection dialog box show all zeros? This is because you haven't yet chosen a selected sequence. Once you choose a selection, it is reflected in the dialog box (as well as in the sequence bar) until you choose a different sequence or insert a different clip.

Making Your Video Selection

If you don't know the timing coordinates, you can simply drag the markers on the sequence bar to choose the portion of the movie you want.

Start by clicking the Start Selection marker (at the far left of the sequence bar) and dragging it to the beginning of the section you want. As you drag the marker, the video changes to show the current movie segment (see Figure 7.12), so you can see where you are.

EDITING MOVIES | 233

FIGURE 7.12:

Defining where you want the movie segment to begin

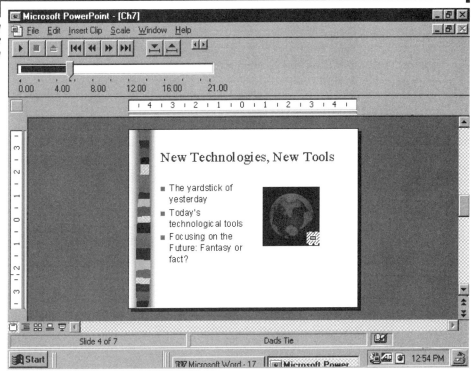

Next, specify where you want the movie to end by clicking Play. As the movie clip continues, anticipate where you want to stop the video. (The film runs at a rate of about 30 frames per second.) When the movie gets to that point, click the End Selection button. Notice that a colored bar shows the segment in the sequence bar you have selected.

If you want to choose a different movie selection, display the Set Selection dialog box and zero out all the timing values. If you want to edit the settings, use the up arrow and down arrow in the From and To boxes to modify the beginning and end points of the segment.

Using Volume Control

Especially in a multimedia presentation, setting the volume to a good healthy balance that neither deafens your audience nor makes them strain is an important part of conveying your message. Volume control is a global Windows setting that you may or may not have already discovered for yourself. Choose Insert Clip ➤ Volume Control to display the Volume Control dialog box (see Figure 7.13).

FIGURE 7.13:
Volume is a delicate balance—you don't want to deafen your audience, but you don't want to go unheard.

You can set the various aspects of volume control by using the slide controls in each of four areas: Volume Control, Wave (this affects sound and movie files you use in your presentations), CD Audio, and Synthesizer files. (The latter three all control additional sound output devices; Volume Control controls the basic sound system of the PC.) When you're finished changing the volume settings, click the Close button in the upper right corner of the window.

You can also display the Volume Control dialog box from any point in Windows 95 by double-clicking the speaker icon in the bottom right corner of the Taskbar.

Returning to PowerPoint

When you've finished editing your video clip in the Media Player and are ready to return to PowerPoint, simply click outside the movie area. The PowerPoint work area is redisplayed and the movie object is shown highlighted, with handles at the corners and along the sides of the object.

Opening a Movie for Editing

Another method of displaying the Media Player and preparing your movie file for editing is to position the mouse pointer on the movie object, click the right mouse button, and choose Open Video Clip Object. The current movie frame is displayed in another popup window to the side of the movie object. The Media Player window appears—smaller, this time—in the upper right corner of the PowerPoint work area.

All the same Media Player menus, tools, and options are available in the smaller window. When you're finished working with the open object, click the close box in the upper right corner of the opened movie window. The window closes and the Media Player is put away.

Cropping the Movie Object

In some cases, you may want to narrow down a portion of your video so you're displaying only the portion you need. Suppose, for example, you want only the top portion of the revolving world showing behind the text on a series of slides. You can crop the video of the world spinning to get only the portion you want.

To crop the movie, right-click on the movie object to open the pop-up menu. Click Show Picture Toolbar, and the tool palette appears (see Figure 7.14). Click the Crop tool. You can now crop the movie object by clicking in its corner (or along its side), then dragging the corner or side to its new position. When the object has the view you want, release the mouse button. Click outside the object to finish and return the pointer to its normal shape.

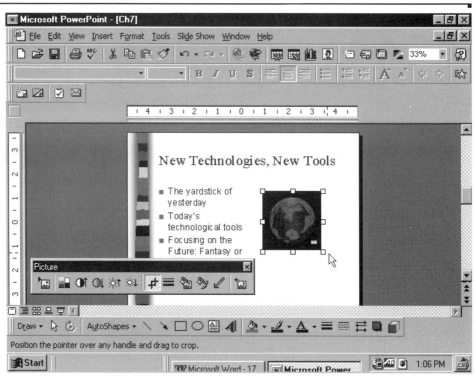

FIGURE 7.14:
You can crop a movie to hide the portions that you don't want your audience to see.

Recoloring Images

Sometimes some of the background color or primary colors of the video may not mesh the way you'd like with the color scheme you've selected for your PowerPoint presentation. The Recolor Picture tool in the Picture toolbar lets you change the colors in the video to either make the color scheme more consistent or create stunning color special effects.

Start by displaying the Picture toolbar (right-click the movie object and choose Show Picture Toolbar). When the toolbar appears, click the Recolor Picture tool. The Recolor Picture dialog box then appears.

To change a color in the picture, click the checkbox beside the color you want to change in the Original column. Next, click the down arrow of the color in the New column and select the new color from the palette that appears. To choose from the larger scheme of colors, click Other Color.

For best results, preview your changes before you click OK and have them recolored in the movie. When you click OK, PowerPoint replaces all occurrences of the selected color in the movie sequence you've selected with the new color.

If you return to the slide and realize that you really don't like the color change, choose Edit ➤ Undo Recolor Picture or press Ctrl+Z to restore the video to its original color scheme.

Chapter Review

This chapter explored the basics of adding movies to your PowerPoint slides, using either movie files from other sources or, if you have the right hardware and software, video input from your TV, VCR, or camcorder. With a mix of video, sound, graphics, charts, and text, your presentation is nearly complete.

The next chapter shows you how to finish up the fine points for presenting, showing you how to set slide transitions and add special effects like animation to your presentation.

Chapter 8

Finishing the Slide Show

FEATURING

What Is a Slide Show?

Adding the Finishing Touches

Building Slides

Creating Hidden Slides

Rehearsing Slide Display Timing

Starting a Screen Show

Presentation Special Features

Chapter 8

Finishing the Slide Show

FEATURING

What Is a Slide Show?

Adding the Finishing Touches

Building Slides

Creating Hidden Slides

Rehearsing Slide Display Timing

Starting a Screen Show

Presentation Special Features

Chapter 8

Finishing the Slide Show

Up to this point in the book, you've concentrated on compiling all the different elements of your presentation. You wrote and edited the text, created and modified the charts, designed and/or imported graphics, added sound, and inserted movie objects. What's left to do besides give the presentation?

A few subtle differences can make a big difference in the way your presentation comes across. These subtle differences—the way your slides make the transition from one to another in the slide show and how quickly or slowly you "turn the page"—are the focus of this chapter. You'll also learn about the new features PowerPoint adds to strengthen your presenting power—things like on-screen drawing, Meeting Minder notes, and presentation conferencing.

If you're not thrilled about standing up in front of a group and giving that presentation, practicing it a few times can help you learn what to expect while you're presenting. You'll be less nervous at show time if you've rehearsed the presentation enough to know it well.

What Is a Slide Show?

In its simplest state, a slide show is an on-screen presentation of slides. When you click the Slide Show button or choose View ➤ Slide Show (and then click the Show button), PowerPoint displays the slides, one at a time, in full-screen view. The selected slide is displayed complete with all text, art, graphs, and any other items you added.

You can display a slide show at any time during the creation process. When you want to see how a single slide will look, how a particular piece of video will appear, or how a sound effect will sound, you can display the slide show in its unfinished form.

Click the Slide Show button and check out how your developing presentation is looking at various stages throughout the creation process. Seeing the slide in Slide Show view gives you a much better idea of how the screen will look, because it gets rid of the clutter of the menu bar and toolbars.

Adding the Finishing Touches

By this stage in the presentation creation process, you've gotten your slides finished to a point you're happy with them. The text is where you want it, the charts appear the way they will in the presentation, and you've conscientiously used the Spelling checker and Style Checker to make sure that the basic content and layout of your presentation look as professional as possible.

If you haven't used the Spelling checker or the Style Checker—or if it's been a while since you did—take a minute and do so before continuing. You'll find both commands in the Tools menu.

While you are focusing on building slides, you are working in an up-close perspective, asking yourself questions like "What would look good on this side of the slide?" or "Is this too much text in a bullet list?" Your attention is given to each individual slide to make sure it meets its goal.

Once you get all the elements in place, your vision becomes more global: you begin thinking of the presentation as a whole. "How much time will this presentation take?" or "How many different transitions should I use in a 25-slide presentation?" or "How do I know how much time to leave for each slide in order to get them all in?" become the questions you're more concerned with now.

The answers to each of these questions help you add the finishing touches to your presentation. In the next section, you learn how to work with features that help your presentation really shine.

PowerPoint "Polishing" Tools

PowerPoint includes a number of features that make the finishing step one of the easiest:

- Dozens of transitional effects like wipes, fades, and dissolves to keep your audience's attention
- A hidden slides feature that lets you include backup slides for more information but display them only when needed
- A rehearsal feature that lets you rehearse the presentation with a recording timer so you can set just the right amount of time for individual slides
- A Slide Meter that enables you to compare your actual presentation timing to your rehearsal timing so you can gauge how accurate your projections were and decide whether you need to make modifications
- An on-screen draw feature that lets you write notes, circle important items, or underline important concepts, using a variety of colors and pen styles
- The Meeting Minder feature, which lets you take notes during the meeting or presentation. You can assign priorities to the notes and even export them to use in other applications
- Presentation conferencing that enables you to give the presentation over your network, so others can log in on the process and participate online

Setting Slide Transitions

A slide transition is the effect PowerPoint uses to remove the current slide and bring in a new one. By default, PowerPoint doesn't assign any special transitional effect—until you specify the transition you want, one slide is simply replaced uneventfully with the next. But PowerPoint can supply dozens of interesting transitional effects, such as fades, wipes, blinds, and checkerboards.

Choosing the Transition

To choose a transitional effect for your slide, first select the slide to which you want to apply the transition when the slide appears. If you are in Current Slide view, the transitional effect will be applied to the current slide. If you are displaying Slide Sorter view, you need to click the slide to which you want to add the transition. You can display the Slide Transition dialog box necessary to add transitions in two different ways:

- You can choose Slide Show ➤ Slide Transition.
- Or, you can click the right mouse button on the slide you want to set the transition for in Slide Sorter view and choose Slide Transition from the pop-up menu that appears.

Figure 8.1 shows Slide Sorter View. You can click the Slide Transition button on the far left side of the special effects bar to display the Slide Transition dialog box. If you know the name of the transition effect you want to apply to a slide, you can choose it from the Slide Transition drop-down list.

FIGURE 8.1

You have two different methods of choosing slide transitions in Slide Sorter view.

ADDING THE FINISHING TOUCHES | **245**

Although PowerPoint lets you work in either Slide view or Slide Sorter view when you're adding transitions to your slides, it's often easiest to work in Slide Sorter view when you're putting together the final elements of your presentation and preparing a slide show. All the tools for the slide show are right there on the Slide Sorter tools row and you can immediately see the effects you create.

The Slide Transition dialog box lets you try out all the different transitional effects on the dog picture before you add them to your slides (see Figure 8.2). Display it by clicking the Transition button in the Slide Sorter tools row or by choosing Tools ➤ Slide Transition.

FIGURE 8.2
The Slide Transition dialog box

When you first display the Slide Transition dialog box, the setting No Transition is displayed in the Effect box. To show the list of potential transitions, click the down arrow (see Figure 8.3).

FIGURE 8.3

Displaying transition choices

What you see in the Effects list isn't all there is: click the down arrow to scroll through the list. The names may not tell you much, however—it's hard to tell exactly what the effect does until you see it in action. You can sample different effects and see what they do by clicking the one you want to view and watching the small preview picture (the little dog) in the lower right corner of the Slide Transition box. Once you try an effect, the picture changes to a key picture. When you try another effect, there's the dog again. This variance makes it easy for you to see exactly what the effect does. If you don't want to work your way through the list to see what each effect does, look at Table 8.1.

TABLE 8.1: SLIDE SHOW TRANSITIONAL EFFECTS

Effect	Description
No Transition	No transitional effect has been applied to this slide
Blinds Horizontal	Horizontal strips close, revealing the next slide

Continued

TABLE 8.1: SLIDE SHOW TRANSITIONAL EFFECTS (CONTINUED)

Effect	Description
Blinds Vertical	Vertical strips close, revealing the next slide
Box Out	Next slide starts as a small box in center of the former slide and spreads outward
Box In	New slide spreads inward from the outer edges
Checkerboard Across	A checkerboard pattern fills in the new slide from left to right
Checkerboard Down	A checkerboard pattern fills in the new slide from top to bottom
Cover Left	The new slide slides in from the right
Cover Up	The new slide slides up from the bottom
Cover Right	The new slide slides in from the left
Cover Down	The new slide slides down from the top
Cover Left-Up	The new slide slides up from the bottom right corner
Cover Right-Up	The new slide slides up from the bottom left corner
Cover Left-Down	The new slide slides down from the top right corner
Cover Right-Down	The new slide slides down from the top left corner
Cut	A quick exchange inward reveals the new slide
Cut Through Black	A quick exchange reveals the new slide after a momentary blackout
Dissolve	The old slide dissolves into the display of the new slide
Fade Through Black	The old slide fades to black and the new slide appears gradually
Random Bars Horizontal	Randomly placed bars reveal the new slide
Random Bars Vertical	Random vertical bars reveal the new slide
Split Horizontal Out	The new slide begins as a horizontal line in the center of the screen and spreads outward
Split Horizontal In	The new slide begins along the top and bottom of the screen and spreads inward
Split Vertical Out	The new slide starts as a vertical line in the center of the slide and spreads outward
Split Vertical In	The new slide begins at the left and right edges of the screen and spreads inward

Continued

TABLE 8.1: SLIDE SHOW TRANSITIONAL EFFECTS (CONTINUED)

Effect	Description
Strips Down-Left	The new slide builds in diagonal strips from the upper right corner to the bottom left corner
Strips Down-Right	The new slide builds in diagonal strips from the upper left corner to the bottom right corner
Strips Up-Left	The new slide builds in diagonal strips from the bottom right corner to the upper left corner
Strips Up-Right	The new slide builds in diagonal strips from the bottom left corner to the upper right corner
Uncover Left	The old slide is removed from the left, revealing the new slide
Uncover Up	The old slide is removed from the top, revealing the new slide
Uncover Right	The old slide is removed from the right, revealing the new slide
Uncover Down	The old slide is removed from the bottom, revealing the new slide
Uncover Left-Up	The old slide is removed from the upper left corner, revealing the new slide
Uncover Right-Up	The old slide is removed from the upper right corner, revealing the new slide
Uncover Left-Down	The old slide is removed from the bottom left corner, revealing the new slide
Uncover Right-Down	The old slide is removed from the bottom right corner, revealing the new slide
Wipe Left	The old slide is wiped off to the left, revealing the new slide
Wipe Up	The old slide is wiped off the top, revealing the new slide
Wipe Right	The old slide is wiped off to the right, revealing the new slide
Wipe Down	The old slide is wiped off the bottom, revealing the new slide
Random Transition	PowerPoint chooses any transitional effect

After you've decided on the transition you want and are ready to exit the Slide Transition dialog box, leave the one you want highlighted and click OK. But if you want to set other options—such as manual or automatic advance or adding sound effects—don't click OK to close the Slide Transition dialog box just yet.

ADDING THE FINISHING TOUCHES   249

Once you've chosen the effect you want from the Transition Effects drop-down box, the slide in Slide Sorter view shows a small icon in the bottom left corner, indicating that you have added a transitional effect (see Figure 8.4).

FIGURE 8.4
After you choose a transitional effect, PowerPoint adds an icon to show that an effect has been applied to the slide.

When you click OK to close the Slide Transition dialog box, PowerPoint displays the slide and its transition in place in Slide Sorter view without going into the slide show.

Choosing Transition Speed

Some transitional effects work better at different speeds than others. All effects are set to a Fast speed at first, but you can change the speed in the Slide Transition dialog box.

For example, the Uncover Up effect moves very quickly to pull the old slide off the screen. You might want to slow it down for your presentation. Start in the Slide Transition dialog box. In the Speed area, choose whether you want Slow, Medium, or Fast. Again, the preview window shows you the effect of the change.

Don't be afraid to mix and match the speeds of transitional effects. Some naturally work faster than others. The speed of the checkerboard effect, for example, might be plenty slow enough for you, but the Uncover or Wipe effects might work too quickly.

Choosing Manual or Automatic Slide Advance

Certain presentations need a fair amount of flexibility built in, with the opportunity to stop and discuss important points or areas that require more elaboration. For this type of presentation, you would use manual slide advance, so you control when each slide is replaced with the next. This way, you can make sure your audience has enough time to register the information before you move on to the next topic.

Other presentations are geared more toward communicating general information, often giving an overview of a company's progress, an introduction to a new product line, or the "look and feel" of a new organization. For these presentations you may choose to use an automatic slide advance, which has a timer and advances the slides automatically after a specified period of time has elapsed.

Both situations are needed at different times, and PowerPoint includes a number of features to support both types of presentations.

Manual Advance

By default, PowerPoint's slides are set to manual advance. You see this in the Slide Transition dialog box, where Only on Mouse Click is selected in the Advance area. When you display the presentation in a slide show, you must click the left mouse button to move to the next slide.

During presentation, an Options button appears in the lower left corner of the display. You can click this button (or you can click the right mouse button anywhere on the slide) to display a pop-up menu of choices. Using these options, you can move to the next (or previous) slide in the presentation or go to a specific slide. If you want to end the presentation, you can click End Show (see Figure 8.5).

ADDING THE FINISHING TOUCHES | 251

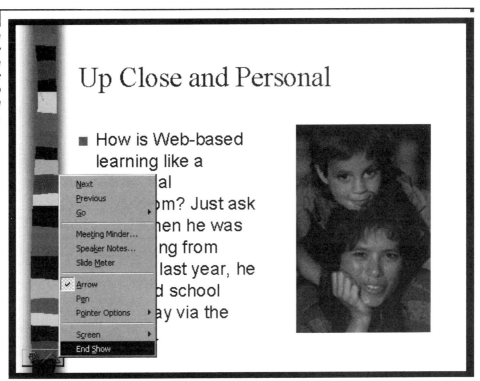

FIGURE 8.5
If you have chosen Manual slide advance, you can use options in the pop-up menu to navigate through the show.

For more about navigating through the various slides in your slide show, see "Moving through a Slide Show," later in this chapter.

Automatic Advance

You can have PowerPoint automatically advance the slides in your presentation by choosing Automatic advance in the Slide Transition dialog box. First click the slide for which you want to enter the automatic advance settings, then, in the Advance options, click Automatically After and enter the number of seconds you want to wait before the slide advances in the Seconds box (see Figure 8.6). The default is 0 (zero).

FIGURE 8.6

Entering automatic settings

> **NOTE**
>
> When you work with automatic slide display, PowerPoint advances the slides for you. In return for this convenient feature, you also lose some control, so it's important that you get the timing just the way you want it before you present if you're going to let PowerPoint advance the slides for you. You can practice and fine-tune the timing of your slide display by using PowerPoint's rehearsal feature. For more information, see "Rehearsing Slide Display Timings," later in this chapter.

After you click OK, PowerPoint assigns the amount of time you entered to the selected slide. (You must set the timing for each slide individually.) The time value is shown below the slide in Slide Sorter view (see Figure 8.7).

ADDING THE FINISHING TOUCHES | 253

FIGURE 8.7
In Slide Sorter view, the timing for automatic advance is shown beneath the slide.

You can change the time allotted for the display of any slide by displaying the Slide Transition dialog box and changing the Automatic Advance value. This modifies the time advance settings for the selected slide, overriding any other settings (such as the ones for Rehearsal mode).

Adding Sound Effects

In Chapter 6, "Adding Sound," you learned the ins and outs of adding sound effects and sound files to your PowerPoint presentations, so we'll just touch on the process here briefly. Remember that even though PowerPoint includes a few sound effects you may want to use in your presentations, there are many third-party libraries of sound effects available that you can add to your slide transitions.

In the Slide Transition dialog box, the Sound area controls whether a sound is added to the transition of your slide. By default, No Sound is selected.

> **TIP**
>
> If you want a sound to play automatically when the selected slide appears, add the sound as a sound effect in the Slide Transition dialog box.

To see what sounds are available, click the Sound down-arrow (see Figure 8.8).

FIGURE 8.8
Scrolling through available sound effects

Scroll through the list until you find the sound you want. If you want to add a sound from disk or CD-ROM, scroll down to Other Sound. When you select that option, the Add Sound dialog box appears, as shown in Figure 8.9. Navigate to the disk and/or folder you need and click the sound file you want to use, then click OK. PowerPoint adds the file name to the list in the Sound area.

CREATING HIDDEN SLIDES | **255**

FIGURE 8.9

Use the Add Sound dialog box to add a new sound to the Sound list.

After you've selected the sound you want in the Sound list, you need to decide whether you want the sound to play only once or repeat. PowerPoint calls this looping.

If you've used a looping sound and want to turn it off at the beginning of the next slide, select the slide on which you want the sound turned off, display the Slide Transition dialog box, and in the Sound area, choose either another sound or Stop Previous Sound.

Creating Hidden Slides

Why create a slide if you just plan to hide it?

In some cases, you may want to create backup slides that offer more information about a specific topic. For example, suppose that it's your job as personnel manager to explain a new benefits program your company is offering. You've got all kinds of data on various programs and benefits.

You're a little concerned that the profit-sharing plan may be confusing to people who are seeing it for the first time. For this reason, you create additional slides showing graphs and bullet lists that can help explain the basic concepts. However, the time you have for giving your presentation is limited, so you only want to show as much information as is necessary. If everyone in the audience already understands the profit-sharing plan, you won't display your backup slides. But if they need a little more of an explanation, you'll have that explanation already prepared and right at your fingertips. *That's* why you can hide slides in PowerPoint.

Hiding a Slide

To hide a slide, follow these steps. In Slide Sorter view, click on the slide you want to hide. Now, click the Hide Slide button in the tools row or open the Slide Show menu and choose Hide Slide. A small box appears around the slide number, indicating that it is hidden (see Figure 8.10).

FIGURE 8.10
The page number is enclosed in a box, indicating that the slide is hidden.

TIP

You can unhide a slide as easily as you can hide one: just click the slide and click the Hide Slide button (or choose Hide Slide again in the Slide Show menu).

Displaying a Hidden Slide

But how do you get to the slide when you need it? PowerPoint knows automatically when you come to a hidden slide. Your presentation will skip right over the slide as though it was never there.

If you want to display a hidden slide (or slides) as you are giving the presentation, just press H. PowerPoint moves directly to the hidden slide.

If you prefer to see what you're doing, you can display the hidden slide by clicking the control button in the lower left corner of the screen. When the pop-up menu appears, as shown in Figure 8.11, click Go To and then click Hidden Slide.

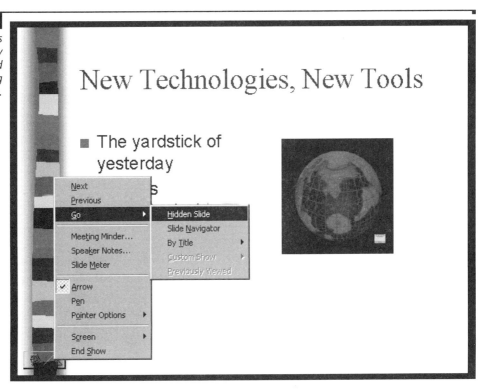

FIGURE 8.11
Use the options button to display the command for displaying hidden slides.

> **TIP**
>
> If the control button does not appear while you are giving your presentation, move the mouse pointer to the lower left corner of the screen. The button will appear.

Rehearsing Slide Display Timing

When you want to rehearse the timing of your presentation, simply click the Rehearse Timings button in the Slide Sorter tools row. PowerPoint displays the slide show, beginning with whatever slide you had selected, and starts a timer in the lower left corner (see Figure 8.12).

FIGURE 8.12
The rehearsal timer

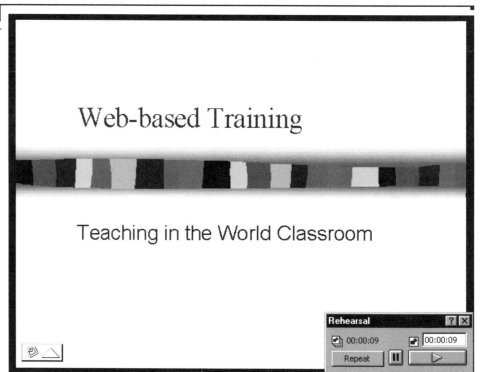

The Rehearsal timer helps you get your spoken presentation synchronized with your slide show. The timing value on the left shows the amount of time expended so far in the presentation; the box on the right shows the amount of time assigned to the current slide. Table 8.2 explains the different buttons in the Rehearsal timer.

TABLE 8.2: REHEARSAL TIMING BUTTONS

Button	Name	Description
Repeat	Repeat	Restarts the timing for the current slide
∥	Stop	Stops timing
▷	Advance	Advances to the next slide and begins timing

While you record the time you spend on each slide, you can go through your notes, pretend to answer questions, or just sit and wait out the amount of time you feel is appropriate. When you are ready to move on to the next slide, click the Advance button. If you want to stop recording, click Stop. To re-time the current slide, click Repeat.

WARNING

The clock in the Rehearsal timer may appear to stop while PowerPoint adds special text effects. PowerPoint is still timing the slide, however; after the special effects have been added, you'll notice that the Rehearsal timer shows that it has added the time.

When you're finished recording the time, whether you've completed the entire slide show or just want to stop rehearsing, PowerPoint tells you the total time your presentation took and asks whether you'd like to record the time settings (see Figure 8.13).

If you want to save the timings, click Yes. The new settings are displayed beneath the slides in Slide Sorter view. To discard the timing settings, click No.

TIP

Another feature, called the Slide Meter, lets you compare the slide timings you set up during rehearsal with the actual timings you use in manual advance in your presentation. Right-click the mouse when in Slide Show View, and you'll see a representation of how your planned and actual timings compare.

FIGURE 8.13

Elapsed time of the presentation

Starting a Screen Show

You may not want to wait until you've finished the entire presentation to display a slide show. Displaying a show as you're creating slides can help you see what you've done and judge the effectiveness of a certain element, font, or color.

You can start a screen show in either of two ways:

- Click the Slide Show button in the lower left corner of the screen.
- Or, choose View ➤ Slide Show.

Even if you don't plan to display your presentation on a computer monitor and will only print it out for a meeting, moving through the slides in sequence can help you make sure you've made the most effective statement possible.

Working with the Set Up Show Dialog Box

There are a number of other options you can set to further customize the way your slide show displays. Open the Slide Show menu and click Set Up Show to display the dialog box in Figure 8.14.

FIGURE 8.14
The Set Up Show dialog box

In the Set Up Show dialog box, you can select the type of show you want to give. PowerPoint gives you a number of options:

- You can have the show display full screen.
- You can display the show in a window so an individual can browse the slides at will.
- You can set up the show to be browsed at a kiosk in full-screen style.

The next set of options enables you to choose whether the show will loop continuously until you press Esc. *Looping* means the presentation will start over as soon as it completes. You can also opt to present the show without narrations and/or without animations.

The Set Up Show dialog box also lets you control which slides are displayed and how they advance. To choose only a few slides for display, enter the beginning and ending slide numbers of the sequence in the From and To boxes. Finally, in this dialog box you can select Use Slide Timings to instruct PowerPoint to control the slide display for you, or choose a Pen Color for your notes and diagrams that you add during the presentation.

For more information on adding notes, arrows, and on-slide scribbles during a presentation, see "Drawing On Screen," later in this chapter.

Moving through a Slide Show

If you jumped right in and started the slide show by clicking the Slide Show button, or if you clicked the Show button in the Slide Show dialog box, you are ready to navigate your way through the slides. The following commands make it easy:

- To move to the next slide, click the left mouse button, press N, or press Enter or Page Down.
- To move to the previous slide, press Page Up or P.
- To cancel the slide show and return to the presentation work area, press Esc.
- If you prefer working with a menu, click the right mouse button anywhere on the slide. A pop-up menu appears. You can then choose the command you want, depending on the direction you want to go (see Figure 8.15).

Using the Slide Navigator

If you want to jump directly to a specific slide—perhaps a slide that you've already displayed—you need the Slide Navigator. Display the slide show pop-up menu by clicking the right mouse button anywhere on the slide when you're giving a slide show. Click Go, and from the pop-up submenu, choose Slide Navigator. The Slide Navigator dialog box appears, as shown in Figure 8.16.

STARTING A SCREEN SHOW   263

FIGURE 8.15

Displaying the Slide Show menu

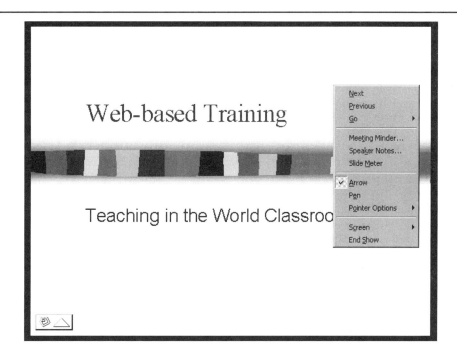

FIGURE 8.16

You can use the Slide Navigator to move to any slide in your presentation.

The Slide Navigator lists the different slides in your presentations by title. The current slide is highlighted, and any slides you've hidden are displayed with the slide number in parentheses. At the bottom of the dialog box, the Last Slide Viewed area shows you the last slide you displayed.

To change to the slide you want, simply click it and then click the Go To button. The Slide Navigator closes and you are returned to the presentation.

MASTERING TROUBLESHOOTING

Tips for Presenters

The more you create and give your own presentations, the more you'll discover the individual challenges and pitfalls your particular industry or business presents. As you're starting out, remember that each situation will have its own unique issues, so it's a good idea to keep a notebook of the tips you discover along the way.

Practice, practice, practice. Especially if you are a first-time presenter or will be presenting in an area or forum new to you, make sure you know your topic—and your presentation—inside and out. Many people prefer to practice in front of a mirror, so they can check out their expressions and gestures. Some people are more comfortable practicing in front of small groups of friends or coworkers. Others videotape the presentation so they can review the result more objectively later. Whatever mode of practice you're most comfortable with, remember to put yourself in the audience and watch yourself from a distance. How are you coming across? Are you enunciating clearly? Do your slides—and slide timings—give your audience a clear picture of what you're trying to say? What can you do to improve your message?

Invite feedback before the event. Few of us like to have our work scrutinized. We don't want to see a red line through a headline we particularly liked or watch someone shake their head while we're giving a presentation. It's not fun to listen to a group of people tell you what's wrong with your work when so few people will take the time to tell you what's right. But toughening your skin and inviting input can dramatically improve the quality and effectiveness of your presentation.

Everyone processes information and reacts to it a little differently. Getting input from a variety of people about what works for them and what doesn't will serve to make your presentation more appealing to a wider variety of people. To some degree, you can control the input you get by asking targeted questions such as, "If you could do one thing to improve the text (or charts or graphics) of this presentation, what would you change?" This makes your reviewer think about a solution rather than just making a broad judgment like, "It stinks!"

> **MASTERING TROUBLESHOOTING CONTINUED**
>
> ***Speak simply.*** Remember that your audience may represent a wide range of education and intelligence levels. Don't shoot for the Mensa crowd, using four-syllable words and obscure analogies. Simple and straightforward is best, especially if you're talking to a high-end audience. Even people who do heavy brainwork for a living appreciate communication that's easy to understand and implement.
>
> ***Show, don't tell.*** A basic philosophy, but probably one of the primary motivations you have in giving the presentation at all. Your presentation—and multimedia in general—gives you the option of creating for your viewer an experience that is much different from a book, a lecture, or a videotape. You've got all the elements—text, sound, video, art—and you can use them interactively to create a totally unique experience. After you finish the first draft of your presentation, display it in a slide show and ask yourself what carries the bulk of your message. If most of your message is in the text, you've missed the boat. Text—the on-screen text in bullets, paragraphs, notes, and titles—and the script you recite (or wing, depending on your style) should be **supporting** what the audience is viewing. With the brain, sight goes right in, but hearing has to be decoded and processed. Don't make your audience read your message. Use your multimedia resources to show it.
>
> ***Start with the end in mind.*** Presentations can be given for all kinds of reasons. Whatever your reasons are—whether you are there to inform, entertain, enlighten, motivate, inspire, or educate—keep your goal in mind throughout the presentation. Your voice, your expression, and your body movements should all be in alignment with your goal. Everything about you communicates something to your audience, so stay focused to make sure that you're sending the right message.

Presentation Special Features

Several of PowerPoint's newest features add to your ability to present. In previous versions of PowerPoint, you had an on-screen drawing feature that let you write notes or circle and underline things to visually emphasize points on the slide during your presentation. The on-screen drawing feature has been enhanced in PowerPoint for Windows 95 so that you can choose colors in a variety of places, making it easier for you to get just the right color contrast for your on-screen notes.

TIP

In some cases, you may want to remove the drawing pointer altogether. Press Ctrl+H to hide the pointer while it is inactive on this slide or press Ctrl+L to hide the pointer for the rest of the presentation. If you hide the pointer and then want to redisplay it later, press Ctrl+L to return the pointer to the display.

PowerPoint includes other features, as well, including the new Meeting Minder—a note-taking utility that allows you to take notes while you present, assign them priorities, and even export them to Microsoft Word so that you can use them again without retyping them.

TIP

For more information on working with Meeting Minder notes, see "Creating On-the-Spot Notes with Meeting Minder," later in this chapter.

Finally, a presentation conferencing feature makes it possible for you to give your presentation over a network, so you can get feedback from a number of sources while you're still in the development stages of your presentation. Or, if you've completed the presentation and need to present to seven top executives scattered across the world, you can actually link everyone up and present in real time through the wonders of telecommunication.

Drawing On-Screen

One of the most interesting things about PowerPoint's display possibilities is the addition of an on-screen marker you can use to annotate your slides during a presentation. Suppose that you are explaining the pecking order of a new division in your corporation and have an organizational chart displayed on-screen. If someone in the audience doesn't understand how a project moves from one department to another, you can use the on-screen drawing feature to help highlight points while you talk.

To start drawing on-screen, press Ctrl+P and start moving the mouse on-screen. Or, if you prefer, you can click the right mouse button to display the slide show pop-up menu and click Pen.

You can choose the Pen Color at several different points. In the Set Up Show dialog box (display the dialog box by choosing Slide Show ➤ Set Up Show), click the Pen Color down-arrow and choose the color you want. If you're already running the presentation, display the pop-up menu, choose Pointer Options, and select Pen Color, as shown in Figure 8.17.

FIGURE 8.17

Choosing a new pen color in the middle of a presentation

Go ahead and scribble on your slides—those on-screen markings aren't recorded. The next time you give the presentation, it will be as good as new.

Creating On-the-Spot Notes with Meeting Minder

In some situations, you may be giving your presentation as part of a small brainstorming session. Your coworkers may be evaluating the presentation itself, giving you pointers or suggesting additional information to include or points you could clarify. Or, you may be gathering information for the next stages of a project, taking notes and deciding on the next logical step in your reach for a particular goal.

Whatever the scenario, PowerPoint now includes a feature called Meeting Minder that makes it easy for you to take notes during the presentation. Once you record the notes, they stay with the presentation (although, by default, they're not visible on your slides). You can, however, export the notes to a Word document, or you can move them to the Notes Pages of your presentation and print them with your slides.

To take notes during a presentation, click the right mouse button and choose Meeting Minder from the pop-up menu that appears. If you're not currently in a presentation, choose Tools ➤ Meeting Minder, and the Meeting Minder dialog box will appear, as shown in Figure 8.18. Enter the notes as necessary in the Meeting Minutes page. When you're finished, click OK to return to the presentation.

FIGURE 8.18

Displaying the Meeting Minder dialog box

NOTE

If you have already entered notes in the Meeting Minder, the notes attached to your current presentation will appear. Otherwise, the Meeting Minder dialog box will be blank.

We've all been there—sometimes meetings turn into exercises in futility, where everyone voices his or her opinion about a topic and nothing really gets done or decided. The Meeting Minder includes a tab for Action Items, where you can record and prioritize the most important issues discussed and the things you most need to take action on.

Adding Meeting Minutes

Especially when you are working in a group, you'll find it helpful to keep track of your project and the tasks it requires. The Meeting Minutes tab of the Meeting Minder can help you keep your thoughts tied to the items you need to act on in order to get the presentation done. Figure 8.19 shows sample notes added to the Meeting Minutes tab.

FIGURE 8.19
Taking notes in Meeting Minutes

Exporting Meeting Minder Notes to Word

Sometimes the information you come up with in a meeting can be really beneficial. Perhaps someone came up with a new slogan, a new topic to introduce, or a new way of handling or solving a particular challenge. If you've captured the notes in the Meeting Minder, you can easily export the notes to Word, so you can circulate the ideas in memos to the necessary people to get things done.

When you want to export Meeting Minder notes, open the Meeting Minder and display the page of notes you want to export. Then click the Export button in the lower right corner of the dialog box. A pop-up box appears, as shown in Figure 8.20.

The first option—Send Meeting Minutes and Action Items to Microsoft Word—is selected by default. When you click the Export Now button, Microsoft Word starts and a new document is opened, with your note text inserted. Remember to save the file by choosing File ➤ Save before you exit Word.

FIGURE 8.20

Exporting Meeting Minder notes to Microsoft Word

When you export the notes from Meeting Minder, the notes from *all* of your presentation slides are exported into the Word file. If you only want to keep some of the notes, you can select and delete any unwanted text with normal text-editing operations.

Presentation Comments and Review

Now in PowerPoint 97, you can add your very own custom "sticky notes" to presentations, reminding yourself of work to be done, changes to be made, or suggestions to be implemented. Later, you can use Microsoft Outlook to e-mail the note to another person on your work team, if you choose.

To add comments to your presentation, make sure you're in Slide View, then open the Insert menu and choose Comment. A small yellow note appears in the upper right corner of the presentation page, with the name of the registered user already entered. A short Review toolbar also appears, with four tools you can use as you add and use notes: Insert Comment, Show/Hide Comments, Create Microsoft Outlook Task, and Mail Recipient (see Figure 8.21). To add the note, simply type your comment. When you're finished, click outside the note area.

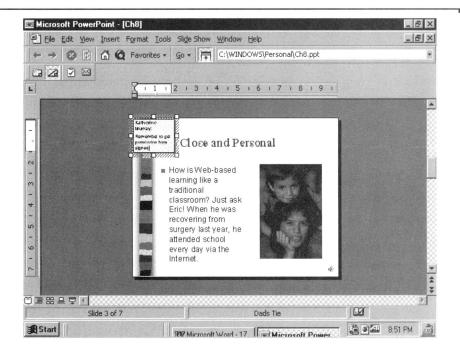

FIGURE 8.21

Adding a sticky note to a presentation page

Presentation Conferencing

If you work on a network, PowerPoint's presentation conferencing feature is available to you. First you need to make sure that PowerPoint knows which computers will be participating. Find out the computer name of all workstations that will be participating by looking in the Identification tab of the Network dialog box. (You'll find the Network icon in the Control Panel.)

Your computer name may be different from your user name. To find out the particulars of your system, consult your network administrator.

When you've got the computer name of all participants, open your presentation and choose Tools ➤ Presentation Conference. A Presentation Conference Wizard will help you set up and run the presentation tailored to your needs (see Figure 8.22). (You'll use the Presentation Conference Wizard to join a conference, as well.) Your presentation starts, and you can work with the pop-up menu as well as add any necessary notes and action items.

FIGURE 8.22

A Presentation Conference Wizard helps you set up and give the presentation conference.

> **TIP**
> If you are not giving a presentation conference but want instead to join one, choose Tools ➤ Join A Conference. You can fully participate in the conference by marking or underlining items with the on-screen pen. Other participants will be able to see your notations and make their own.

Chapter Review

This chapter has introduced you to the ins and outs of presenting your PowerPoint Slide Show. PowerPoint makes displaying your slides easy, and, if you are working in Slide Sorter view, all the tools you need are there on the screen within easy reach. New presentation features like the Meeting Minder and Presentation Conferencing make it easy for you to enhance the concept, content, and charisma of your presentation by collecting feedback from a variety of sources.

The next chapter explains how you can customize the color selections in your presentation to produce just the right mix of color for the effect you want.

PART III

Quintessential PowerPoint

LEARN TO:

- *Work with color in your presentations*
- *Print slides and handouts*
- *Turn your presentation into a Web site*
- *Manage multimedia files*
- *Rehearse, present, and evaluate information*

Chapter 9

Coloring Your Presentation

FEATURING

How Do You Use Color?

A Shortcut to Color Choices: Templates

Making a Fast Color Change

Changing Entire Color Schemes

Working in Black and White

Recoloring Clip Art

Working with Slide Backgrounds

Coloring Your Presentation

Life is colorful—there's no denying that. If you want to bring life into your presentations, color is one of the most effective and enlivening tools you have, whether it's in the form of photographs, video, or background illustrations.

If you use color well, you can dazzle your audience. If you aren't particularly adept at mixing and matching colors, you could drive your viewers batty (or, worse, give them headaches). Recognizing that we're not all equipped with a natural instinct for putting colors together, PowerPoint includes sets of colors known as *color schemes* with each template or presentation design. However, even though the colors for the background, text, graphics, and clip art are already set, you can change any or all of the colors on your own. You can also easily change your color presentation to a black-and-white presentation to see what your slides will look like when printed on a single-color printer.

This chapter explains how you can do a variety of things with color, including choosing a new color in a color scheme, creating your own colors, and using special illustrations for background color in your presentation.

How Do You Use Color?

Using color to your best advantage is one of the surest ways you have of grabbing and holding your audience's attention. Even though PowerPoint sets up the colors for you automatically, here are a few examples of situations in which you might want to change the colors PowerPoint assigns:

- You want to change selected words in a bulleted list to highlight them, as Figure 9.1 shows. (For example, you might change the key words from white to yellow so they stand out against the background.)

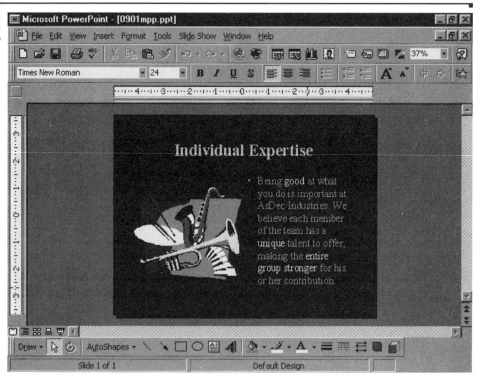

FIGURE 9.1
You can change the color of selected words to highlight them.

- You could change the background of the slide to better complement the main colors in a color photograph you're using on the current slide.
- You may want to choose a different color for the headline text to distinguish it from the main text.

- You might create a custom-drawn logo that you want to fill with a color not included in the original color scheme.

Changing colors isn't just about color—you can also change the pattern, texture, and shading of the colors you use to create a myriad of effects.

A Shortcut to Color Choices: Templates

If you haven't yet taken advantage of the templates that come with PowerPoint, look them over now. The templates—also known as presentation designs—have all the colors preset for you. You can display the variety of templates and presentation designs available by choosing File ➤ New and clicking the Presentation Designs tab. To see the basic colors of the different designs, click the design file once to display it in the Preview window (see Figure 9.2). When you've got the one you want, click OK.

FIGURE 9.2
You can scroll through the presentation designs to choose the color scheme you like.

Templates also can help you find which colors go together—you can learn from the combinations put together by the developers of the software. If you find a set of colors you like, your color problems are over: PowerPoint has done it for you. Turn to Chapter 2 for more information on choosing and using templates.

PowerPoint 97 now includes a "consistent color" feature that helps you keep the same colors in your various Office programs. When you copy a shape from Word to PowerPoint, for example, you can be sure the green rectangle you created in Word is the same color green in PowerPoint.

Making a Fast Color Change

When you know what you want to change and are ready to change it, two options allow you to make your color choices quickly. If you're changing text, choose the Format ➤ Font command and change the color in the Font dialog box. To change the color of the inside or outside of a text box, graphic object, or chart, you can use either the Format ➤ Colors and Lines command or select the color tools in the Drawing toolbar, located by default along the bottom of the presentation window.

Changing Text Color

The most common color change involves changing the color of text. To change text color, highlight the text you want to change and choose Format ➤ Font to open the Font dialog box. Click the Color down arrow to see the color choices you have for changing the text (see Figure 9.3). If you aren't happy with the choices you have, display more colors by clicking More Colors.

If you just want to highlight a word, position the cursor in the word before you choose Format ➤ Font. You don't need to select it. PowerPoint will change the color of the word at the cursor position.

After you've selected the color you want, click OK. PowerPoint applies the new color to the selected text.

MAKING A FAST COLOR CHANGE | 283

FIGURE 9.3

Changing text color with Format ➤ Font

Changing Object Color: Inside

To change the color of an object, first click it to select it, then click the Fill Color tool in the Drawing toolbar.

The Fill Color tool displays a pop-up color menu with a variety of choices, as shown in Figure 9.4. You can select from the displayed colors (representing only a small part of the entire selection available). To change the shade, pattern, texture, or background color, click Fill Effects. If you want color choices other than those shown in the displayed palette, click More Fill Colors. When you make your selection, the inside of the object selected changes to the new color.

FIGURE 9.4

Displaying the menu for Fill Color

You can also use the Format menu to change the color of an object. Select the object, then choose Format ➤ Colors and Lines to change the internal and external colors of the object. To change the entire color scheme of the presentation, choose Format ➤ Slide Color Scheme.

Changing Object Color: Outside

The Line Color tool changes the lines in the object. If you've selected a graphic, chart element, or text box, the line that surrounds the object changes, not the contents. This means that if you click a piece of clip art and expect to see all the lines in the drawing change when you choose red in the Line Color palette, you're going to be disappointed. Only the border of the object will change.

TIP

What does No Fill mean? In the Fill Color pop-up menu, No Fill means that the selected object takes on the color of the background—or is transparent. In other words, when you've selected a text box in which the text appears to be placed right on the background of the slide (as opposed to appearing in a colored box layered on top of the background), No Fill has been selected as the Fill Color. To do away with the line surrounding the object, choose No Line in the Line Color pop-up menu.

Again, you can choose the color or other option you want from the displayed pop-up menu; PowerPoint changes the selected object to reflect the modifications you made.

What If You Want More Colors?

Whenever you have displayed the Font dialog box to change text color, the Fill Color pop-up menu to change the internal color of an object, or the Line Color pop-up menu to change the lines surrounding an object, you have the option of selecting More Colors.

Clicking More Colors displays a "honeycomb" of available colors from which you can choose (see Figure 9.5). The Colors dialog box contains a wide array of color choices. The current color is highlighted in the palette and appears in a preview box in the lower right corner of the dialog box.

The Standard tab of the Colors dialog box broadens your color horizons, but there are still more colors to see. You can define your own color by choosing the Custom tab. This lands you squarely in the world of custom color definition.

Creating Custom Colors

It's not likely that you'll search through all of PowerPoint's color schemes without finding the one you want. If you're particular about the color you need (or if you're trying to replicate something that needs to be a certain color, such as a company logo, or an important piece of art), however, you do have the option of mixing a custom color.

When you choose the Custom tab of the Colors dialog box, you're presented with a mixing board on which you can create a new color, as shown in Figure 9.6.

FIGURE 9.5

Choosing a color from the Colors dialog box

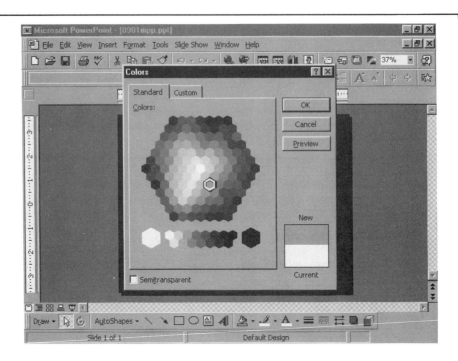

FIGURE 9.6

Defining a custom color

The crosshair shows the current color as well as the levels of red, green, and blue it contains and its hue, saturation, and luminance settings. You can create a custom color in either of two ways:

- Click the color scale at any point where it displays the color you want
- Manually adjust the Red, Green, and Blue settings by entering new numeric settings

To choose a new color by clicking the color scale, just position the pointer on the color you want and click the mouse pointer. The New area of the box in the bottom corner of the dialog box changes to reflect your choice, while the Current area continues showing the current color.

If you want to adjust the settings by altering the amount of red, green, and blue in the mixed color, click on either the up- or down-triangles beside the color you want to change, or else type in a new value. As you make the change, the crosshair moves to show the color you are selecting, and the New area of the box reflects your choice in comparison with the color you have chosen to replace (the Current color).

NOTE

Although you'll probably find it much easier to use the crosshair cursor to change color mixes, typing in values lets you duplicate a specific color, such as "dialog box gray" (192 192 192).

When you've got the color you want, click OK to add it to the selection of colors at the bottom of the Fill Color pop-up menu.

Changing Entire Color Schemes

The color scheme of your presentation defines the color of eight different elements in your presentation:

- Slide Background
- Title Text
- Smaller Text and Lines
- Fill colors
- Three different accent colors for chart elements

One of the greatest things about using a color scheme is that you can easily search and replace one color with another. If you want to replace all blue green with olive, for example, you can do that with a few quick clicks of the mouse.

Viewing and Changing the Current Color Scheme

A presentation that you've begun already has its own color scheme. How do you find out which it's using?

Open your presentation and choose Format ➤ Slide Color Scheme. The Color Scheme dialog box appears, as shown in Figure 9.7. The Color Schemes area shows you what color schemes are currently available—the one currently in use has a border around it, indicating that it is selected. Take a few minutes and consider the variety of colors used. Do they give you enough contrast? Do you like the colors shown for chart elements? For text? Is the background color the color you want? If not, you can change a color or create your own mix.

Want to see which color is assigned to which element? Click the Custom tab. The Scheme Colors area shows you which color is used for title text, for text and lines, for the background, and so on.

By default, you have several different color schemes—color and black-and-white— you can use right away. You can create up to a total of sixteen schemes for each presentation. For more information on creating your own color scheme, see "Creating a Custom Color Scheme," later in this chapter.

To choose a different color scheme for your presentation, click the one you want and click either Apply to apply the new colors to the currently displayed slide only, or Apply to All to apply the color to all slides in the presentation. PowerPoint makes the change and returns you to the presentation.

CHANGING ENTIRE COLOR SCHEMES | 289

FIGURE 9.7
The Standard tab of the Color Scheme dialog box

Creating a Custom Color Scheme

If you want to create a custom color scheme, click the Custom tab in the Color Scheme dialog box. You'll see the basic set of colors you can choose to create the new color scheme (see Figure 9.8).

To choose a new color for an element, select the element you want to change (for example, Title Text) and then click the Change Color button. The Title Text Color dialog box appears—it's the same dialog box you saw when you selected the Custom tab of the Colors dialog box. Choose the new color for the title text by clicking the color in the honeycomb, or create a new color on the Custom tab, as explained in the Creating Custom Colors discussion earlier. Click OK to return to the Color Scheme dialog box.

When you're finished making changes to the color scheme, you can save it by clicking the Add as Standard Scheme button. This saves the color choices you have made and displays the new color scheme in the Standard tab of the Color Scheme dialog box.

PART
III

Quintessential
PowerPoint

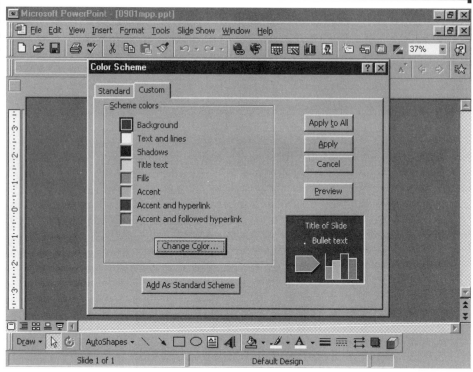

FIGURE 9.8

Choosing colors for a custom color scheme

To make the color changes in the presentation, click Apply to All to change the title text color for the entire presentation or click Apply to change the color for the currently displayed slide only.

Using Apply to All to Globally Replace a Color

There may be times when you are mostly happy with a color scheme but want to replace a certain color.

Apply to All, available in the Color Scheme dialog box, will seek out every occurrence of a color, even an accent color used for a text item, and replace it with the new color you have chosen.

For example, suppose that you like using a particular shade of pink against a sky blue background. However, after getting raised eyebrows from your coworkers ("Do you think Henderson is going to go for *hot pink*?"), and a little doubt of your own, you change your mind about the color. Maybe you'd better use something a little more traditional.

To change that color throughout your presentation, display the Custom tab of the Color Scheme dialog box, click the color, and choose the Change Color button. Then choose the new color you want to replace the hot pink with and click Apply to All. PowerPoint then finds the hot pink in the presentation and replaces it with the color you selected.

If you have assigned a color to more than one element, you must change the color for each type of element individually.

As you work with color schemes, you'll realize how drastic a change you can make with a few clicks of the mouse. You can take a finished presentation and completely change its look with a simple change of background or text color. This is helpful if you travel to different locations to present in places where the lighting is not within your control. You can quickly change from lighter to darker backgrounds to suit the lighting conditions.

You can use accent colors to apply color to any special elements on your slides—items you draw yourself, pen color, object borders, even the background for clip art or charts—without using a color that's already being used for something else. This gives your presentation a consistent look and feel and helps you fine-tune your color choices.

Working in Black and White

To convert any color presentation to black and white you need only click the B&W View button on the Standard toolbar.

Why would you use black and white? For starters, you can produce a presentation with simpler hardware requirements: you can print out the slides, copy them to transparencies, and give the presentation with just an overhead projector. Or you may want to double-check the appearance of the handouts for your presentation. Or perhaps your ultimate goal is not to actually give a presentation at all but to explain your message with handouts. Even if none of these scenarios apply to you, having a good balance of dark and light colors gives your slides and printouts a more polished, professional look.

When you click the B&W View button, the presentation screen changes to black and white. A small Color View window appears in the upper right corner of the presentation that shows the presentation's original color scheme (see Figure 9.9).

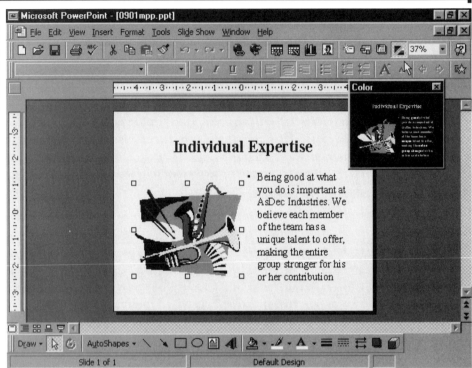

FIGURE 9.9

When you show the presentation in black and white, a Color View window shows you the slide as it appears in color.

When you're working with the Color Scheme dialog box, you can choose a black-and-white color scheme from the Standard tab. Just click the color scheme and click OK.

Setting Black-and-White Options

You still have many color options, even in a black-and-white presentation. Many shades of gray are available in the Fill Color and Line Color pop-up menus. You also have the option of choosing black text on a white background or white text on a darker background.

To see the options you have for black and white, click the object you want to work with in the black-and-white slide. (If you haven't activated B&W View, do so now.) Now, right-click the object to open its pop-up menu. Choose Black and White. Another menu appears, as shown in Figure 9.10.

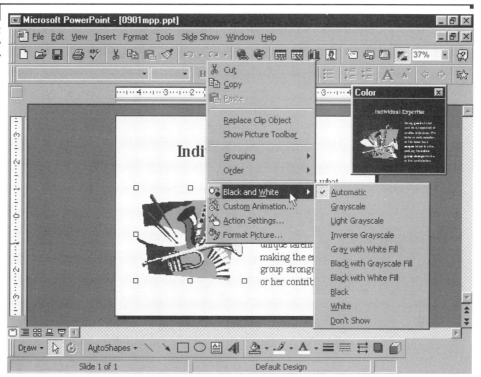

FIGURE 9.10
Choosing options for black-and-white display

This menu appears whether you have selected a text object, graphic, or chart. As explained in Table 9.1, the different options enable you to control just the right mix of grays, blacks, and white.

TABLE 9.1: BLACK AND WHITE OPTIONS

Option	Description
Automatic	Automatically sets the black and white scale as the slide is converted from color to black and white
Grayscale	Displays the selected object in shades of dark gray
Light Grayscale	Displays the object in shades of light gray
Inverse Grayscale	Displays the object with its colors inverted, so light gray becomes dark gray and dark gray becomes light gray
Gray with White Fill	Outlines the selected object with gray and fills it with white
Black with Grayscale Fill	Displays lines in black and shows other object elements in gray
Black with White Fill	Outlines the object in black and fills the internal area with white
Black	Draws and fills the entire object with black
White	Draws and fills the entire object with white
Don't Show	Hides the selected object

Do I Need a Black-and-White Color Scheme or Just a Black-and-White View?

Whether you need a change in color scheme or just a grayscale view of the color scheme depends on your final product. If it's your goal to produce a black-and-white presentation, either for print or for screen display, your best bet is to use a black-and-white color scheme. This enables you to easily control the different grays, blacks, and white used for the different elements in your presentation. If you prefer, you can use the Custom tab to create your own black-and-white palette.

If you're more interested in checking out how the presentation will look in print than you are in creating the most effective on-screen look, use the B&W View button. When you're working in color, it's easy to distinguish between shades. When everything is converted to shades of gray, subtle differences may be harder to see. You can control the grayscales to make the contrast greater by experimenting with the black-and-white options in the pop-up menu.

Recoloring Clip Art

Those of us who were at the candy machine when art talent was passed out are really grateful for clip art. It makes our presentations sparkle, adds humor, and generally provides interesting and informational effects we'd have a tough time creating on our own.

But sometimes the art doesn't come in just the way you want it. You really wish that trumpet were green instead of yellow. Or you want the tree to be orange instead of green.

PowerPoint's Picture toolbar makes it easy to recolor clip art. Click the object; then, if the Picture toolbar does not display, right-click the object to open its pop-up menu. Now choose Show Picture Toolbar. To change the colors, choose this toolbar's Recolor Picture tool, as shown in Figure 9.11. This displays the Recolor Picture dialog box. You can either select multiple items to recolor or simply exchange all of one color (for instance, white, like the white keyboard and drum) with another color to change them all at once. You don't have to ungroup the object unless you want to apply recoloring to only specific items in the group. If you don't ungroup, the color change will be applied to all items in the group with the same color.

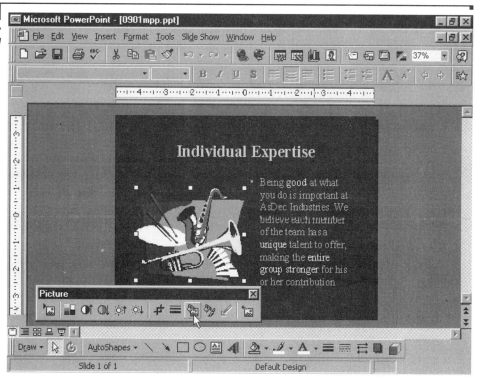

FIGURE 9.11
Choosing the Recolor Picture tool

The Recolor Picture dialog box appears, as shown in Figure 9.12.

FIGURE 9.12

You can recolor the fill or line color of the selected object.

Indicate whether you want to change the Colors or Fills of the object in the lower left corner of the dialog box. Fills affects only the internal color fills—lines are not affected by the change. If you choose Colors, you can change any color in the picture.

Next, click the checkbox of the color you want to change. In the Original column, you see the color of the object as it was before you changed it. In the New column, choose the new color you want to use.

To change the trumpet from yellow to green, for example, you'd select Colors as the Change option; then scroll down to the yellow color, click its arrow, and select green from the pop-up color palette that appears. The preview window shows the change. When you're happy with the recoloring of the object, click OK.

TIP

You can use Recolor Picture to change colors in any object—even photographs and video. If the object you select has more than 64 colors, PowerPoint will warn you that it will list only the first 64 colors in the image.

Working with Slide Backgrounds

Like a color scheme, the choice of a slide background sets off your presentation. Substantial offerings are available in PowerPoint 97.

Start with the presentation you want to change, and choose Format ➤ Background. The Background dialog box appears, as shown in Figure 9.13.

FIGURE 9.13
The Background dialog box

To choose a different color for the background, click the down arrow in the selection box, just beneath the Background Fill display. As you see in Figure 9.14, a pop-up menu appears, similar to the one you see when you click the Fill Color or Line Color tools in the Drawing toolbar.

FIGURE 9.14

Choosing a new color for the presentation background

Using the color scheme colors displayed in the pop-up menu, you can create a unique effect with little effort. The color options speak for themselves: your background will be set to the color you choose.

Another option in the pop-up menu, More Colors, displays the honeycomb palette that we've discussed before in which you can choose just the color you want. Make your choice and click OK to return to the Background dialog box.

The Fill Effects option displays a dialog box with four tabs—Gradient, Texture, Pattern, and Picture—which are fun to work with and can produce really dramatic effects. But be warned: this is your *background*. You don't want to distract your audience from your central message.

TIP If you want to blank the background—removing any graphic elements, logos, or other artwork you may have positioned there—click the Omit Background Graphics from Master checkbox on the bottom of the Background dialog box.

Shaded Backgrounds

When you choose the Gradient tab in the Fill Effects dialog box, you can choose how you want the background shaded (see Figure 9.15). The color of your choice is blended with black, white, or another color of your choice along a continuous gradient, producing the effect of day fading to night across the screen (or a variation on that idea). You can either pick your colors or choose from a menu of preset combinations. When you've got a color combination you like, choose the orientation of the gradation (for example, horizontal, vertical or diagonal) and click OK.

FIGURE 9.15
Creating a shaded slide background

Textured Backgrounds

Textures can produce a really cool effect—try them at least once. You can choose from a wide variety of textures that look like wood, stone, cloth, or even waterdrops.

To see the textures, click the Texture tab in the Fill Effects dialog box, as shown in Figure 9.16. You can scroll down to see many more choices.

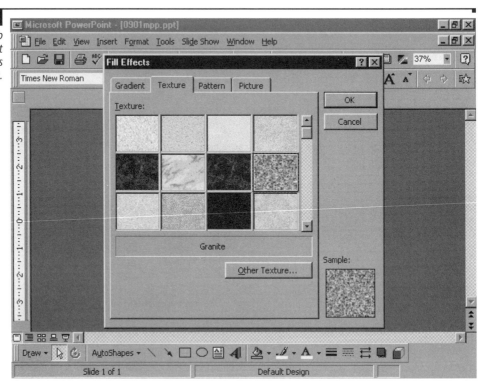

FIGURE 9.16
The Texture tab shows you what PowerPoint textures look like.

You can also add textured backgrounds not included in PowerPoint to your presentations. Click the Other Texture button to display the Select Texture dialog box, and navigate to the drive and folder that stores the background file you want to use. Click the file you want and click OK to add the file. The file is then added to the Texture tab in the Fill Effects dialog box and is available for future presentations.

After you've selected the texture you want, click OK. PowerPoint then applies the new texture to the sample shown in the Background dialog box so you can decide whether you want to apply it to your presentation.

Patterned Backgrounds

When you choose the Pattern tab, you create a pattern by combining two colors of your choice according to any one of 48 different pattern options, as shown in Figure 9.17.

FIGURE 9.17
The Pattern tab enables you to add a pattern to your presentation background.

You can choose the colors you want as the Foreground and Background choices. Try reversing them or choosing other colors to experiment with the effects.

TIP

Make your selection and click Preview to assess the change before you actually make it. The background changes (you can see it even though the Pattern Fill dialog box is still open on the screen). If you like the look, click OK. If you don't, change it and Preview again.

When you've made your choices, click OK to return to the Custom Background dialog box.

Picture Backgrounds

The final tab in the Fill Effects dialog box lets you use a picture from another source as your background. Click Select Picture, as shown in Figure 9.18, to go to the Select Picture dialog box, similar to the Open dialog box. Choose the drive, folder and file type you want. All Pictures includes most graphic file types, or you can choose the specific type you want (.jpg, .tif, .gif, etc.), or All Files.

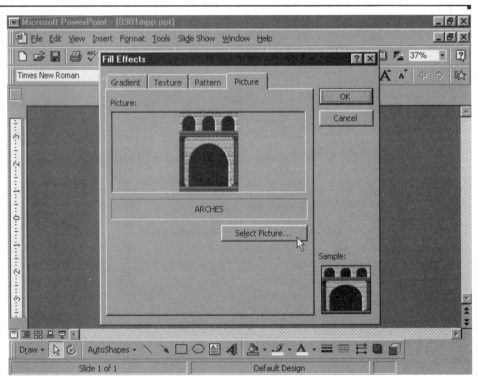

FIGURE 9.18:
With the Picture tab you can import backgrounds from outside Powerpoint.

Chapter Review

PowerPoint makes it easy for you to leave the color choices to the professionals. But when you want to make color decisions or further customize your presentation by adding a shaded, textured, or otherwise customized background, you can easily make changes to PowerPoint's color schemes. The Color Scheme dialog box gives you the power to easily make subtle updates or sweeping changes to a large group of slides.

This chapter has explored the various ways in which you can modify and enhance your use of color in your presentations. The next chapter will help you prepare the handouts you'll print to accompany your presentations.

Chapter 10

Printing Slides and Handouts

FEATURING

Why Print Your Presentations?

Getting Started

Checking Page Setup for Slides

Printing the Presentation

Printing Slides and Handouts

Even though your audience may be dazzled by on-screen effects and riveted by interesting video and colorful designs, there's something convincing about having something printed in their hands.

Think about it. When you're considering buying a new car, you might dial up an online service and look at a few pictures of new cars. You might even send away for a CD-ROM demo disk from a car manufacturer that shows your favorite models in any color you imagine, with any number of options you envision. You might even receive a custom presentation originally produced in PowerPoint. But until you've got some sales literature in your hands—something you can take to your desk and look through at your own pace (perhaps again and again), you're probably not going to feel comfortable writing that check.

When you're creating a presentation, the printouts you create along with the presentation can be almost as important as the presentation itself. The handouts you create do the presenting for you when you're not around to do it yourself.

Today's affordable color printing technology makes it easier than ever to produce slides and/or handouts in full color, close to what appears on the screen. This chapter introduces you to the benefits of printing and describes procedures for printing slides and handouts to accompany your PowerPoint presentations.

Why Print Your Presentations?

You may wonder why you need to take the time to print handouts. Won't the audience see what you're doing? Why would they want the same thing in their laps? Here are a few ways you can benefit from creating handouts to accompany your presentation:

- In some cases, the presentation you give may *be* the printed presentation. If you don't have the means to display the presentation for a group on the screen, you can still print and copy the slides onto transparencies. Or you could create a set of slides, printed and either bound or stapled, to hand out. The actual presentation, in this case, is really made with the printed pages. (If you can make color printouts, so much the better.)

- Your printed presentation can travel farther than you can. Suppose that you are giving a presentation on a new product line to the top fifteen sales managers in your company. They are flying in from all over the country, representing a sales force of over 100 representatives nationwide. Each of these managers will attend your presentation and then go back to their regions, prepared to brief their salespeople. With printouts, the managers can show the slides to the salespeople, answer questions, and stay much closer to your original message because they've got it right there with them and aren't relying on memory to get it right.

- Printouts are easy advertising. If you're competing for attention with a number of other vendors, you can use your printouts not only to remind people of your message but to get your contact information into their hands. Make sure the logo is on all those slides—and put the company name and numbers in the header or footer. A little corporate ID can go a long way.

- If you are working on a group project and need feedback from coworkers before you continue, you can print handouts of the presentation and invite written comments from the other people on your team. You can then mull over the changes you want to make based on the comments made on the printouts and easily implement any necessary revisions.

If you are working on a group project and are hooked up to a network, you can use PowerPoint's presentation conferencing feature to give the presentation to several people on your team at the same time. Team members can use the pen feature to write comments on the slides so you get immediate written feedback without printing. To find out more about presentation conferencing, see Chapter 8, "Finishing the Slide Show."

Getting Started

PowerPoint gives you a number of choices for your printouts: color or black-and-white, single slides or several slides per page. You can also add frames around the slides, or scale the slide to fill the entire page. You'll make all these choices in the Print dialog box.

The type of printer you have will, to some degree, affect the kind of printout you can make. If you have a single-color printer, for example, the chances that you're going to get a color printout are pretty remote! Check out the type of hardware you have available before you invest a lot of time in planning your printouts.

Printing Decisions You Need to Make

Before you start the printing process, consider the answers to the following questions (because sooner or later, PowerPoint will want to know what to do about each of these issues):

- Will you be producing the presentation both on-screen and on paper?
- How large do you want the slides to be?
- Do you want the slides to be printed in Portrait or Landscape orientation? How about your notes, handouts, and outlines?
- How many copies do you want?
- Will you print to a file or to the printer?
- Do you want to print only the current slide, the complete presentation, or a selected range of slides?

"Orientation" is a typographical term used to describe the way the item is printed on the page. Portrait refers to the standard, 8½-by-11-inch format; landscape refers to the lengthwise, 11-by-8½-inch format. If you're printing a single slide on a page and want it to fill the available space, choose Landscape orientation.

- PowerPoint uses the options you choose in the Page Setup and the Print dialog boxes to get the answers it needs for these questions. The next section explains how to check the setup of the slides for your presentation.

A Few Printing Ideas

- When you need to conserve space in your printouts, print slides three to a page. Make sure you use the header and footer to convey any important contact information about your business or project, and number your pages so your readers won't get lost.
- Print sets of full-page slides and put them in folders or envelopes for your sales managers to deliver to their salespeople. Back in their regions, they can use the printouts to create transparencies for their own training sessions.

Use PowerPoint's Pack And Go Wizard to send copies of your actual on-screen presentation back with the sales managers. For more information about Pack And Go, see Chapter 11.

- Print slides with notes pages to help others give the presentation at a later time independent of you.
- If color printing is at a premium in your office, print the first—or cover—slide in color; then print the rest in black and white. (If color is available for all slides, of course, your output will look much better.)
- Unless you're dealing with guarded information, print hidden slides, too, when you print the presentation. That way, audience members who need the additional information can look through it on their own time.

Checking Page Setup for Slides

One of PowerPoint's biggest benefits is its flexibility. You can choose Page Setup options for your slides before you begin, while working on a presentation, or after you finish. Whenever you change the slide size or choose a different orientation, PowerPoint changes the current presentation to reflect your selection.

Display the slide setup options by choosing File ➤ Page Setup. The Page Setup dialog box appears (see Figure 10.1).

FIGURE 10.1
The Page Setup dialog box

Choosing Page Size

The first option in the Page Setup dialog box is Slides Sized for. You use this option to tell PowerPoint how large an area you've got to work with. You can choose from the following choices:

- On-screen Show (the default)
- Letter Paper (8.5 by 11 inches)
- A4 Paper (210 by 297 mm)
- 35mm Slides
- Overhead
- Banner
- Custom

To choose a page size, click the down-arrow to display the drop-down list box and click the page size you want. When will you use the different page sizes? The sizes for

35mm Slides and Overhead are slightly different—Overhead is a bit smaller. With Custom, you can enter the dimensions you want to print. A4 paper is European letter-sized paper, and can be used only if your printer is equipped for it.

You may also be able to change the Paper Size and Orientation for your particular printer by using the Options button in the Printers dialog box, but if you plan to use an irregular page size, be sure to specify it by clicking the Custom option in the Page Setup dialog box.

Changing Slide Width and Height

You can also change the Width and Height yourself, if you're concerned about meeting a particular measurement. When you choose one of the other page sizes, the Width and Height settings change automatically. Change the Width or Height settings by adjusting the values in the box, either clicking the up or down buttons or typing a new value.

If you make changes and then decide to return to the default settings, open the Slides Sized for box and click On-screen Show. The values are returned to normal.

You may never need to worry about the preset size of the slides in your presentation. As a general rule, though, if you use a custom paper size, make sure that for a slide printout you leave at least a one-inch margin all around the edge of the slide to leave room for binding, and stapling. If you're planning on printing notes, you don't need to calculate and resize the slide in the Width and Height box; PowerPoint will do that for you at print time.

Choosing Orientation

The Page Setup dialog box gives you two different options for the orientation settings. When printing slides, you might want to use one kind of orientation (slides are typically printed in landscape orientation), but when printing handouts, you might prefer the more traditional portrait.

When you click a different orientation setting, the Width and Height settings are adjusted automatically to reflect the change (see Figure 10.2). The shape of the background will change, but otherwise the slide's appearance on-screen will not change.

FIGURE 10.2
Changing the orientation

When you're finished with all the Page Setup settings, click OK to return to Slide view. Now you're ready to tackle printing basics.

Numbering Slides

By default, PowerPoint does not put a page number on your presentation slides. To add one, choose Insert ➤ Slide Number. If no text box is currently activated, a message reminds you that if you want to add the number on only the current slide, you must select the text box in which you want the number added (see Figure 10.3).

To add the slide number to every page in the presentation, you must add the number to the header or footer. You can display the Header and Footer dialog box by choosing View ➤ Header and Footer (see Figure 10.4).

CHAPTER 10 • PRINTING SLIDES AND HANDOUTS

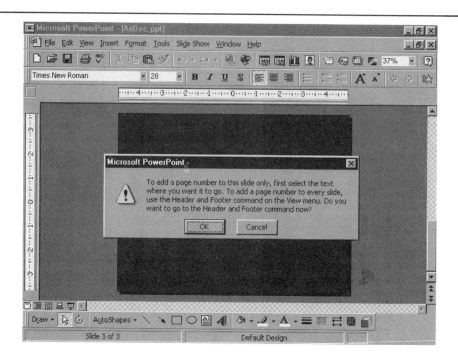

FIGURE 10.3

The message box that appears when you choose Insert ➤ Slide Number

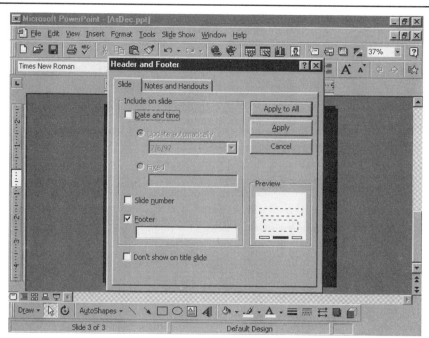

FIGURE 10.4

The Header and Footer dialog box

To add the slide number on the slide, click the Slide Number checkbox in the Include on Slide area. The box in the lower right corner of the Preview window darkens to show you where the slide number will be printed.

Click Apply to apply the slide number to the current slide or Apply to All to put slide numbers on all slides in the presentation.

Adding Headers and Footers

While you're here, you might as well think about the types of headers and footers you want on your slides and handouts. The header and footer on your slides can give important information about your company, your project, or yourself. You might include your company name or logo, the time and date, the name of the presentation, or other important information in the header or footer.

Adding the Date and Time to Slide Printouts

The first option in the Header and Footer dialog enables you to add the date and time to your slide. Start by clicking the Date and Time checkbox. The Update Automatically and Fixed options become available. To add a date that changes to reflect the date on which you print the presentation, click the Update Automatically option and choose the date and time style you want from the list that is displayed (see Figure 10.5).

FIGURE 10.5
Select the date and time you want from the Update Automatically list.

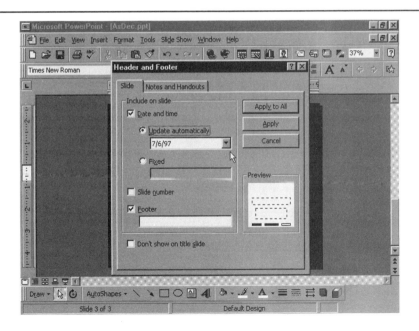

If you want to enter a date that remains the same no matter what the current date is, choose Fixed, then enter the date you want to appear. The Preview box shows the position in which the date and time will be printed.

If you don't want the slide number or time and date to print on the title slide of your presentation, click the Don't Show on Title Slide checkbox in the bottom left corner of the Header and Footer dialog box.

Adding a Footer to Slide Printouts

A footer is the information that prints at the bottom of the printed page. In PowerPoint, you can add a footer to both your slide printouts and your notes and handouts.

To add a footer, simply click in the Footer checkbox. The text entry area becomes available, and you can type the information you want to include in the footer.

Be sure to include only necessary information in the footer. Cramming too much information into the footer will detract from the effectiveness of your printouts.

When you're finished making choices for the slide printouts, click Apply to All to apply the new settings to the entire presentation or Apply to apply them only to the current slide.

Adding Headers and Footers to Notes and Handouts

The second page of the Header and Footer dialog box enables you to make choices about the way your notes and handouts print (see Figure 10.6).

Only three basic differences exist between the Notes and Handouts tab and the Slide tab:

- You can enter text to the Header line
- The Page Number option appears in place of the Slide Number option
- The Apply button is missing (you can only apply these settings to the entire presentation)

Make your choices for the date, time, page number, header, and footer you want on your notes and handouts; then click Apply to All. You won't see the header or footer as you work with the presentation, but they will be there when you print.

FIGURE 10.6

The Notes and Handouts tab of the Header and Footer dialog box

Printing the Presentation

In most cases, printing is a pretty simple process. If you've got all your settings specified and your printer set up, a quick print will probably take nothing more than pressing Ctrl+P and pressing Enter.

First, make sure you've got the right printer selected to receive your PowerPoint file. Choose File ➤ Print or press Ctrl+P to open the Print dialog box shown in Figure 10.7.

FIGURE 10.7

The Print dialog box

Selecting Your Printer

The first item at the top of the Print dialog box is the Name box, where you should see the name of your printer. If a printer other than the one you plan to use appears in the Name box, click the down-arrow beside the box and choose your printer from the displayed list.

NOTE

If you don't see your printer listed in the Name list, you'll need to use the Windows Control Panel to add the printer driver for your particular printer.

To set options for your particular printer—like the paper size or orientation—click the Properties button to the right of the Name box in the Print dialog box.

Choosing Print Options

The print options in the Print dialog box are fairly straightforward. Once you make sure you're ready to run with the right printer, you can choose which slides you want to print, select how you want them printed, and specify the number of copies you want.

The Print Range options control which slides in your presentation are printed. The first option, All, prints all the slides (notes, handouts, whatever) in the presentation. The Current Slide option prints only the slide that was selected when you displayed the Print dialog box. If you have created any custom shows for the presentation, the Custom Show box lets you print the materials for the custom show you want. The Slides option lets you choose a range of slides. To print slides 2 through 4, for example, you would enter in the Slides box:

2-4

To print two different ranges of slides, like pages 2 through 4 and pages 7 and 8, you could enter those specifications in the Slides box like this:

2-4,7-8

NOTE

Don't add spaces before the second range (7-8 in the example above) or around the hyphens.

What Do You Want to Print?

When you've decided which slides you want to print, you need to think about the format in which you want them printed. Each slide in PowerPoint can contain many different types of information and can be printed different ways. Table 10.1 describes each of these different print choices.

TABLE 10.1: PRINT OPTIONS	
Option	Description
Slides (with Animations)	Prints each slide with the additional animated item
Slides (without Animations)	Prints only the completed animated slide with all items in place
Handouts (2 slides per page)	Prints two slides per page: one above the other if Portrait is selected; one beside the other if Landscape is selected
Handouts (3 slides per page)	Prints three slides per page: one above another if Portrait is selected; one beside another if Landscape is selected
Handouts (6 slides per page)	Prints six slides per page: two across and three down if Portrait is selected; three across and two down if Landscape is selected
Notes Pages	Prints the slide at the top of the page and the Notes Page in the lower portion
Outline View	Prints only the text of the presentation in outline form, as it appears in Outline view

To choose the item you want to print, click the down-arrow in the Print What: box. The drop-down list shown in Figure 10.8 appears. Scroll through the list, if necessary, and then click the item you want and PowerPoint enters it in the Print What: box.

How Many Copies Do You Want?

You'll also need to decide how many copies of the presentation (or the range of slides you've selected) you want to produce. Type the number in the Copies: box or click the up or down button to increase or decrease the amount.

The first time you print a presentation or slide, print only one copy. This gives you the opportunity to check what you've done without investing a great amount of paper in a first draft. When you've got the slide the way you want it, go ahead and make multiple copies.

If you want PowerPoint to collate—print in order—the multiple copies you've elected to make, be sure that the checkmark appears in the Collate box. To copy multiples of the same page (for example, print ten copies of page 3 before you move on to ten copies of page 4), remove the checkmark.

PRINTING THE PRESENTATION | 321

FIGURE 10.8

Choosing what you want to print in the Print What: box

How Do You Want the Page Printed?

The final set of print options controls some of the more subtle print choices you may make concerning the way the slides are printed. Here's a quick overview of when you might use these additional options:

- If you've created hidden slides in your presentation (slides that are used as backup—not displayed automatically), PowerPoint enables the Print Hidden Slides option at the bottom right of the dialog box. If you want a printout of the hidden slides, click this checkbox.
- To convert the color slide to black and white tones, click Black & White. This removes any grayscale shading for the best possible black-and-white print.
- If gray areas make your printouts hard to read, click Pure Black & White to eliminate the gray tones.

- If you are working with an irregular page size and are concerned about the size of the slide at print time, click Scale to Fit Paper. PowerPoint adjusts the size of the slide to fit the paper size. If you click Scale to Fit Paper when you're working with a letter-sized page, PowerPoint enlarges the slide to stretch almost to the edges of the page.
- Especially if you are using a black-and-white printout, you may want to frame your slides so readers can easily see where the edge of the slide falls. Click Frame Slides to print the slides enclosed in a thin frame.

Printing to a File

Another decision you need to make is whether you'll be printing to a printer or a file. You might want to do this, for example, to use the color printer that's only available in the office down the hall. You could print your PowerPoint slides to a file, take them down the hall, and print them on that printer—whether or not that computer has PowerPoint. If you want to print to a file, click the Print to file button.

When you click OK to print the file, PowerPoint displays the Print to File dialog box so that you can enter a file name for the resulting file. Enter a name and click Save. PowerPoint then prints the presentation to the file and saves it with the name you specified.

Finally...Printing!

Once you've got all the options set the way you need them, you can print your presentation by following these simple steps:

1. Display your presentation.
2. Open the File menu.
3. Choose Print.
4. Choose the range and number of copies (and any other options).
5. Click OK.

In a matter of moments (depending on the speed of your printer), you'll have the printouts in your hands.

The fastest way to print your presentation is to click the Print button in the Toolbar. PowerPoint sends the presentation directly to the printer using the current defaults.

How Did It Turn Out?

Once you've got the printed product in your hand, it's a good idea to take a few minutes and review what you've produced. Here are a few questions to help you determine whether your printouts look the way you want them to:

Did you use the right colors? If you printed in color (or even if colored screens were converted to black and white output), make sure that the colors you've chosen are not too light. Light blue text will print as very light gray, for example, so against a white background, this isn't the best choice.

Would the slide look better if it were framed? Add frames before the next print by clicking Frame Slides in the Print dialog box.

Is the page cluttered? Remember that open space is as important as the text and graphics on your page. Use it to draw the reader's eye to a certain area on the page.

Would your printed presentation be better for readers if you provided room for notes? You can print Notes Pages so that a reduced version of the slide leaves room for audience notes.

Do the headers and footers contribute to the printout? Perhaps you need to reduce the amount of text in either the header or the footer. Display the Header and Footer dialog box by choosing View ➤ Header and Footer, then make your changes.

Chapter Summary

In this chapter, you learned the basics of making page setup choices and print decisions. Specifically, you learned how to choose the size of the page, the width and height of the slide, and the orientation. You also found out how to select a printer, choose the number of copies and pages to print, and set additional print options.

Chapter 11

Web Publishing with PowerPoint

FEATURING

Web Basics

Creating Links

Displaying the Web Toolbar

Saving Your Presentation as an HTML File

Posting Your Web Page

Chapter 11

Web Publishing with PowerPoint

Just a few short years ago, the term *Web publishing* didn't exist. The Internet was just becoming known to the masses; the World Wide Web was hot on its heels. But the idea of using the Internet was intimidating enough—who would have thought that just a few years later we would be publishing our own materials and posting them on the Internet, ready for a world-wide audience to view?

PowerPoint 97 makes publishing on the Web as easy as creating a presentation. You use all the same tools, templates, and transitions. Multimedia, animation, sound, colors, all the same elements you've been learning to use for presentations throughout the course of this book can be used on your Web pages, as well. This chapter shows you how to turn your presentation into a Web site. But first we'll take a look at some Web basics.

Web Basics

The Internet is a new world—and the World Wide Web is a unique continent in that new world. The Web is a user-friendly way to locate and explore information on the Internet. But there's still a learning curve involved. This section introduces you to some basic information about the Web.

Web Terms

If you are just beginning to learn about the Internet, you may be unfamiliar with some of the terminology you'll see in this chapter. Let's start out by defining a few terms:

- **Internet.** The Internet is a world-wide network of computer networks. More computers are signing on every day.
- **World Wide Web.** The World Wide Web provides a graphical way for Internet users to access information. Users can navigate through pages of information by clicking links that take them to other Web page with related information. The metaphor of the web is taken from the effect of the linking from page to page, forming a world-wide web of information channels.
- **Internet Service Provider (ISP).** Before you can gain access to the World Wide Web, you must have Internet access. You can get an account with an Internet Service Provider in your area or use one of the Internet accounts available through online services such as CompuServe, America Online, or MSN.
- **Web Page.** A screen of information published on the World Wide Web. Individuals or companies may have single pages or multiple pages in their Web sites.
- **Links.** Links are "hot spots" on the Web page that take the user to other pages when clicked.
- **URL.** An acronym for Universal Resource Locator, a URL is the address of a Web page (for example, http://www.revisionsplus.com/kbm).
- **Web Browser.** A software program that enables you to view and navigate Web pages. Two examples of popular Web browsers are Internet Explorer (available free from Microsoft) and Netscape Navigator.

What Does a Web Page Look Like?

If you haven't yet begun exploring the World Wide Web, you may be surprised to find that a Web page looks basically like any other computer program on your computer's monitor. Depending on the Web browser you use, you will probably see the familiar Windows interface, so you won't have much trouble finding your way around.

The difference surfing the Web offers over a typical program, however, is how far information can take you. Links can take you all over the world and back again, enabling you to find in a single afternoon information that might otherwise take months to gather. If you were using a program, the information would be finite—you'd have no way to discover information beyond that programmed into the software. The Web offers you the world—and a continually expanding world, at that.

Figure 11.1 shows an example of a Web page. The Web browser being used is Internet Explorer 4.0. In the toolbar at the top of the window, you see a number of tools that enable you to navigate the Web. The Back button returns you to the last page you visited; the Forward button moves you forward to another link in the sequence you are traveling. The Stop button stops a page from loading; the Search button opens a search window so you can search for topics, keywords, people, or things. The Favorites button opens a menu of Web pages favorites (you add Web sites to the Favorites folder yourself, so the contents of this menu will be different for each person). The toolbar also gives you the means of printing the page, reading your e-mail, and more.

These are the commands for Internet Explorer; Netscape Navigator includes similar buttons and commands in a slightly different interface. Other browsers are modifications on the same theme, but all have the tools to enable you to find, navigate to, and use information on the Web.

FIGURE 11.1

An example of a Web page

When you click the first button on the Web page, **Info for Publishers**, it takes you to another page of linked information (see Figure 11.2). Some pages may have links built into photographs, icons, text phrases (linked text is highlighted in a different color and the pointer will change to a hand icon when you place the pointer over linked text).

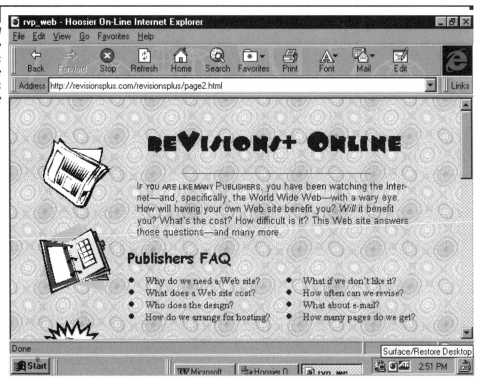

FIGURE 11.2
The page displayed when you click the Info for Publishers button on the reVisions Plus home page

You can scroll down through the page by pressing PgDn or clicking the down arrow on the scroll bar to the right of the work area. Most Web pages include additional navigation buttons at the bottom of the page so you can easily move among other pages in the site.

You can download Microsoft's Internet Explorer free of charge by going to Microsoft's Web site at http://www.microsoft.com/downloads.

Creating Links

In order for your Web page visitors to be able to move from one page to another, you must provide links for them. You can create a link using a button, a shape, a picture, or text. First create the item you want to use as the link. For this example, we will use AutoShapes. An entire palette of Action Buttons has been provided in the AutoShapes so you can add predrawn buttons to your Web pages (see Figure 11.3).

FIGURE 11.3

AutoShapes include Action Buttons for Web pages, but you can use other shapes, images, or text as well.

When you choose the button you want to draw and then drag the shape on the slide, the Action Settings dialog box appears (see Figure 11.4). PowerPoint wants to know what you want to have happen when the user clicks the button. By default, the mouse click will follow a hyperlink to the next slide. Click OK to establish the link.

FIGURE 11.4

After you create the button, the Action Settings dialog box appears, ready for you to establish the link.

NOTE

When you use AutoShapes' Action Buttons, PowerPoint makes guesses about what you want to link to in the Action Settings dialog box. When you create your own buttons or link to clip art or text, however, you must establish the link yourself. In the Action Settings dialog box, click Hyperlink to and click the down arrow to display a list of choices. Click the one you want and click OK.

Continue adding buttons as needed to link up the pages in your presentation. When you are finished, preview the presentation by choosing Slide Show ➤ View Show.

Displaying the Web Toolbar

While you are working on the presentation and creating your Web pages, it will be helpful to display the Web toolbar. You can do this two different ways:

- You can choose View ➤ Toolbars ➤ Web Toolbar.
- *Or* you can click the Web toolbar button in the center of the Standard toolbar.

The Web toolbar then appears beneath the toolbars in your PowerPoint work area (see Figure 11.5). If you prefer, you can suppress all toolbars except the Web toolbar by clicking the Show Only Web Toolbar button in the center of the Web toolbar. The effects of this are shown in Figure 11.6.

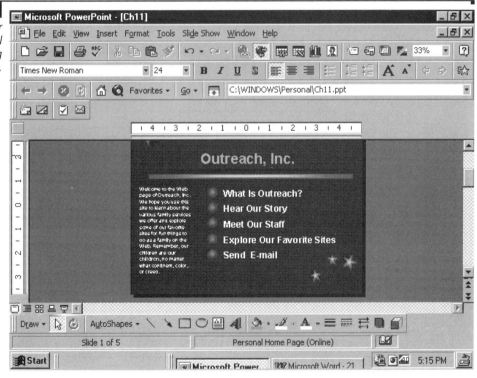

FIGURE 11.5
The Web toolbar gives you additional tools for working with your Web page.

FIGURE 11.6

You can choose to hide all toolbars except the Web toolbar by clicking the Show Only Web Toolbar button.

Saving the Presentation as an HTML File

After you have completed your presentation and made sure all the links work the way you want them to, you are ready to save the presentation as an HTML file.

What is HTML? HTML is an acronym for HyperText Markup Language, the set of tags that controls the formatting of documents for the World Wide Web. When you save a file as an HTML file, PowerPoint adds the HTML codes necessary to format the pages for the Web.

Begin with your presentation open on the screen. Choose File ➤ Save as HTML. The Internet Assistant begins to lead you through the process of saving your presentation as a Web page.

The Internet Assistant

The Internet Assistant is a type of wizard that walks you through the various steps in completing your Web page. When the first page appears, click Next to start the process.

You are first asked whether you want to use a layout you've already created or start a new one. When you click New, the wizard gives you a choice of Standard or Browser Frames. Select the style you like and click Next.

You then need to choose the type of graphics you will use—GIF or JPEG. You can also make a choice as to whether you will use animations and you can give visitors the option of downloading the PowerPoint Animation Player so they can view your animations. Click Next to continue.

The next screen asks you about screen resolution. The capabilities of monitors vary, and for best results you should plan for your Web site to be viewed on the lowest standard, 640 by 480. Make your choices and click Next.

Now you can enter your e-mail address and other Internet information. You can also choose to allow users to download your information. Click Next.

Next you can choose the colors for the links, text, and background. You can choose to use either your browser's colors or choose custom colors. You also have the option to make the buttons transparent. Click Next.

Now you can choose where to put the buttons on your Web page—above, below, to the right, or to the left of the page. Click Next to reach the final page.

The last page of the wizard asks you for the HTML folder in which you want to place the HTML files. You can either create a new folder or click Browse to navigate to the folder you want to use. Click Finish to complete the process.

The next screen asks you whether you'd like to save all these choices you've made as a file so you can use the same selections again later. If you want to save them, enter a name for the file and click Save. If not, click Don't Save.

PowerPoint displays the HTML Export in Progress window so you can see the progress as the program prepares the file for the Internet. When the process is finished, click OK to return to the presentation screen.

Posting Your Web Page

The way in which you post your Web page to the Internet depends in part on the software your ISP gave you for such things. Before you can upload your Web page, you need to have the following:

- Space on a Web server
- Procedures for uploading Web files
- The software needed for uploading Web files

Some Internet Service Providers give you a set amount of space as part of your monthly subscription. My ISP, for example, gives each subscriber one Web page—with only 1 graphic (gee, thanks, guys)—for free. If I want to add more than one graphic (by the way, a graphic is a single button, or a piece of clip art, or a line, etc.), I have to pay for extra space. I found it cheaper and less hassle to open an account with a Web service provider, which is a different animal from an ISP. For a set monthly fee, I get many megabytes of Web storage space, which means I can create as many Web pages as I want to, for my own business, for clients, for whoever needs it. Two Web service providers I've worked with are ForSite (www.forsite.net) and Netfinity (www.netfinity.com).

Next you need to know the procedure for uploading your Web files. Some Web service providers support Microsoft extensions, which means you can use Microsoft's Web Publishing Wizard (you can download this free of charge from Microsoft) to publish your HTML files to the directory on the Internet reserved for your Web page. Other providers require that you use FTP or another utility to place the files where they need to go. Contact your ISP for details.

Finally, you need the software required to upload the files. Again, if you can use the Web Publishing Wizard, you can download it from Microsoft's Web site (www.microsoft.com). The first place to start is your service provider, however. If they don't give you the software you need, they can tell you where on the Internet to find it so you can use a program you know is compatible with their software setup.

MASTERING TROUBLESHOOTING

Trouble with the Web Publishing Wizard?

Not all Internet Service Providers enable you to upload Web pages using the Web Site Publishing Wizard from Microsoft. You may have to look for other avenues. One method that I use works faster and more reliably on my system with my ISP than the Web Wizard: I use CuteFTP from ftp://ftp.cuteftp.com/pub/cuteftp/. First I create the presentation for the Web site; then I choose File ➤ Save as HTML and enter the necessary folder name and click Save. PowerPoint saves the file to the HTML documents for the pages in the folder I specified.

When the save process is finished, I exit PowerPoint and start CuteFTP. (Note: There are many other FTP utilities available on the Internet or perhaps bundled in with the software provided by your ISP. I use CuteFTP because it's easy to use and reliable.) I then upload all the files from the folder to the folder on the Internet that is reserved for my site. It's a simple process that takes 10 minutes or less for most Web sites I publish.

Chapter Summary

In this chapter, you have learned how to turn your PowerPoint presentation into a Web page. Using the features built into PowerPoint 97, you can easily add buttons, create links, and come up with a layout that will help readers navigate your site easily.

The next chapter explains some of the unique challenges of working with sometimes-cumbersome multimedia files. You'll learn how to compress, link, embed, import, export, and prepare your presentations for the road.

Chapter 12

Working with Multimedia Files

FEATURING

The Big File

Linking and Embedding Files

Importing and Exploring Files

Running a Presentation on a Computer without PowerPoint

Working with Multimedia Files

The presentation files you create in PowerPoint—and the graphics, video, sound, and slides they include—will be as different as the audiences you present them to. As you begin creating PowerPoint presentations, you'll discover that managing your files as they accumulate and preparing them for use both in your office and abroad are important jobs.

In this chapter, you'll learn about the nature of PowerPoint files and find out how to best work with them. You'll learn about the different multimedia files you may work with and find out how to link and embed objects in your PowerPoint presentations. Additionally, you'll discover how to import and export files and get ready for a multimedia presentation on the road with the Pack And Go Wizard.

The Big File

Rest assured that your PowerPoint files will be large. Huge, maybe. The basic text won't cause the presentation to take up a lot of room, but the slide backgrounds, graphical elements, and especially multimedia objects such as video clips and sound bytes can push a file into the enormous range. The greater the number of multimedia objects you use, the larger the presentation file. If your computer has sufficient memory and disk storage space, you may not be worried about file size right now. But once you get a number of files on your system, you may be feeling the pinch.

Windows 95 Compression

If you are concerned about preserving disk space (or need to copy a large presentation to disk, which can be a pretty challenging endeavor), you may want to use some kind of compression utility. Windows 95 comes with its own compression utility—called DriveSpace—which will save you considerable hard disk space. You start DriveSpace by choosing Programs ➤ Accessories ➤ System Tools ➤ DriveSpace. Figure 12.1 shows the opening screen of DriveSpace.

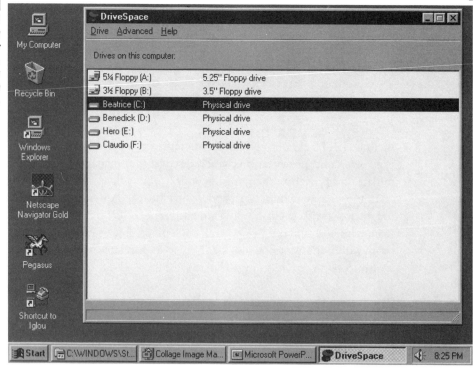

FIGURE 12.1

Windows 95 comes with a compression utility called DriveSpace, which you access from the System Tools menu.

WARNING

In some cases, file compression can cause irregularities when you're playing back multimedia objects. For example, you may hear slight hitches in the narrator's voice as the computer expands and reads a compressed audio file from disk. For best results, if you compress your presentation files, practice the presentation a number of times before you give it live. This way, you'll know what to expect and can determine whether file compression will cause any loss of quality in your presentation.

You may already use a different commercial compression program—like Stacker or DoubleSpace—that compresses your hard disk storage space. Whether you use the Windows DriveSpace utility or another one, compressing files saves you valuable storage space on disk.

TIP

If you are taking your presentation on the road, you can use PowerPoint's Pack And Go Wizard to gather all the files you've used in the presentation—the basic presentation file as well as all sound, video, and graphics files you have used—and compress them into a package saved on disk. Start the Pack And Go Wizard by choosing File ➤ Pack And Go.

Compression Techniques

When you use a program to compress a file, the program writes the file to disk in such a way that it takes up less room on your storage media—whether that's your hard disk or a diskette. Different types of compression are available, but the common denominator is that they look for repeating patterns in data. If the compression software finds a repeating pattern in the file, the repeated data is removed and a direction tells the program to return to the first occurrence of the data when the file is accessed.

When you're compressing video data, you may be working with other compression standards. The JPEG (Joint Photographic Experts Group) method of compression determines which colors are used most in an image file and those are the ones that are updated in each frame; the colors used less frequently are dropped and updated intermittently. This results in a controlled loss of clarity, but it is barely noticeable to the viewer—in some cases, not at all noticeable.

MPEG (Motion Picture Experts Group) compression takes JPEG a bit further by analyzing the current frame to anticipate what is most likely to be displayed in the next frames. This requires less actual processing of each frame because, for example, the background drawn in the current frame is used for the anticipated frames, instead of the background being redrawn for every frame.

> Windows 95 has a Disk Troubleshooter that gives you a list of options to try if you find yourself running out of disk space. To find out more about the options, choose Help from the Windows Start menu, click the Index tab, type **Disk Troubleshooter**, and press Enter.

A caveat, however: Be sure to read up on all available compression utilities before you buy. If you have a system administrator or a technical support person handy, ask his or her advice (or permission) before installing such a program. Especially with Windows 95, you don't want to try anything untested and unproven—playing Russian roulette with your hard-won data isn't a safe bet.

Yet another option—hardware, not software—is a new item called a ZIP drive. A ZIP drive (available from Iomega through computer mail order houses like PC Connection) is a small drive with 100MB removable disks that plugs into your computer's parallel port. It shows up on your system as just another usable drive, but it's much, much more. A ZIP disk stores up to 100MB of information, while your typical 3.5-inch high-density disk stores only 1.2MB. (If you're worried about where your printer will attach, don't be—the printer cable plugs right in to the other end of the ZIP drive, giving you the benefit of massive amounts of storage space and not making you choose between disk storage and printing capabilities.)

Another way you can conserve space—especially at the "save-it-on-disk" end—is by using a zipping utility such as PKZIP or NortonZip. These utilities compress a file (or a set of files) into a single file. This reduces the size and allows you to copy the file to floppy disk. When the disk arrives at the receiving end (whether you or the delivery person are doing the transporting), the person using the file simply uses a partner utility (PKUNZIP or NortonUnZip) to expand the file back into its usable form.

Working with Files

All that having been said, you know you're going to have to work with those files, not just compress them and store them away.

Windows 95 changed the organizational strategy of the way files are stored. We no longer have the "directory" and "subdirectory" concept at work; now everything is "folder" and "folder within a folder" terminology. No matter. The most important thing about the way you store your files is that it makes sense to you and you know how to find the files you need with a minimum of toil and trouble.

Here are some guidelines for basic file organization you should know before you get started working with files:

- Don't lump too many different files in one "catch-all" folder. If you have a number of multimedia files for a particular presentation, create a different folder for each object type. For example, have a Sound folder, a Video folder, an Art folder, and a Presentation folder.
- If you don't have the folders you need, create them.
- Use folders within folders to help organize files clearly.

Planning File Organization

Most likely, you've already got some kind of organization going on your computer. You've probably been using Windows Explorer and saving, copying, renaming, and deleting files in various folders. Figure 12.2 shows an example of the Windows Explorer.

FIGURE 12.2

The Windows Explorer organizes files into folders.

Take a moment and look through the way you currently organize your files. Hopefully, you'll see some method there. You may be organizing files one of these ways:

- by client
- by application
- by project
- randomly

If you are organizing your files by client, you would have a folder named for the client you are working with (for me, a client folder would be SYBEX). Inside the folder, you would store all files related to that client, such as text files, illustrations, outlines, memos, etc. If the number of files inside the folder warrants a subdivision, you can create additional folders inside the CLIENT folder to help organize those files. (I might, for example, create the subfolders TEXT, FIGURES, MEMOS, and OUTLINES.)

If you were organizing folders by application, you might create one folder for your POWERPOINT files, one for your WORD files, and yet another for your EXCEL files.

If you are organizing your files by project, you approach the task from a different angle. When preparing for an annual meeting, for example, you might name a folder MEETING97. Then, everything related to that meeting—PowerPoint presentations, sound files, video, art—would go in the MEETING97 folder. Again, if the file load makes division practical, you can add folders within MEETING97 to clarify the organization and make files easier to find.

The one way you don't want to store files is randomly. The temptation may be very great—especially at first, when you haven't created many presentations—to just dump the file in whatever folder comes up when you click File Save. Fight it. Get organized from the beginning, as it's much easier than cleaning up messes later.

What Kind of Files Will You Use?

The "multi" in multimedia guarantees that you'll be working with a variety of different objects in your presentations. PowerPoint supports a number of files in different formats related to the object you're working with. Basically, the files you'll be using fall into the following categories:

- **Text files.** Text files you import might include Microsoft Word tables or outlines, text copied from another open Windows application like Works or Notepad, or a WordPad document you insert as an object on the slide. Figure 12.3 shows a table from a Microsoft Word document used in a PowerPoint presentation.

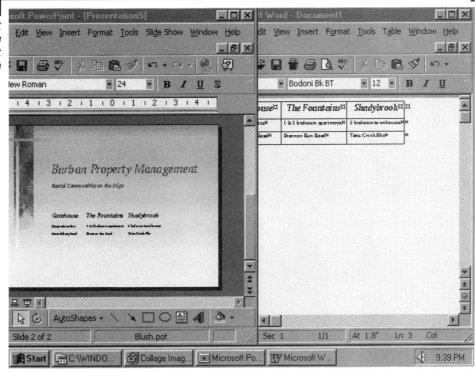

FIGURE 12.3
Using a Microsoft Word table in a PowerPoint presentation

- **Art files.** You might use clip art or custom art files from a variety of sources and in a variety of formats. The format of the art file depends to a certain extent on the program that created it—some art programs create bitmapped images, which are images drawn as a pattern of dots on the screen. Photographs, for example, are bitmapped images. You can see the individual color dots in the enlarged photo on the slide in Figure 12.4.

The other type of art file you might work with is a vector image. Instructions in the vector image's file tell the computer how to recreate the object on the screen; as a result, the art is based on mathematical calculations and not on dots, which gives you a smooth art object that's easy to modify.

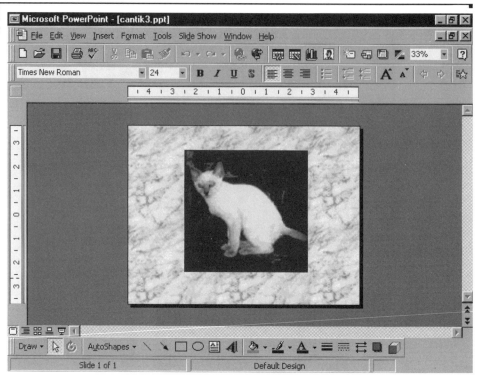

FIGURE 12.4
A bit-mapped image

- **Video files.** The video formats you'll be working with will most likely be AVI (which stands for Audio Video Interleaved—a standard that mixes sound and video) or JPG, a format that compresses video data based on recognizing the patterns of color used in the video file.

- **Sound files.** When you either record or acquire sound files for use in your presentations, you'll be working with either MID or WAV files. For more information on working with MID and WAV sound files, see Chapter 6, "Adding Sound."

- **Presentation files.** One of the multimedia objects you add in your PowerPoint presentation may be another PowerPoint presentation. PowerPoint files end with the extension .ppt, and you use Insert ➤ Object to add the presentation file as an object.

> You can add a single PowerPoint slide as an object by choosing Insert ➤ Object and selecting Microsoft PowerPoint Slide from the Object Type list.

Linking and Embedding Files

All Windows programs have the capability of linking and embedding objects. OLE (object linking and embedding) is the ability to include in your current application objects you create in other programs and then update them from within that application or have them updated automatically when you change the object. Whether or not this technology works for you probably depends on how much memory and disk storage your computer has available. In most cases, linking and embedding won't be a problem—although it may work slowly in terms of screen updates.

Linking and embedding objects is particularly important when you're working with presentations graphics because many of the elements you rely on to provide information in your presentation may be created in other programs. For example, you might use a financial report created in Microsoft Works to compare the results of several sales regions, a logo created in Windows Paint as part of the on-screen demo, or incorporate sound into your presentation. All of these items and more can be linked or embedded in your presentation.

Linking vs. Embedding

When you link an object to your PowerPoint file, you create a connection between the object, which you insert in your presentation, and the program in which you created it. Then, when you update the file in the original program, the linked version of the file is updated as well. For example, suppose that you are linking the Microsoft Works spreadsheet to your PowerPoint file. When you make changes to the spreadsheet later, during a Works work session, the changes are automatically updated the next time you start PowerPoint.

When you embed objects, the data becomes part of the new document, and if data in the sponsoring program is updated, the changes are not reflected in the embedded object. You can, however, move directly to the sponsoring program by double-clicking an embedded object. You saw an example of this in Chapter 7, when you learned about editing video files. When you double-click a video object on your PowerPoint slide, you are taken directly to the Media Player, where you can edit the clip as necessary and then return to the PowerPoint presentation.

For example, if you inserted a section of a Microsoft Word report into PowerPoint as an embedded object and then wanted to modify it, you would double-click the object and Word would open with the outline displayed. When you made the changes and closed Word, the changes would be reflected in the embedded outline.

Linking and embedding objects in your PowerPoint files not only saves you from duplicating effort—you don't have to enter something in one program and then retype it in PowerPoint—but you also cut down on your margin for error. Linking and embedding can help you ensure that you've used the most up-to-date information you've got on hand in your PowerPoint files.

Linking Objects

To link an object in PowerPoint, first display the slide on which you want the object to appear. Then open the Insert menu and choose one of the following items:

- Picture
- Text Box
- Movies and Sounds
- Chart
- Object
- Hyperlink

In this case, because we're talking about inserting objects, select Object on the Insert menu. The Insert Object dialog box appears, as shown in Figure 12.5.

The options in this dialog box are set assuming that you are going to create a new object. To link an existing file to the presentation, click the Create from File option. When this option is active, the Link checkbox appears to the right of the Browse button, as Figure 12.6 shows. The Link checkbox controls whether the object is linked or embedded—unchecked, the object will be embedded; checked, the object will be linked.

If the file you want to link is not in the open folder, click the Browse button. The Browse dialog box, similar to the File Save dialog box, appears so that you can navigate through folders as necessary to locate the file you want.

LINKING AND EMBEDDING FILES | 351

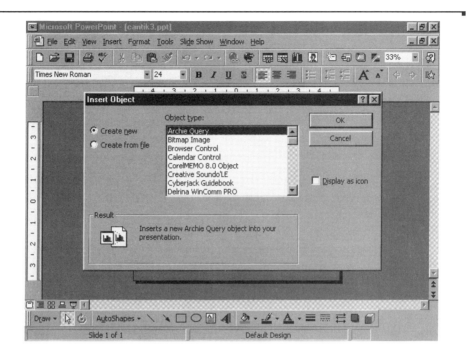

FIGURE 12.5

The Insert Object dialog box

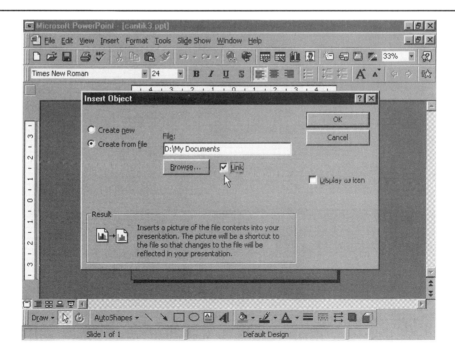

FIGURE 12.6

Preparing to link an object

PART
III

Quintessential
PowerPoint

If you are looking for a specific type of file but don't remember where you've stored it, you can use PowerPoint's search capabilities to locate it for you. If you know the name of the file, type it in the File Name: box at the bottom of the Browse dialog box, then click Find Now. If you don't know the name, use the choices in Files of Type to narrow your search. PowerPoint will search the folders you've specified and display the results of the search in the window in the center of the dialog box.

If you've used the Browse command to locate the file, select the file you want and click OK to return to the Insert Object dialog box. The name of the file you selected now appears in the File text box.

To establish a link between the original file and the object you are inserting in your PowerPoint file (remember, this means that the file will be updated to reflect any changes you make in the original file), click the Link checkbox. If you want the object to appear as an icon and not as a file or object in itself, click Display As Icon. You might do this, for example, if you are inserting a report in your presentation that you would want to cover in a meeting only if questions were asked. If you linked the report as an icon, you would have the option of displaying it or not, as the situation required.

You can change the icon used to represent the object. Click Display As Icon; then click the Change Icon button. A small pop-up dialog box gives you the chance to choose the icon you want to use. Click OK to return to the Insert Object dialog box.

When you've made your selections and are ready to return to the presentation, click OK. The Insert Object dialog box closes and the object appears on the current slide.

Embedding Objects

Embedding objects is a similar procedure. Again, you display the Insert Object dialog box by choosing Insert ➤ Object. You can choose either Create New, and select one of the options from the Object Type list, or select Create From File and locate the file you want to embed.

This time after clicking Create From File, don't select the Link checkbox. PowerPoint will copy the object into the PowerPoint file without maintaining the data links to the original file. This means that when the original object is updated, the changes won't be reflected in the PowerPoint object. You can, however, edit the object you've embedded in PowerPoint by double-clicking the object. This takes you right to the program associated with that file type.

Importing and Exporting Files

There will be times when you want to use files created in other applications in your PowerPoint presentations. If you have been working with an earlier version of PowerPoint, for example, you may want to use the files you've already created as the basis for your PowerPoint 97 files.

Importing Presentations

To use a file from an earlier version of PowerPoint, Choose File ➤ Open. Display the folder or drive in which the file is stored. Select the file you want to use and, in the Files of Type text box, choose Presentations and Shows. PowerPoint will automatically convert the file, and when you prepare to save the file, the program will remind you that it was previously saved in a different version and ask for confirmation before continuing.

Exporting Presentations

Exporting a presentation is nothing more than saving it in a format different from the usual PowerPoint 95 format. To export a file, you use the File menu's Save As command. The Save As dialog box appears. Choose the drive or folder in which you want to store the file, then enter a file name and choose the format you want in the Save as Type: text box.

PowerPoint allows you to choose between many formats to save your presentation, including:

- Presentation (the default PowerPoint 97 format)
- Windows Metafile
- Outline/RTF
- Presentation Template
- Powerpoint Show
- Previous versions of PowerPoint
- GIF (.gif graphics file)
- JPEG (.jpg graphics file)

After you've made your choice, click Save. PowerPoint then saves the file in the format you specified.

Running a Presentation on a Computer without PowerPoint

If you need to run your presentation on a computer without PowerPoint on it, look no further. PowerPoint 97 includes the new Pack and Go Wizard, an automated utility that assembles the different pieces of your presentation into one neat little package that you can then run on another computer, even one without PowerPoint.

You might do this, for example, when you have been working on a presentation for a client and want them to double-check it before the corporate meeting. Or you might send a self-running demo of a new product to a potential client. For any number of purposes, the Pack and Go Wizard can help you get your presentations out and about, where they can communicate your message with or without PowerPoint.

Using the Pack and Go Wizard

To use the Pack and Go Wizard, start with the presentation you want to use open on the screen. Next, open the File menu and choose Pack and Go. The first screen of the Pack and Go Wizard appears, as shown in Figure 12.7.

FIGURE 12.7
The Pack and Go Wizard lets you put the pieces of your presentation together and take them on the road.

The next screen of the Pack and Go Wizard asks you which presentation (or presentations) you want to pack. The active presentation is shown first. Click Next to continue.

You can package multiple presentations in one Pack and Go file by clicking Other Presentation(s) and then clicking the Browse button. Choose the files you want to include by pressing Ctrl and clicking the files you want to package.

Next, the Pack and Go Wizard asks you where you want the packaged presentation to be stored. If you will be sending multiple copies of the packaged presentation out to different clients, you may want to keep a copy on your hard disk so you can make copies easily. If you are packaging the presentation just this once—perhaps so you can take it home and spend some time reviewing it after the kids go to bed—you can get away with creating a copy on Drive A.

The Pack and Go Wizard will then ask you whether you want to include linked files and/or embedded fonts in the presentation. These will require some extra space—some linked files, especially sound or video files, may take a large amount of space—but for your client to see the full impact of the presentation, consider packing all elements you included in the original.

The final step involves determining whether you need to include the PowerPoint Viewer, a utility that enables users who don't have PowerPoint to view the presentations on their computers. The Include PowerPoint Viewer option is checked by default.

The Viewer included in the Pack and Go Wizard works only on computers running Windows 95 or Windows NT. PowerPoint includes a different Viewer disk—enclosed in your software package—that will run the presentation on earlier versions of Windows.

The final step is to click Finish. PowerPoint then gathers all the file elements, compresses them, and stores them in the location you specified.

Now the PowerPoint Viewer includes password protection for presentations you run on kiosks. You can also hyperlink to other presentations or to an established Web site.

Running the Presentation

When it's time to run the presentation on the remote computer, start Windows 95, insert the disk containing the presentation in drive A, and display the drive window. Locate the PowerPoint file produced by the Pack and Go Wizard, and double-click it. After a few moments, your presentation will begin, showing the colors, page layouts, special effects, transitions, and any multimedia features you used in the original.

Chapter Review

In this chapter, you learned some of the particular challenges you face in working with multimedia files. Although they can be enormous, you can juggle multiple files gracefully with a little forethought and organization. Additionally, you learned how to link and embed objects in your PowerPoint files, and learned about the Pack and Go Wizard, which assembles all the different pieces of your presentation into one neat package. The next chapter finishes off the book by taking you right up to the point of no return: live presenting.

Chapter 13

You're On! Giving the Presentation

FEATURING

What Is a Finished Presentation?

What Are Your Options for Presenting?

Effective Rehearsal Techniques

PowerPoint Case Studies

You're On! Giving the Presentation

Throughout the course of this book, you've created a wide variety of elements that fit together to produce an interesting, informative, and effective presentation. Whether your presentation is for a brainstorming group of four or five coworkers, or a room full of sales associates from all over the Midwest, the moment of truth comes when you actually step in front of that group and start the show. This chapter helps you double-check the effectiveness of your plan by reminding you of your presentation options, guiding you through a trial run, and suggesting ways for you to evaluate the entire presentation and fine-tune any remaining details. At the close of this chapter, you'll see examples of how different people have used PowerPoint to meet very different presentation needs.

What Is a Finished Presentation?

When you're working on a presentation, and especially when you're up against a tight deadline, you may feel like your presentation will never be done. Like a book, a video, a corporate report, or anything else, there's always room for improvement.

Therefore, you may find yourself continually updating and improving your presentation, even after you've given it a couple of times. Just think of all that's gone into it—by the first time you give your presentation, you've done all of the following things:

- You've created the presentation design, using one of PowerPoint's templates or by starting with a blank presentation and choosing background, text color, and design.
- You've written the basic text for your presentation message, using the AutoContent Wizard or constructing your own from scratch.
- You've checked for spelling errors in your text with the Spelling Checker.
- You've planned, created, and revised any charts you'll use to illustrate data trends and relationships.
- You've used PowerPoint Central or ValuPack to locate fresh new movies, sound, and art.
- You've incorporated logos, background art, or illustrations, by using AutoClipArt to find appropriate clip art or by importing or creating graphics.
- You've added multimedia objects where applicable, including sound, video, and animated objects.
- You've checked for consistency in your presentation's use of visuals, punctuation, and spelling with the Style Checker.
- You've added slide transitions and timed the display of slides.
- You've planned printed materials, including notes pages, handouts, and full slide prints.

What Are Your Options for Presenting?

Many presentations aren't given in the boardroom. They occur on the desk of a prospective client, in the lunchroom, or in the convention hall. Often, you may not be the sole focus of all eyes in the room, but must compete with other presentations in other booths, all vying for the same attention.

Perhaps you won't even be face-to-face with the people you're presenting to. You can arrange to give your presentation online, using PowerPoint's conferencing capabilities. When you give your presentation over your company's network, you can elicit direct responses from all participants and control the timing and progression of slides.

NOTE

For information on setting up and giving an online presentation conference, see Chapter 8, "Finishing the Slide Show."

In another scenario, you may simply be creating the presentation, packing it up with the Pack And Go Wizard, and sending the disk off to your client(s) so they can load and review it themselves. You don't have to stand up in front of anyone; you won't even be around to hear the comments from the peanut gallery. The presentation, in this case, must speak for itself.

Finally, rather than standing up with a computer monitor (for small groups) or a large projection screen (for larger groups), you might be using a slide or an overhead projector. In that case, you won't be standing alone with a monitor in front of your audience; instead, you will be working with a slide projector or an overhead and transparencies. Even if you aren't giving a slide show with special transitional effects, the quality, color, and content of your slides will be extremely important. For low-budget presentations, you can create the slides yourself by printing the slides in color on printer-ready transparencies. For higher-budget presentations, you can have slides professionally prepared by a copy center that creates slides.

PowerPoint 97 includes a number of options that help you further customize the way you present your work. Consider using these features as you give your presentation:

- **View on two screens.** Now you can link your computer to two screens so you can see your notes and on-screen tools on one computer monitor while displaying the presentation on the other.

- **Kiosk presentations.** If you are planning on setting up your presentation to run continuously as a loop or you want to allow individual users to navigate through the presentation at their own pace, you may want to set up the presentation to run kiosk-style. You can also add voice-over narration that plays continuously during the presentation.

- **Custom shows.** You don't need to create a new presentation every time you want to present one, especially not if you already have one that includes slides you'd like to use. You can choose a subset of any set of slides to show in a customized presentation, rearranging them in a new order if necessary, and with any slides you want to add. Further, even though you may be reordering slides at will and creating multiple custom shows from subsets of various existing presentations, you won't be affecting those presentations. PowerPoint keeps it all straight for you.

- **Improved Meeting Minder.** The new, improved Meeting Minder records your notes and action items as you go through your presentation. You can simply keep the Meeting Minder dialog box open on the screen and add to the notes as needed.
- **Enhancements to presentation conferencing.** PowerPoint 95 introduced presentation conferencing, a feature that enables you to give your presentations over the company network or over the Internet and gather feedback from participants. PowerPoint 97 improves presentation conferencing by giving you the options of giving presentations over Windows NT networks, intranets, Novell networks, and the Internet. A wizard guides you through the process of setting up the conference and making the connection.

Effective Rehearsal Techniques

When you've got all the pieces in place, timed out the slides, and added any transitional effects, you're ready to take a trial run. Here are some pointers.

Even If It's Informal, Practice

If your presentation is one you're giving to coworkers around the lunch table, you may want to practice with one other trusted friend as an advisor. You could do a blind presentation, where you simply give the presentation as you would to any audience member, and ask your friend afterwards a series of questions to see whether she "got the message." Or, if you want her to watch for a certain aspect of your presentation, you can tell her what you're trying to accomplish before you begin so that she knows where you're going and can tell you afterward whether your presentation got there.

Choose a Diverse Trial Audience

If you are designing a presentation you will be presenting to a variety of different clients—for example, a corporate ID piece that introduces your training service to large corporations—practice the presentation with many different types of people. Ask people of different age groups and experience levels for their suggestions and observations. Be open to constructive criticism, and be committed to making the best possible representation of your company before you take it on the road.

Include Setup in the Trial Run

Don't forget to practice setting up and arranging your materials. If you will be unpacking a laptop, setting up a docking station and speakers, and laying out printed booklets, brochures, and business cards, practice those things so that you know the whole routine from start to finish.

Go Straight through, from Start to Finish

Even if you forget something or stumble through a transition, keep going. The experience of moving through the entire presentation is more important that doing the same part over and over again until you get it right.

When You're Finished Giving the Trial Presentation, Evaluate

Don't just pack everything away; consider what you've just done. You can use the following questions to help you gather information about your presentation:

What Parts of Your Presentation Need to Change?

Foremost in your mind, once you've finished the trial run, should be what you need to change about your presentation. Avoid the temptation to be overly critical or to tell yourself that the glitches don't matter, that no one will notice. The glitches do matter, and someone is sure to notice. If you resolve to make your presentation the best it can be, the quality will show in your work and in the way you present yourself. Look clearly at what works and what doesn't in your presentation and improve it as necessary.

Will Anything Make You More Comfortable Presenting?

Sometimes something as simple as a word change can make a sentence a whole lot easier to say. Think through your trial run and, at any points that you hesitated or lost momentum, ask yourself whether a change would make the presentation clearer. A different word, the addition of clip art, a new chart, a different title—each of these small changes might make a big difference in how easily you present the slide.

What Does Your Audience Think?

If you went through the trial run in front of a group, ask your audience whether anything needs to be clarified. Make a list of any suggestions or changes your audience members suggest. Then, later, when you review your notes, you can decide whether—and how—to implement any of the changes they've suggested. Although input from others is important, you are the one who understands best what you're trying to communicate. Weigh each suggestion against your message and make sure it fits before you change anything.

Especially if you will give your presentation again and again, any investment you make now in targeting and fine-tuning the presentation will be well worth it in the long run.

PowerPoint Case Studies

As you've seen again and again throughout this book, one of the best features PowerPoint offers is its flexibility. Whether you'll be presenting to one person or a party of a hundred, you can create an attention-getting presentation that communicates with vibrant color and vitality the concept you're trying to get across. This section gives you a cross section of examples, showing how PowerPoint can be used in a variety of presentation situations.

The Small Group

Linda is responsible for introducing a new product line at her publishing company. After researching the potential market, Linda has created a presentation to show how her department's brainchild—a new line of instructional videos—is a good risk for budget dollars.

The presentation itself consists of 20 different slides—some bullets, and some builds—with charts showing industry trends compared to current statistics on video sales and projections for the future. A sample video clip and voice-over by a celebrity narrator are part of the presentation itself. Animation is used to zoom in the logo and colors and styles have been chosen to convey an upbeat, modern tone.

Linda will be presenting to a small group of departmental managers in a conference room, so she'll use a large-screen PC monitor to do the actual display. In addition, she has printed handouts with a full-color copy of the opening slide as the front cover, Notes Pages to highlight important points, and handouts including a small reproduction of each slide.

On the Road

Brian works for an insurance company. Part of their new computerized system allows Brian to take his laptop to prospective clients, dial up the home office, and run a professionally made PowerPoint presentation from the company mainframe.

This high-quality piece gives the client a taste of what's possible with that insurance provider.

When Brian cannot access the mainframe, or when communication lines are busy or slow, he can use a prepackaged version of the presentation to show the client. In this case, he loads the presentation from the disks he created with the Pack And Go Wizard, and he can show the presentation on his laptop or, if he's included the PowerPoint Viewer on the disk, he can leave the disks with the client to review at his leisure.

To reinforce his message, Brian prepares a printed handout showing all the slides in the presentation, along with notes providing the phone numbers of the various insurance departments at his agency. His name, number, and e-mail address, and his company's Web site, are printed as a footer at the bottom of each page so the client can easily find the information to contact him.

The Corporate Meeting

Don has been working on the corporate meeting for almost six months. He's planned the site, polled the prospective attendees to find the most available date, taken care of everything from reservations to catering to parking, and has now inherited the task of overseeing the production of the main presentation. His assistant did much of the assembly work on the presentation, even finding appropriate video in the company archives and digitizing it for use in PowerPoint. Don hired a writer to produce the text, an artist to do custom graphics, a musician to create a piece of music to introduce the presentation, and a camera operator to produce a video of the CEO welcoming everyone to the meeting, superimposed on flashing images of employees at work.

Even though Don won't be presenting himself, it's in his best interest to make sure the presentation is as polished and professional as possible. He has his chosen presenter run through the slide show again and again, looking for possible glitches and practicing until they reach a certain comfort level. With all the video projection and sound equipment in place, Don runs through the presentation the morning before the meeting to note potential hang-ups that he could anticipate and solve from behind the scenes.

As part of the presentation, the writer has prepared not only a printout of all slides in handout form, along with Notes Pages and an outline, but a corporate report written in Microsoft Word with slides from the PowerPoint presentation illustrating it. A professionally done cover shows the company's logo (used as animation in the slide show) and the document is spiral bound. Once the presentation is completed, they publish it to a folder and upload it to the Internet, so clients worldwide can view the presentation given at the company meeting.

> **NOTE**
>
> Larger meetings require larger plans and larger investments—usually both in terms of time and money. Depending on the size of your meeting, you may be renting a meeting hall, getting the right production equipment, and making sure you're getting a professional quality sound system. There's lighting—and the control of it—to worry about, as well as where to put the podium, and whether the sound system will carry to the back of the auditorium.

Chapter Summary

This chapter completes your journey through *Mastering PowerPoint 97*. By looking at the various ways people present with PowerPoint, you can get some idea as to what will work best for you, how to evaluate what you've done, and how you can present more effectively in the future. PowerPoint makes it easy to express, review, and revise your ideas, while wowing your audience with color, style, the latest multimedia technology, and professional printouts. One way or another, PowerPoint can help you make sure your message hits home.

Appendix A

Installing PowerPoint 97

Installing PowerPoint 97

Whether you purchased PowerPoint as part of the Microsoft Office suite or as a stand-alone program, the installation procedures are similar. The main differences are between installing from floppies and installing from a CD. I'll present the main steps in this appendix, with brief discussions of what to expect.

Before you install the program, take a few minutes to back up your system to tape, floppies, or other media. At the very least, make sure you have copies of all your important files and programs. Also, if you will be installing PowerPoint from floppies (as opposed to CD), make backup copies of the program disks to store in a safe place.

The Installation Process

After backing up your system and, if you have them, the program floppies, close any programs you have running, insert the CD or the floppy labeled Disk 1 in the appropriate drive, and then open the Start menu on the Windows Taskbar and choose Run. The Run dialog box appears, as shown in Figure A.1.

FIGURE A.1
The Run dialog box

In the Open: line of the Run dialog box, type **a:\setup** or **d:\setup** (depending on whether you're installing from a floppy drive or from your CD-ROM drive), and click OK to start installing PowerPoint. If you are installing from a different drive (for example, a second floppy drive that's referred to as *b:*), substitute the appropriate letter for *a:* or *d:* above, then click OK to start the installation process.

If you are installing the program for the first time, PowerPoint displays an introduction screen. Click Continue. You are then asked to enter your name and organization. Fill in your information and click OK. A confirmation screen appears, showing you what you have entered. If the information is correct, click OK to continue. If not, edit the information as necessary.

NOTE

If you are installing a PowerPoint upgrade, which means that you have an earlier version of PowerPoint on your system, PowerPoint displays a message telling you that the Setup utility is searching the existing copy to make sure you're eligible for the upgrade.

If you are installing from CD, you will next be asked for your CD-Key. This is the number located on the back of your CD package. (If you are installing from floppy, you will not have this step to complete.)

On the next screen, PowerPoint displays your Product ID. Write down this number for safekeeping, in case you have trouble with PowerPoint and need to contact technical support.

NOTE

Once you've installed PowerPoint, your Product ID will also appear in the About PowerPoint dialog box, which you can display any time you are using the program by choosing Help ➤ About. Having your Product ID written down somewhere outside the program, however, is a good preventive measure, in case you experience a program crash and cannot get back into PowerPoint.

The Install program then makes sure you've got enough storage space on your hard drive and gives you the option of selecting the directory in which your PowerPoint files will be stored. If you want to change the directory in which PowerPoint stores its files, click the Change Directory button and, when prompted, enter the name of the directory you want to use for PowerPoint files.

The next screen, shown in Figure A.2, lets you choose the type of installation, so that you may control how much space the program takes on your hard drive. *Typical* installs the full program; *Compact* (available only if you're installing from floppy disks) installs only minimum options; and *Custom* allows you to install only the options you want. An additional option, *Run from CD-ROM*, which is available only if the install program has recognized that you are installing from a CD, installs only what PowerPoint needs in order to run from the CD. Of all the installation options, this one conserves the most storage space on your hard disk, but it also means you will need to insert the CD into your CD-ROM drive almost every time you use the program. Click the installation option you want and click OK. Installation begins and you can simply follow the prompts to complete the process.

FIGURE A.2
Types of installation available

Adding and Removing Options

Later, if you want to go back and add or remove items, change the installation settings, or reinstall the entire program, you can run Setup again. Rerunning Setup will not destroy any data files you have created; it will simply allow you to reinstall program files or add features you skipped the first time you installed PowerPoint.

If you run Setup after PowerPoint has been installed, you'll see three different options: Add/Remove, Reinstall, and Remove All. Add/Remove enables you to add or remove individual PowerPoint features; Reinstall begins the installation process again; and Remove All removes all PowerPoint files from your hard disk. Remove All, by the way, is the best way to go about uninstalling the program, because it hunts down and modifies any internal settings that refer to PowerPoint within your Windows system files.

NOTE

If you are rerunning Setup and have not previously used PowerPoint's On-Line Registration option to register your copy of PowerPoint with the Microsoft powers-that-be (registering allows you to use their customer service operation and to be eligible for discounted upgrades), you will also see the option that suggests you do this now.

Appendix B

Modifying Program Defaults

Modifying Program Defaults

Because one of PowerPoint's primary goals is to be easy to use right off the bat, many options have been preset for you. These options determine, among other things, the way the screen works, how printing is handled, which dialog boxes appear automatically, whether text is replaced when you type or inserted when you type, and how many Undos you'll allow. As you become proficient with PowerPoint, you may want to change some of the program defaults.

To change the program defaults, you'll go to the Options dialog box (choose Tools ➤ Options), which has numerous tabs containing various categories of options, as shown in Figure B.1. In this appendix I'll discuss each of the options available in this dialog box.

General Options

The first tab in the Options dialog box is the General tab (Figure B.2). The options on this page control items displayed in dialog boxes and menus, as described below:

- **Provide feedback with sound to screen elements.** This option plays Microsoft Office 97 sounds when PowerPoint performs designated functions or displays certain types of objects. If you don't have Office 97 sounds installed on your system, you can get them by choosing Help ➤ Microsoft on the Web ➤ Free Stuff, and clicking on the Sounds folder.

- **Recently used file list.** Check this to be able to specify the number of files displayed in the recently used file list.

- **Macro virus protection** keeps an eye out for viruses infecting your files.

- **Link sounds with file size greater than *x* Kb.** You can speed the processing of sounds if you tell PowerPoint to break large sound files into smaller segments and then link them together. Experiment with different settings for this option to see if it makes any appreciable difference in the playing of sounds.

GENERAL OPTIONS 375

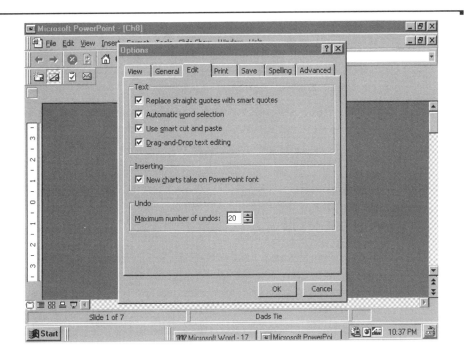

FIGURE B.1
The Options dialog box

FIGURE B.2
The General tab

Edit Options

The Edit tab of the Options dialog box (shown in Figure B.3) contains the settings in effect when you're editing the text in your PowerPoint presentation. Here are the basic function of these different options:

- **Replace straight quotes with smart quotes** automatically replaces straight quotation marks (also called double primes) with curly quotation marks—open quote marks at the beginning of the word or phrase, and close quote marks at the end.
- **Automatic word selection** causes PowerPoint to automatically highlight the whole word at the cursor position. This can be really useful or really annoying, depending on what you're trying to accomplish, so remember this feature exists, and come back to it to change it as needed.
- **Use smart cut and paste.** This feature, which operates in Slide View or Outline View, removes extra spaces you may have accidentally included at the beginning or end of a phrase or sentence when you swiped the mouse across it to select it for cutting. Additionally, this feature will add any necessary spaces when you paste text into a presentation.
- **Drag-and-Drop text editing** enables you to select and drag text and graphics from one point to another in your presentation. Without this feature enabled, you are limited to using Cut, Copy, and Paste commands.
- **New charts take on PowerPoint font** assigns the current PowerPoint font to charts you import.
- **Maximum number of undos** lets you set the number of operations you can reverse.

View Options

The View options control the elements displayed on the screen during your PowerPoint work session. The top group of options affect the PowerPoint work area; the bottom group determine what you see during a slide show.

- **Startup dialog** determines whether the Startup window appears when you begin PowerPoint.
- **New slide dialog** displays the New Slide dialog box.

FIGURE B.3
The Edit tab

- **Status bar** controls whether or not the status bar appears at the bottom of the PowerPoint work area.
- **Vertical ruler** determines whether or not it's the vertical ruler that is shown when you choose View ➤ Ruler to display the rulers.
- **Popup menu on right mouse click** controls whether the popup menu—which includes Slide Show navigation and enhancement commands—appears when you click the right mouse button during a slide show.
- **Show popup menu button** determines whether the menu button appears in the lower left corner of the Slide Show screen.
- **End with black slide** displays a black slide at the end of the presentation rather than restarting the presentation at the opening slide.

Printing Options

The Printing options, shown in Figure B.4, enable you to control how PowerPoint handles printing.

- **Background printing** lets you turn on background printing.
- **Print TrueType fonts as graphics.** This prints fonts in graphical mode.
- **Print inserted objects at printer resolution.** Enable this option to have PowerPoint print objects you place on presentation slides in the highest resolution your printer can handle.

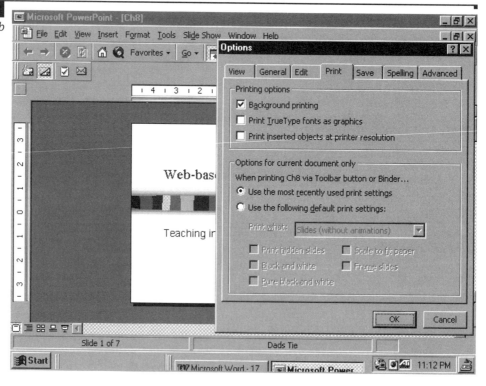

FIGURE B.4
The Print tab

Save Options

The Save options, shown in Figure B.5, control how and when your files are saved.

- **Allow fast saves.** With this option enabled, you save time because only the changes are recorded whenever you save the presentation during a session; the full file is saved only when you close the presentation or exit the program. (You can override a fast save in specific instances by using the shortcut Ctrl+S to save your presentation. Ctrl+S always saves the full file.)
- **Prompt for file properties** asks for more information about the file during a save.
- **Full text search information** provides for full-text searches.
- **Save AutoRecover info every *x* minutes** saves the file at the interval you specify.
- **Save PowerPoint files as ???** enables you to set the default file format for saved files.

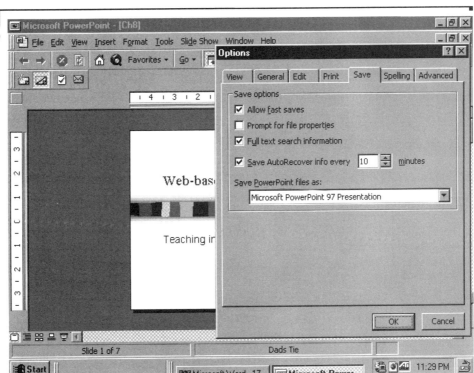

FIGURE B.5
The Save tab

Spelling Options

The Spelling tab, shown in Figure B.6, enables you to specify spelling preferences in three basic areas.

- **Check spelling as you type.** In this area, you can choose whether to let PowerPoint correct spelling mistakes as you type, or to hide spelling errors until you spell check them later.
- **Suggest.** In this area, you can click Always to activate the spell checker's suggested spellings list. (If you don't click Always, the spell checker will never suggest.)
- **Ignore.** The options in this area tell the spell checker whether or not to bother with flagging words in uppercase (if you use a lot of acronyms you won't want to be bothered by the spell checker flagging every single one of them) or words with numbers (same reasoning: lots of high-tech company names and product names include numerals).

FIGURE B.6

The Spelling tab

Advanced Options

The Advanced options, shown in Figure B.7, control the quality of graphic images.

- **Render 24-bit bitmaps at highest quality.** By default, this option is turned on. It gives you the best resolution for highly detailed graphics with a mix of colors.
- **Export pictures.** This option enables you to choose whether to export your pictures in the quality that is best for printing or best for viewing.
- **Default file location** lets you enter the drive and folder where you want to store your presentation files. (Note that even if you enter a default folder in this area, however, you can specify another folder or drive when you use File ➤ Save.)

FIGURE B.7
The Advanced tab

Appendix C

Tips for the First-Time Presenter

Tips for the First-Time Presenter

Presenting can be a harrowing experience, even if you've been doing it for years. When you are first faced with the prospect of creating and presenting a presentation, the experience may seem overwhelmingly intimidating. Here are some tips that will help you target, produce, and present your first presentation with a reduced level of anxiety:

- **Ask questions.** When you are first commissioned to do the presentation, ask plenty of questions. Find out who the audience is, what the general age range might be, what the overall tone of the presentation should be, and what the audience most needs to know from your presentation.

- **Keep a folder of styles you like.** If you have the opportunity to see presentations done by other people, take advantage. Keep a notebook or folder of what you liked and what you didn't. Ask yourself, What works, and why? What would you change if you were doing the presentation? Notice audience reaction and keep samples of the printed materials to see what the presenter felt was most important to include in printed form.

- **Become an informed watcher.** You don't have to limit your input to traditional presentations. Even with something as seemingly unrelated as watching television, you can learn something about the presentation you're preparing: What commercials catch your eye, and why? What shows hold your interest, and what elements contribute to their success? Make mental notes about what keeps and holds your attention and use that as you craft your own project.

- **Try a variety of styles.** If you have time to prepare a couple of samples, try using two or three of PowerPoint's different presentation designs to see what's most effective. Pass the samples around to get the opinions from others in your office or work group, as well—the more feedback you get in the early stages, the better.

- **Keep it simple.** When preparing the basic content of your presentation, try to keep to a series of simple concepts. The temptation to cram a wide range of information into a 30-minute presentation may be great, but remember that your ultimate goal is to be heard and understood. If you throw too much information at your audience at once, they may not remember the most important points.

- **Over-prepared is better than under-prepared.** Practice doesn't necessarily make perfect, but it certainly makes you better. The more time you spend preparing yourself, the better armed you'll feel at the moment of truth. In addition to spending time honing your presentation, double-check to be sure that you've got all the equipment, printouts, and space you need. Early in the creation process, make a list of items you'll need the day of the presentation. Several days before you present, review that list and make sure you haven't missed anything.

- **Make yourself comfortable.** Remember that jitters are just that—jitters. Once you begin the presentation and see how your audience is responding, much of the stage fright will pass. Taking care to make sure you're comfortable, however, will give you an edge. Wear clothing in which you feel competent and sure of yourself, make sure the conference room or stage is set up so you can move around the way you need to, be yourself as much as possible, and give yourself plenty of time.

- **When you discover something that works, use it again.** You don't have to create your next presentation from scratch if you hit on something that works well in your first presentation. Make sure you save the file and, if applicable, use it as a template for future presentations.

Appendix D

High-End PowerPoint

High-End PowerPoint

One of the best things about Microsoft Office 97 is the addition of VBA, or Visual Basic for Applications, which enable you to stretch the features of the Office programs to meet your own customized needs.

Programmers can work in Visual Basic to create a variety of add-on features that tailor Office to their own needs. Among other things, you might be interested in creating the following items with Visual Basic:

- Custom dialog boxes
- Data-entry forms
- Specialized command buttons
- Macros to perform repeated tasks

All of the Office applications include VBA implementation, and PowerPoint is no exception. You can use the Visual Basic Editor to create the add-in programs and develop specialized data-entry forms using the built-in utility Microsoft Forms.

Glossary

Glossary

Accent colors
Colors in the selected color scheme used to highlight presentation elements like gridlines, data labels, bullets, underlines, and custom-drawn shapes.

Anchor point
The point at which text is "anchored" to the text box. Change with the Text Anchor command in the Format menu.

Animation effects
Special effects you can add to PowerPoint objects, enabling them to move or be drawn on the screen in a manner you specify.

Annotations
Notes added to your slides during a presentation.

Arrowheads
The small arrow symbols on the end of the arrow line tool in the graphics tool box.

Attributes
Specific text options, such as font size, style, and color.

AutoClipArt
A wizard-like feature that enables PowerPoint to pick out appropriate clip art for you, based on the content of your presentation.

AutoContent Wizard
An automated utility that prepares presentations by asking you a series of questions about the type of presentation you want to create.

AutoCorrect
A feature of PowerPoint that automatically corrects misspellings.

AutoLayout
A predrawn slide type with its text, graphics, and/or clip art areas already set. You choose an AutoLayout selection when you choose a slide type in the New Slides dialog box.

AutoShapes tool
A shape palette from which you can choose one of 24 predrawn shapes.

AVI files
An acronym for Audio Video Interleaved, which refers to a multimedia file format that stores both audio and video data in the same file.

Axis
The horizontal or vertical line (the X axis and Y axis, respectively) along which the data items are plotted in a chart.

Background
The colored, textured, or blank backdrop on which all slide elements are placed. You can also use photographs or other custom graphics as presentation backgrounds.

Backup
The process of making a copy of a file or disk for storage.

Bar graph
A type of graph that uses bars in a variety of styles, such as traditional, stacked, and 3-D, to represent values of selected data series.

Bitmap
A type of graphic that is actually a pattern of dots, or pixels, on the screen.

Build slides
A slide show feature that lets you add text one item at a time, as in a bullet slide or slide with numerous text entries.

Bulleted lists
A list of (usually) indented text items, each started with a small graphical element called a bullet character.

Buttons
Command buttons—such as OK, Cancel, and Print—that allow you to carry out actions with the mouse.

Cells
The intersection of a row and column on the datasheet, in which you enter values and data labels.

Checkboxes
A small space in a dialog box that enables you to turn an option on and off by clicking in the space.

Clip art
A type of prefabricated art you can insert as is in your PowerPoint slides. PowerPoint comes with a 125-piece clip art library and you can add additional clip art from other programs and third-party vendors.

Clipboard
The invisible Windows clipboard, used to store copied or cut data.

Color scheme
A preset scheme of colors PowerPoint uses with templates. Colors are preselected for background, text, charts, and accent items. You can modify either entire color schemes or individual colors in PowerPoint.

Comments
You can add comments in the form of "sticky notes" to your presentation slide by opening the Insert menu and choosing Comments.

Conferencing
Makes it possible to give your presentation on the network, with a number of participants making notations on-screen.

Data marker
The small marker used in a line or scatter chart to show the data point.

Data series
The values included as a series in a graph.

Datasheet
The spreadsheet-like box in graph mode in which you enter data values and labels.

Demote button
Indents the entered text one level when you're working with text in Outline view or in a text box.

Drawing tools
The set of art tools along the left edge of the work area.

Drawing+ tools
A secondary set of drawing tools that appears when you choose Toolbars and select Drawing+. These tools enable you to set various drawing options and rearrange, flip, and rotate graphics objects.

Expand Slide
A feature that will break a slide that has many bullet points into different slides.

Graduated patterns
A shaded or mixed pattern that uses two colors and gradually fades one into another.

Grouping objects
The process of combining lines or objects into a single object.

Handles
Small black squares that appear along the perimeter of a selected object.

Handouts
A special print format that allows you to print two, four, or six presentation pages per printed page.

Home page
The first page of a Web site is said to be the home page.

HTML
An acronym for HyperText Markup Language, HTML is the coding language used to prepare documents for the World Wide Web.

Internet
A worldwide network of computer networks.

Image editing
The capability of modifying images—including photos and clip art—that you import into your PowerPoint presentations.

Importing data
The process of making data from another application part of a PowerPoint presentation.

Justification
The alignment of text in a text box. You can choose left-justified, centered, right-justified, or fully justified text.

Landscape orientation
Printing the page in 11-by-8½ format.

Layering
The process of placing one object on top of another to create the desired effect. Use with Send to Back and Bring to Front commands in the Format menu.

Legend
The key to a chart, explaining chart data sets and color and pattern codes.

Multimedia
Video, graphics, sound, and text—multiple media—integrated into your presentations.

Narration
With PowerPoint 97 you can record your voice to play along with your presentations.

Object
Any text, chart, or graphic item that can be selected and manipulated with the selection tool.

Online help
The help system accessible by pressing the F1 key.

Organization chart
A type of chart that illustrates a corporate structure or project flow, starting with a main level and breaking into subordinate levels.

Orientation
Describes the way the page is printed or displayed. Landscape prints horizontally (11 by 8½) and portrait prints vertically (8½ by 11).

Outline view
A view mode in PowerPoint that allows you to enter and edit text in outline fashion.

Portrait orientation
Prints the page in 8½-by-11 format.

PowerPoint Central
A new feature of PowerPoint 97 that enables you to get the latest sound clips, graphics, templates, and more from Microsoft's Web site.

Presentation Conferencing
A feature that enables you to give presentations to a group over a corporate network (intranet) or over the Internet, or by distributing disks.

Rehearsal feature
Lets you use the Rehearse Timings button (in Slide Sorter view) to plan out and practice the amount of time you need for each slide.

Rotating
In graphics mode, you can rotate a selected item in any angle.

Rulers

The rulers appear along the left and top borders of the work area, measuring in inches the size of the selected element. Display them by choosing View ➤ Ruler.

Slide show

An on-screen display of slides in a presentation.

Slide Sorter View

A view in which you can display thumbnail sketches of the slides in your presentation.

Spelling checker

Checks the spelling in your presentation.

Summary Slide

A new feature of PowerPoint 97 that creates a slide that is based on the content of slides you have selected.

Templates

Predesigned presentation files you can use as the basis for your own presentations.

Tip of the Day

A pop-up window that explains a new tip every time you start PowerPoint.

Transitional effects

The special effect used to remove the current slide and show the new slide. A transitional effect might be a fade, wipe, dissolve, or other effect.

Views

PowerPoint gives you several different ways to see your presentation: Slide view, Slide Sorter view, Outline view, and Notes Pages view, and Slide Show.

Web page

A document, displayed on the Internet's World Wide Web, that is linked to other documents via hyperlinks in text, buttons, or images.

Work area

The central area of the screen on which you create slides for your presentation.

X axis
The horizontal axis in most chart types.

Y axis
The vertical axis in most chart types.

Zoom in
The process of magnifying the screen area to get a closer look at an object or layout.

Zoom out
Reducing the page area and displaying the page from a more distant vantage point, enabling you to see more accurately how items are placed on the page.

Index

NOTE: Page numbers in *italics* refer to figures or tables; page numbers in **bold** refer to primary discussions of the topic

—Numbers—

3-D objects, AutoShapes as, 173
3-D tool (Drawing toolbar), *169*
8-bit, 198
16-bit, 198

—A—

About PowerPoint dialog box, 369
accent colors, 390
Action Items, in Meeting Minder, 269
Action Settings dialog box, 331, *332*
Add Sound dialog box, 203, *204*, 254, *255*
Adobe Photoshop, 165
advertising, printouts as, 308
alignment of text, **103–104**, *104*
America Online, 23
anchor point, 390
animation, 390
    for art objects, **187–188**
    for graphs, **148**, *149*
    sound for, 188, **205–206**
    for Web page, 335
Animation Effects toolbar, *46*, 188
annotations, 390
    of help, 34
    of slides during presentation, 266
Apple QuickTime for Windows, 218
Apply Design dialog box, 98
area graphs, 119, 126
Arrow Style tool (Drawing toolbar), *169*
Arrow tool (Drawing toolbar), *169*, 186
arrowheads, 390
arrows, for art, 177
art. *See also* clip art
    AutoShapes, **171–174**, *173*
    drawing, **165–171**
    files of, 347
    grouping and ungrouping objects, **178–179**, *178*, *179*
    importing, **162–164**
    layering objects, **180**, *181*
    line color and style, **185–186**

planning, **166**
right-click for editing options, *176*
sources, 162
for web page, 335
art editing, **175–177**
with Format Picture dialog box, **176–177**, *177*
art library, 171
art objects
animating, **187–188**
vs. clip art, 163
color and fill effects of, **181–185**, *182*
sizing, **55**
attributes, 390
audience
and presentation design, **26**
for rehearsal, **364**
and text, 71
Auto Repeat, for video, 230
Auto Rewind, for video, 230
AutoClipArt, 26, **154–155**, 390
AutoClipArt dialog box, *154*, 154
AutoContent Wizard, 7, *8*, *12*, **18–19**, 34, **37–41**, *38*, 390
benefits of, 44
in New Presentation dialog box, 39
opening screen, *39*
for text entry, *81*, **81–82**
AutoCorrect, 9–10, *10*, **86**, 391
AutoLayout, 391

automatic colors, 181
automatic slide advance, **251–253**, *252*, *253*
AutoRecover, 379
AutoShapes, **171–174**, *173*
groups, **172–173**
options for, **173–174**
for Web page link, 331
AutoShapes menu (Drawing toolbar), *168*
AutoShapes popup menu, *172*
AutoShapes tool, 391
AVI (Audio Video Interleaved) file format, 218, 348, 391
PowerPoint enhancement of, 220
space requirements, 197
axes, 391
setting chart options, 128

B

background color
blank, 299
of graph, 146
of object, 285
of slides, **297–302**
Background dialog box, **297–298**, *297*
background printing, 378
backgrounds, 391
patterned, **301–302**, *301*
picture, **302**, *302*
shaded, **299**
textured, **300–301**

backups, 391
balanced outline, 92
bar graphs, 119, 125–126, 391
bitmapped graphics, 165, 347, *348*, 391
   importing, *163*
black slide, option to end with, 377
black and white
   color scheme vs. view, **294**
   converting color presentation to, **291–294**, *293*
   printing color as, 321
Blank presentation, in PowerPoint dialog box, 34
Blinds transitional effect, 246–247
block of text, changing indent of, 101
.BMP files. *See* bitmapped graphics
bold text, 109
borders of objects, color of, **284–285**
Box transitional effect, 247
brevity, 68
brightness of art, *177*
Bring Forward, for art object, 180
Bring to Front, for art object, 180
browsers, Web, 23, 328
bubble charts, 119
Build slides, 391
Bullet dialog box, 111–112, *112*, *113*
bulleted lists, 392
bullets, **111–112**, *112*, *113*
buttons, 392
By Column button (Graph toolbar), *133*, 135
By Row button (Graph toolbar), *133*

—C—

Carnegie Coach button, in AutoContent Wizard, 39
case studies, **364–366**
CD-Key, 369
CD-ROM Today, 218
cell in datasheet, 122, 392
center tab, *102*
center-aligned text, 103, *103*
Change Icon dialog box, 223
Chart menu
   ➢ Chart Options, *128*, 128, 139
   ➢ Chart Type, 124
Chart Objects button (Graph toolbar), *133*
Chart Options dialog box
   Data Labels tab, 141
   Gridlines tab, 144, *145*
   Titles tab, *140*
Chart Type button (Toolbar), 124, *125*, *133*
Chart Type dialog box, 126–128, *127*
   Custom Types tab, 127, *128*
charts *See* graphs

ChartWizard, in Excel, 118
Checkerboard transitional effect, 247
clarity of text, 68
clip art, **154–189**, 392
   adding, 54
   vs. art objects, 163
   on CD-ROM ValuPack folder, 20
   finding specific, *159*, **159**
   keywords for, 154, 161
   licensing regulations for, 166
   new slides for, **156–157**, *157*
   organizing, **159–161**
   recoloring, **295–297**
Clip Gallery. *See* Microsoft Clip Gallery
Clip Properties dialog box, 161, *161*
Clipboard, 84, 392
closing datasheet for graph, 124
cluttered pages, 323
Collapse Selection button (Outline View toolbar), *78*, 92
collapsing
   outline, **90**, *91*
   single slide, **92**
collated copies, 320
color, **279–303**
   Apply to All to globally replace, **290–291**
   of art objects, **181–185**, *182*
   converting presentations to black and white, **291–294**, *293*
   custom, **285**, *286*, **287**
   design issues, **70–71**
   fast change, **282–287**
   for graphs, **146–147**, *147*
   of line for art, **185–186**
   for object fill, **283**
   of object lines, **284–285**
   of pen for on-screen drawing, 266
   for slide backgrounds, **297–302**
   in templates, **281–282**
   of text, **110–111**, *110*, **282**
   uses for, **280–281**
   in video, 219, **236–237**
color palette
   Fill Effects option, 147
   for Office 97 applications, 111
Color Scheme dialog box, Standard tab, 23, *24*, 288, *289*
color schemes, **23–24**, *24*, 279, 392
   changing, **287–291**
   creating custom, **289**, *290*
   search and replace, 288
Colors dialog box, 285, *286*
   Custom tab, 285, *286*, 287
   Standard tab, *185*
column graphs, 119
columns in datasheet
   deleting, 123, *123*
   sizing, 124
comments for presentations, **271**, *271*, 392

Common Tasks toolbar, *46*
Common Tasks window, *9*
compact install, 369
comparisons, graphs for, 117
compression. *See* file compression
CompuServe, 23
   forums for graphic utilities, 164
computer name, of workstation, 272
conferencing, **272–273**, 308, 392
   enhancements to, 362
consistency, masters for, 19
continuity, **27**
contrast, design issues, **70–71**
control bar, displaying below movie, 230
Control Toolbox toolbar, *46*
copies, setting number to print, **320**
Copy button (Graph toolbar), *133*
copy and paste, to import chart data, 130
copying graphs, 131
corporate identity, 26
corporate meeting, presentation for, **365–366**
Cover transitional effect, 247
cropping, 177
   movie object, **235**, *236*
.CSV files, importing, 129–130
current page miniature, in Outline view, 16, *16*

Current Slide view. *See* Slide view
Custom Animation dialog box, 148, *149*, **187**, 187
   to assign sound, *205*, 205
   Effects tab, *188*
   for movie object action, 225–227, *226*
   Play Settings, 225–227, *226*
custom color, **285**, *286*, **287**
custom install, 369
Custom Shows feature, *12*
custom slide shows, 361
   printing, 319
custom toolbars, creating, 47, *48*, 49
Customize dialog box, 47
Cut button (Graph toolbar), *133*
cut and paste, for text, **84**
Cut transitional effect, 247
CuteFTP, 336
cutting graph, 131

— D —

Dash Style tool (Drawing toolbar), *169*
data for charts, importing, **128–130**
data compression. *See* file compression
data entry. *See also* text entry
   in graph datasheet, 123

data labels, setting chart options, 128
data marker, 393
data panel, 26
data series, 393
Data Table button (Graph toolbar), *133*, 136
datasheet for graph, **121–124**, *121*, 393
  closing, 124
  creating from graph, 136, *137*
  data entry in, 123
  deleting rows and columns, 123, *123*
  labels for, **122**
  setting options, 128
date, in headers or footers, **315–316**
decimal tab, *102*
Decrease Font Size button (Formatting toolbar), 108
default settings, modifying, **374–381**
deleting
  datasheet rows and columns, *123*, 123
  tabs, **103**
Demote button (Outline View toolbar), *77*, 393
design issues
  balanced outline, 92
  cluttered pages, 323

color and contrast, **70–71**
continuity, **27**
effective graphs, **125–126**
for graphs, **117–118**
planning art, **166**
sound, 193, **211–212**
for text, **68–71**
for video, **219–220**
.DIB files, importing, *163*
directory, 344
  for PowerPoint install, 369
Disk Troubleshooter, 344
Dissolve transitional effect, 247
doughnut graphs, 119
downloading Internet Explorer, 23
drag and drop
  to move text, 85
  for text editing, 376
Draw menu (Drawing toolbar), *168*
  Order, 180
Drawing+ tools, 393
drawing, **165–171**
  beginner's guide to electronic, **170–171**
  on-screen, **266**
  vs. painting, **165–166**
drawing pointer, hiding, 266
Drawing toolbar, *9*, *46*
drawing tools, **167–171**, *167*, *168–169*, 393
  Shift key with, 170
DriveSpace, *342*, 342–343

E

Edit Category List dialog box, *160*, 160–161
Edit menu, *44*
- Clear, 131
  - All, 122
- Copy, 131
- Import File, 130
- Paste, 131
- Select All, 84

Edit menu (Media Player), 229
Edit Video Clip Object command, 228
editing. *See also* graph editing; text editing
  art, **175–177**
  movie, **277–237**
Eject tool (Media Player toolbar), *230*
electronic drawing, **170–171**
embedded objects, **352**
  inclusion in packaged presentation, 355
  vs. linked, **349–350**
embossing text, 110
End Selection tool (Media Player toolbar), *230*
.EPS files, importing, *163*
evaluation, of rehearsal, **363–364**
Excel graphs, **118–119**
Expand All button (Outline View toolbar), 90

Expand Selection button (Outline View toolbar), *78*
Expand Slide feature, *12*, **92**, **96**, *97*, 393
exporting
  files, **353**
  Meeting Minder notes to Word, **270–271**, *270*

F

Fade transitional effect, 247
Fast Forward tool (Media Player toolbar), *230*
fast saves, 379
feedback, 264
file compression
  techniques, **343–344**
  for video, 218
  in Windows 95, **342–343**
File menu, *44*
- New, 19, 38
- Pack and Go, 354
- Page Setup, 310
- Print, 317
- Save, 58
- Save As, 353
- Save as HTML, 334

File menu (Media Player), 229
file properties, prompt for, 379
files, **344–353**
  default format for saved files, 379
  importing and exporting, **353**

linking and embedding, **349–353**
organization planning, **345–346**
printing to, **322**
searching for, 352
size of PowerPoint, **341–342**
types of, **346–348**
viewing when opening, 14
Fill Color button (Drawing toolbar), *169*, 181, 283, *284*
Fill Color button (Graph toolbar), *133*
fill effects
   of art objects, **181–185**, *182*
   for slide background, 298
Fill Effects dialog box, 181, *182*, **302**, *302*
   Gradient tab, **299**, *299*
   Pattern tab, 147, *148*, *183*, 183, *301*, 301–302
   Picture tab, 184
   Texture tab, 183, *184*, 300
Find Clip dialog box, **159**, *159*
first-line indent, 102
folders, 344
   for PowerPoint install, 369
Font Color tool (Drawing toolbar), *169*
Font dialog box, 106, *107*, 108
   for text color change, *282*, 283
   for text effects, 110
   for text style, 109

fonts, 74
   for bullets, 112
   changing, **106**
   for graph, **142**, *143*, 376
   size for specialty, 109
footers. *See* Header and Footer dialog box
Format AutoShape dialog box, 173–174, *174*
   Colors and Lines tab, 185, *186*
Format Axis dialog box, 137, *138*
Format Axis Title dialog box, 140, *141*
Format button (Graph toolbar), *133*
Format Chart Title dialog box, *143*
Format menu, *45*
   ➤ Apply Design, 98
   ➤ Background, 297
   ➤ Bullet, 111
   ➤ Colors and Lines, 185, 284
   ➤ Font, 106
   ➤ Line Spacing, 104
   ➤ Slide Color Scheme, 23, 288
Format Painter (Standard toolbar), 111
Format Picture dialog box, **176–177**, *177*
formatting. *See also* text formatting
   Paste Special for, 85
Formatting toolbar, *9*, *46*
ForSite, 336
Fractal Design Painter, 165

frames
  for graph, 131, *132*
  printing, 323
Free Rotate tool (Drawing toolbar), *168*
Frequently Asked Questions (FAQs), 21
full text search, 379
function keys, F7 for spell check, 86

G

GIF file format, 335
  importing, *163*
GIFConverter, 164
graduated patterns, 393
graph area, marked on slide, *120*
graph editing, **130–138**
  data arrangement changes, *134*, **134–135**, *135*
  X and Y axes, **136–138**
graph enhancements, **138–149**
  animation, **148**, *149*
  color, **146–147**, *147*
  data labels, **141**, *142*
  font, size and style, **142**, *143*
  gridlines, **143–145**
  legend, hiding and displaying, **145–146**
  patterns, 147, *148*
  rotating text, **140**, *141*
  text box, **146**
  text changes, **139–142**
  title, 139
graph frame, 131, *132*
graph toolbar, *132, 133*
graphics. *See* art
graphs, **117–149**. *See also* datasheet for graph
  creating, **119–124**
  design ideas, **117–118**, **125–126**
  fonts for, 376
  importing data, **128–130**
  overview of types, **119**
  selecting type, **124–128**
gray tones, black and white printing to eliminate, 321
gridlines in charts, **143–145**
grouping, objects, **178–179**, *179*, 393

H

handles, 393
handouts, 26, 393
  adding headers and footers, **316–317**
  need for, 308
  as print option, *320*
hanging indent, 102
hardware, 7
  for sound, **198–202**
  upgrading for sound, **200–202**
  for video, **217**

Header and Footer dialog box, 313, *314*, **315–317**
    adding date and time, **315–316**
    Notes and Handouts tab, *317*, 317
height of slide, for printing, **312**
help, **34–36**
    Microsoft on the Web, **36**
    Office Assistant, 10, *11*, *35*, **35**
Help menu, 45
Help menu (Media Player), 229
hidden slides, 255–257, *256*
    displaying, **257**
    printing, 321
    in Slide Navigator, 264
home page, 394
horizontal gridlines, 143, *144*
HTML files, 394. *See also* Web pages
    saving presentation as, **334–335**
Hyperlink To Slide dialog box, 94
hyperlinks (links), 94, 328
    creating, **331–332**

I

icons
    customizing for movie object, *223*, 223
    linked object as, 352
image editing, 394. *See also* art editing
Import File button (Graph toolbar), *133*

Import File dialog box, 130, *131*
importing, 394
    art, **162–164**, *163*
    chart data, **128–130**
    files, **353**
    ungrouping art object after, 179
Increase Font Size button (Formatting toolbar), 108
indents
    for outline, *80*
    for text, **101–102**
Insert Clip menu (Media Player), 229
    ➢ Volume control, 234
Insert Hyperlink dialog box, 94
Insert menu, *45*, 350
    ➢ Movies and Sound, 206, *207*, 220
    ➢ New Slide, 53
    ➢ Object, 222
    ➢ Picture, 163
        ➢ Clip Art, 157
    ➢ Slide Number, 313, *314*
Insert Movie dialog box, 220, *221*
Insert New Slide button (toolbar), 53
Insert Object dialog box, *222*, 222, 350, *351*, 352
Insert Picture dialog box, *164*, 164
Insert Sound dialog box, 206
Insert WordArt tool (Drawing toolbar), *169*

inserting
   sound objects, **206**
   text from Microsoft Word, **79**
installing PowerPoint, **368–371**
   running Setup after, 370–371
Internet, 328, 394
   direct link with Microsoft ClipArt Gallery, 162
   logging on to, 36
Internet Assistant, **335**
Internet Explorer, *329*, 329
   downloading, 23
   web site, 330
   and window appearance, 32
Internet Service Provider (ISP), 23, 328
   Web page space from, 336
italics text, 109

—J—

Jasmine, 217
JPEG (Joint Photographic Experts Group) files, 218–219, 343, 348
   importing, *163*
   for Web pages, 335
justification, 394
justified text, 103

—K—

keyboard, for text selection, 84
keywords, for clip art, 154, 161
kiosk presentations, 361

—L—

labels
   in charts, **141**, *142*
   entering in datasheet, **122**
landscape orientation, 309, 394
laptops, for presentation, 364–365
layering, **180**, *181*, 394
layout of slides, changing, **98–99**
left aligned text, 103, *103*
left tab, *102*
legend for graph, 394
   hiding and displaying, **145–146**
   setting options, 128
levels of text, size of, **80**, *81*
licensing regulations, for clip art, 166
line color, for art, 177, **185–186**
Line Color tool (Drawing toolbar), *169*, 284
line graphs, 119, 126
line spacing, **104–105**
Line Spacing dialog box, *105*
Line Style tool (Drawing toolbar), *169*

Line tool (Drawing toolbar), *169*
linked objects
   creating, **331–332**, **350**, *351*, **352**
   vs. embedded, **349–350**
   in Excel spreadsheet, 118–119
   inclusion in packaged presentation, 355
   movie as, 223
links (Web pages), 94, 328
   creating, **331–332**
logging on to Internet, 36
logos, 26
looping, 262
   sound, 255

M

macro virus protection, default setting for, 374
manual slide advance, 250, *251*
masters, **19**
   art on, 166
   changing color of, 111
Media Player (Windows 95), 196, *197*, **228–235**, *229*
   displaying, 235
   menus, *229*
   returning to PowerPoint from, 235
   setting video options, **230**

Meeting Minder, **267–271**, 362
   exporting notes to Word, **270–271**, *270*
Meeting Minder dialog box, *268*, 268
meeting minutes, in Meeting Minder, *269*, 269
menu bar, *9*
menus, **44–45**
microphone, 208
Microsoft Clip Gallery, 54–55, *55*, 160
   Clip Art tab, *155*, 155, *157*
   direct link to Internet, 162
Microsoft Graph 97, 118
Microsoft Network, 23
Microsoft on the Web, **36**
Microsoft Word, inserting text from, **79**
MIDI files, 195, **197–198**
minor gridlines, 144
modem, 22
Move Down button (Outline View toolbar), *78*
Move Up button (Outline View toolbar), *77*
movie icon, **222–224**
movie objects
   cropping, **235**, *236*
   resizing and moving, **224**
movies
   adding to slides, **220–224**
   choosing time to play, **225**

editing, **227–237**
as linked files, 223
playing, **224–227**
posters for, **220**
timing coordinates to clip segment, **231**
moving
movie objects, **224**
tabs, **103**
text box, **52**
text with drag and drop, 85
text in Outline view, **92–93**
through slide show, **262**
MPEG (Motion Picture Experts Group), 218–219, 343–344
multimedia, 7, 394
multimedia files, **341–356**
Multimedia Properties dialog box, *201*, 201–202
multimedia-ready PC, **198–202**
music tracks, *12*

N

narration, 394
recording, **208**
voice-over, 196
Netfinity, 336
Netscape Navigator, 329
Network dialog box, Identification tab, 272
New Presentation dialog box, 8
Presentation Design tab, 19, *281*
Presentations tab, 19–20, *20*, 38
template selection, 19, *42*
New Slide button (status bar), 53, 78
new slide creation, **53–55**, *54*
in Outline view, **78–79**, *79*
New Slide dialog box, *53*, 53, 119, *120*
default setting for display, 376
slides with clip art, *156*
New Toolbar dialog box, 47
Next Mark tool (Media Player toolbar), *230*
No Fill, 285
NortonZip, 344
notes
adding headers and footers, **316–317**
printing slides with, 310
Notes pages, as print option, *320*
Notes Pages view, *13*, *15*, **18**, *18*, *70*, 70
Notes Pages View button, *16*
notetaking. *See* Meeting Minder
numbering slides, **313**, **315**

O

object-oriented graphics, 165
objects, 395
changing fill color, **283**
Office 97 applications, color palette, 111

Office Assistant, 10, *11*, *12*, *35*, **35**
Office Assistant button (Graph toolbar), *133*
OLE links, broken by image conversion, 179
on-screen drawing, **266**
online help, 395
Open dialog box, 34
Open Video Clip Object command, 235
opening files, view when, 14
Options dialog box, 374
   Advanced tab, 85, *381*, 381
   Edit tab, 85, **376**, *377*
   General tab, 374, *375*
   Print tab, *378*, 378
   Save tab, *379*, 379
   Spelling tab, *380*, 380
   View tab, **376–377**
Options dialog box (Media Player), 230, *231*
organization chart, 395
orientation of printing, 309, **312–313**, *313*, 395
Outline view, *13*, **15–16**, *16*, *56*
   for AutoContent Wizard, *40*
   collapsing outline, **90**, *91*
   creating new slide, **78–79**, *79*
   creating summary slide, *93*, **93**, *94*
   moving text in, **92–93**
   as print option, *320*

text editing in, **90–94**
text entry in, **76–79**, *77*
Outline View button, *16*
Outline View toolbar, *77–78*
outlines, balanced, 92
Oval tool (Drawing toolbar), *169*

—P—

Pack And Go Wizard, 224, 310, 343, **354–355**, *354*
Page Setup dialog box, **310**, *311*
page setup for slide printing, **310**, *311*
   orientation, **312–313**, *313*
   page size, **311–312**
   width and height of slide, **312**
Paint Shop Pro for Windows, 164
painting, vs. drawing, **165–166**
paragraph spacing, **106**
Paste button (Graph toolbar), *133*
Paste Special command, 85
pasting graphs, 131
patterns
   for backgrounds, **301–302**, *301*
   for graphs, 147, *148*
PC speaker, 195, 199
.PCT files, importing, *163*
pen color, for on-screen drawing, 266
Pick a Look Wizard, and color, 110
picture backgrounds, **302**, *302*

Picture toolbar, *46*
pie graphs, *119, 126*
PKZIP, *344*
Play tool (Media Player toolbar), *230*
playing, movies, **224–227**
plug-and-play, *7, 201*
PNGSETUP.EXE file, *224*
point, *105*
popup menus
   display option with right-click, *377*
   for navigating slide show, *262, 263*
portrait orientation, *309, 395*
posters, for movie, **220**
posting web pages, **335–336**
PowerPoint
   Clip Gallery to organize clip art, *157*
   getting starting, **7–10**
   highlights, *12*
   installing, **368–371**
   running presentations without, **354–356**
   running Setup after install, *370–371*
   starting, **32–34**
   upgrading, *369*
PowerPoint Animation Player, *335*
PowerPoint CD-ROM, ValuPack folder, *12*, **20–21**, *21*
PowerPoint Central, *12*, **21**, *21*, *395*
   multimedia clips from, *218*
PowerPoint dialog box, *33, 34*
PowerPoint files, size of, **341–342**
PowerPoint screen, *9, 9, 33*
PowerPoint Viewer, *355*
.ppt file extension, *348*
practice, *264*. *See also* rehearsal
Presentation Conference Wizard, *272, 272*
presentation conferencing, *395*. *See also* conferencing
Presentation Designs templates, *8*. *See also* templates
   vs. Presentations templates, *42*
presentation files, *348*
presentations. *See also* slide shows
   black slide at end as option, *377*
   converting color to black and white, **291–294**, *293*
   determining tools for, *26*
   finished, **359–360**
   highlighting all text, *84*
   options for sharing, **360–362**
   printing, **59–60**, **317–322**
   reasons to print, **308**
   running without PowerPoint, **354–356**
   saving, **58–59**
   saving as HTML file, **334–335**
   special features, **265–273**
      comments and review, **271**, *271*

conferencing, **272–273**
drawing on-screen, **266**
Meeting Minder, **267–271**
storing on disk, 224
tips for creating, **24–27**
uses, 6
Presentations templates, vs. Presentation Designs templates, 42
presenters, tips for, **264–265**, **384–385**
Preview window, of New Presentation dialog box, *281*, 281
Previous Mark tool (Media Player toolbar), *230*
Print button (Toolbar), 322
Print dialog box, *59*, **317–322**, *318*
numbering slides for, **313**, **315**
printed objects, resolution for, 378
printers, selecting, **318**
printing, **307–323**
decisions for, **309**
to files, **322**
hidden slides, 321
page setup for slides, **310**, *311*
presentations, **59–60**, **317–322**
range of slides, **319**
reasons for, **308**
Scale to Fit Paper option, 322
slides with notes pages, 310
printouts
reviewing, 323
transparencies from, 310

.PRN files, importing, 129–130
processes, graphs for, 117
Product ID, 369
Promote button (Outline View toolbar), *77*

Q

quality
of multimedia, file compression and, 343
of video, 219
quotation marks, 376

R

radar graphs, 119
Random Bars transitional effect, 247
Random Transition effect, 247
range of slides, printing, **319**
raster graphics, 165
Recently used file list, default setting for, 374
Recolor Picture dialog box, 236, *295*, *296*
Recolor Picture tool (Picture toolbar), 219, 236
Record Narration dialog box, 208, *209*
recording sound, **206–211**
narration, **208**
volume of, 208

Rectangle tool (Drawing toolbar), *169*
registration of PowerPoint, 371
rehearsal, **362–364**, 395
   evaluation of, **363–364**
   of slide display timing, **258–259**, *258, 260*
remote location, presentation at, 356, 364–365
resizing *See* sizing
resolution, for printed objects, 378
Reviewing toolbar, *46*
Rewind tool (Media Player toolbar), *230*
right aligned text, *103*, 103
right tab, *102*
rotating, 395
   chart text, **140**, *141*
rows in datasheet, deleting, 123, *123*
rulers, 396
   display, **100–101**, *100*
Run from CD-ROM, as install option, 370
Run dialog box, *368*, 368
running presentations
   on remote computer, 356
   without PowerPoint, **354–356**

—S—

sampling, 196
saving
   default settings for, *379*, 379
   presentation as HTML file, **334–335**
presentations, **58–59**, 96
sound recording, 211
Scale to Fit Paper, when printing, 322
Scale menu (Media Player), 229
scanned photos, paint program to touch up, 165
scatter (XY) graphs, 119
screen display, viewing presentation on two, 361
screen resolution, for Web page, 335
screen show. *See* slide show
Scroll Backward tool (Media Player toolbar), *230*
Scroll Forward tool (Media Player toolbar), *230*
searches
   for files, 352
   full text, 379
Select Objects tool (Drawing toolbar), *168*, 179
selecting
   graph type, **124–128**
   printers, **318**
   text for editing, **84–85**
Send to Back, for art object, 180
Send Backward, for art object, 180
sequence bar, to selection video portion, 232–233, *233*
sequence scale, for movie, 228

sequence of slides, 96
Set Selection - Time Mode dialog box (Media Player), 231, *232*
Set Up Show dialog box, **261–262**, *261*
setup, including in rehearsal, 373
shaded backgrounds, **299**, *299*
shadow text, 110
Shadow tool (Drawing toolbar), *169*
shadows, for AutoShapes, 173
Shift key, with drawing tools, 170
Show All button (Outline View toolbar), *78*
Show Formatting button (Outline View toolbar), *78*
Show Titles button (Outline View toolbar), *78*, 90
size, of art image, 177
size of text
   changing, **106**, 108, *108*
   for graph, **142**, *143*
   for text levels, **80**, *81*
sizing
   art objects, **55**
   columns in datasheet, 124
   graphs, 131
   movie objects, **224**
   text box, **52**
Slide Layout dialog box, *99*
Slide Meter, 259
Slide Navigator, **262**, *263*, **264**

slide show, 396
   finishing touches, **242–255**
   hidden slides, 255–257, *256*
   manual or automatic advance, **250–252**, *253*
   rehearsing slide display timing, **258–259**, *258, 260*
   slide transitions, **243–250**
   sound effects, **253–255**
   Spelling checker, 242
   moving through, **262**
   option to end with black slide, 377
   starting, **57**, *58*, **260–264**
   timing, 71
   what it is, **242**
Slide Show button, *16*
Slide Show menu, *45*
   ➢ Custom Animation, 148, 205
   ➢ Record Narration, 196, 208
   ➢ Slide Transition, 202
Slide Show view, *13, 15*
Slide Sorter view, *13*, 15, **17**, *17*, 56, *57*, 396
   choosing slide transitions in, *244*, 244–245
   Hide Slide button, 256
   Rehearse Timings button, 258
   text editing in, **95–96**
Slide Sorter View button, *16*
Slide title, in Outline view, *16*
Slide Transition dialog box, 202–203, *203*, 245, 245–248, *246*
   Automatic advance, 251, *252*

slide transitions, **243–250**
   speed of, **249–250**
Slide view, *13*, **14–15**, *14*
   from AutoContent Wizard, *41*
   drawing tools in, *167*
   text entry in, *73*, **73–75**
   transitional effect in, 244
Slide View button, *16*
slides
   adding movies to, **220–224**
   collapsing and expanding single, **92**, **96**, *97*
   hidden, 255–257, *256*
   layout change, **98–99**
   with marked graph area, *120*
   numbering, **313**, *315*
   as print option, *320*
   sequence of, 96
small group, presenting to, 364
smart cut and paste, 376
smart quotes, 376
sound, **202–204**
   for art animation, 188, **205–206**
   default for linking file segments, 374
   design issues, 193, **211–212**
   as feedback for operation, 374
   as finishing touch, **253–255**
   glossary, **195–196**
   hardware for, **198–202**
   recording, **206–211**
   upgrading hardware for, **200–202**
   video with, 220
   volume of, 208
   WAV and MIDI sound files, **197–198**
sound card, 195, 199
sound files, 195, 348
   adding from other sources, **202–204**
   on CD-ROM ValuPack folder, 20
   property rights, 198
   sources for, 204
sound objects, 195
   inserting, **206**
Sound Recorder, *196*, 196, **210–211**, *210*
Sound Selection dialog box, 208, *209*
spaces, in cut and paste, 376
spacing, for lines and paragraphs, **104–106**
speaker notes, 18
   in Slide Sorter view, 96
speakers (hardware), 200
special effects, and clock in rehearsal timer, 259
specialty fonts, larger sizes for, 109
Spelling Checker, 74, 83, **85–86**, 242, 396
   options for, *380*, 380
Spelling tool (toolbar), 86
Split transitional effect, 247
stacked bar charts, 119

Standard toolbar, *9, 46*
Start menu, ➤ Programs, ➤ Microsoft PowerPoint, *32, 33*
Start Selection tool (Media Player toolbar), *230*
starting PowerPoint, **32–34**
Startup dialog, display option, *376*
Status bar, *9*
   display options, *377*
"sticky notes," **271**, *271*
Stop tool (Media Player toolbar), *230*
Strips transitional effect, *247*
style checker, **86–90**, *242*
Style Checker dialog box, *87, 87*
Style Checker Options dialog box
   Case and End Punctuation tab, *87, 88*
   Visual Clarity, *88, 89*
Style Checker Summary dialog box, *89*
style of font, for graph, **142**, *143*
style of line, for art, **185–186**
styles, **109–110**
   picking up and applying, **111**
subscript, *110*
subtitle, *51, 52*
summary slide, *12, 396*
   creating in Outline view, **93**, *93, 94*
Summary Slide button (Outline View toolbar), *17, 17, 78*

superscript, *110*
supplemental information, hidden slide for, *256*

—T—

tabs, **102–106**
   deleting, **103**
   moving, **103**
templates, **19–20**, **41–42**, *43, 396*
   benefits of, *44*
   and color, *110*
   in PowerPoint dialog box, *34*
text
   changes in graph, **139–142**
   color of, **110–111**, *110*, **282**
   design rules for, **68–71**
   inserting from Microsoft Word, **79**
   key points for, **71–72**
   rotating on charts, **140**, *141*
text box
   adding to graph, **146**
   moving, **52**
   and ruler display, *100–101, 101*
   sizing, **52**
Text Box tool (Drawing toolbar), *169*
Text Color button (Drawing Toolbar), *110*
text cursor, *74*
text editing, **83–96**
   AutoCorrect, **86**
   cut and paste, **84**

in Outline view, **90–94**
   moving text, **92–93**
   selecting text for, **84–85**
   in Slide Sorter view, **95–96**
   undoing, **85**
text entry, **49–52**, *50*, *51*, **72–80**
   AutoContent Wizard for, *81*, **81–82**
   in Outline view, 16, **76–79**, *77*
   in Slide view, *73*, **73–75**
   style checker, **86–90**
   within shape, 174
text entry box, *75*
   adding, **75–76**
text files, 346
text formatting, **98–112**
   alignment, **103–104**, *104*
   bullets, **111–112**, *112*, *113*
   color, *110*, **110–111**
   effects, **110**
   font and text size, **106**
   indent changes, **101–102**
   layout change to adjust, **98–99**
   line and paragraph spacing, **104–106**
   picking up and applying styles, **111**
   ruler display, *100*, **100–101**
   styles, **109–110**
   tabs, **102–106**
text levels, size for, **80**, *81*
text wrap, 74

textured backgrounds, **300–301**
tick marks, 137
time, adding to header or footer, **315–316**
timing
   rehearsing for slide display, **258–259**, *258*, *260*
   of slide show, 71
tip of the day, 396
title, 49, *50*
title of graph, 139
Title Text Color dialog box, 289
titles, setting chart options, 128
tone of presentation, **25–26**
   audience and, 71
   continuity in, 27
   text font and, 106
toolbars, **45–49**, *46*
   creating custom, 47, *48*, 49
   suppressing all but Web toolbar, 333, *334*
Tools menu, *45*
   ➤ AutoClipArt, 154
   ➤ AutoCorrect, 9–10, *10*, **86**
   ➤ Expand Slide, 96
   ➤ Join a Conference, 273
   ➤ Meeting Minder, 268
   ➤ Options, 374. *See also* Options dialog box
   ➤ PowerPoint Central, 21
   ➤ Presentation Conference, 272
   ➤ Replace Fonts, 108
   ➤ Spelling, 86

ToolTips, 9
  for Drawing toolbar, 167, *168*
transitional sound effects, 202
transitions, 396. *See also* slide transitions
transparencies, 361
  from printouts, 310
trends, graphs for, 118
TrueType fonts, printing as graphics, 378
.TXT files, importing, 129–130
typical install, 369

— U —

Uncover transitional effect, 247
underlining, 110
undo
  maximum number of, 85, 376
  for text editing, **85**
Undo button (Graph toolbar), *133*
ungrouping objects, **178–179**, *178*
  for layering commands, 180
uninstalling program, 371
Universal Resource Locator (URL), 328
upgrading
  hardware for sound, **200–202**
  PowerPoint, 369
URL (Universal Resource Locator), 328

— V —

ValuPack folder, on CD-ROM, *12*, **20–21**, *21*
VBA support, *12*
vector images, 347
vertical gridlines, 143, *144*
vertical ruler, display options, 377
video, **215–237**. *See also* movies
  benefits of, **216–217**
  on CD-ROM ValuPack folder, 20
  design issues, **219–220**
  file formats, **218–219**
  hardware for, **217**
  recoloring images, **236–237**
  sources of, **217–218**
video capture board, 217
video files, 348
View buttons, *9*
View Datasheet button (Graph toolbar), *133*
View menu, *44*
  ➤ Datasheet, 124
  ➤ Header and Footer, 313
  ➤ Master, ➤ Slide Master, 111
  ➤ Outline, 76
  ➤ Ruler, 100
  ➤ Slide Show, 57, 260
  ➤ Slide Sorter, 95
  ➤ Speaker Notes, 96
  ➤ Toolbars, 47
    ➤ Web Toolbar, 333

views, **13–18**, 396
  black and white vs. black and white color scheme, **294**
  changing, **56**
  uses for, 15
  when opening existing file, 14
virus protection, default setting for, 374
Visual Basic for Applications (VBA), 388
Visual Basic toolbar, *46*
visual continuity, 27
voice narration, *12*, 196
voice recognition, 200
volume, of sound recording and playback, 208
volume control, **234–235**, *234*

— W —

waveform (WAV) files, 195, **197–198**
  on PC speaker, 199
Web browsers, 23, 328
Web features, *12*
Web pages, 8, 328, 396
  appearance, **328–330**, *329*
  links, 94, 328, **331–332**
  posting, **335–336**
Web Publishing Wizard, 336
Web service provider, 336
Web sites
  Clip Gallery connection to, *162*, 162
  for Internet Explorer, 23, 330
  updating PowerPoint Central from, 21
  for Web service providers, 336
Web toolbar, *46*, *333*, 333, *334*
Web toolbar button (Standard toolbar), 333
white space, 323
width of slide, for printing, **312**
Window menu, *45*
Window menu (Media Player), 229
Windows 95
  file compression, **342–343**
  multimedia support, 7
windows, appearance as Web browsers, 32
Windows Explorer, *345*
Wipe transitional effect, 247
wizards, 18. *See also* AutoContent Wizard
  Pack And Go, 224, 310, 343, **354–355**, *354*
  Pick a Look, 110
  Presentation Conference, *272*, 272
  Web Publishing, 336
.WK* files, importing, 129–130
.WMF files, importing, *163*
word, automatically highlighting entire, 376
Word (Microsoft), exporting Meeting Minder notes to, **270–271**, *270*

WordArt toolbar, *46*
work area, 396
workstation, computer name of, 272
World Wide Web, 328
   access to, 22–23

—X—

X axis, for graph, **136–138**, 397
.XL* (Microsoft Excel) files, importing, 129–130
XY (scatter) graphs, 119

—Y—

Y axis, for graph, **136–138**, 397

—Z—

ZIP drive, 344
Zoom controls, 83, 397
   for graph in edit mode, 134

Mastering™ the

FOR BUSINESS

Stay Ahead of the Learning Curve...

The books to choose for comprehensive, accurate coverage of virtually any popular program. Mastering titles demonstrate basic to advanced skills through real-world examples. Recognized as the highest quality computer books on the market.

Mastering Microsoft Office 97 Professional Edition (2nd Ed)
Lonnie E. Moseley, David M. Boodey
ISBN: 0-7821-1925-5, $39.99

Mastering Access 97 (4th Ed)
Alan Simpson, Elizabeth Olson
ISBN: 0-7821-1924-7, $44.99
CD included

Mastering Microsoft FrontPage 97
Susann Novalis
ISBN: 0-7821-2027-X, $49.99
CD included

Mastering Excel 97 (4th Ed)
Thomas Chester, Richard H. Alden
ISBN: 0-7821-1921-2, $34.99

Mastering Word 97 (4th Ed)
Ron Mansfield
ISBN: 0-7821-1926-3, $34.99

Opportunities

AND TECHNICAL USERS

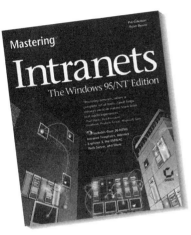

**Mastering Intranets
The Windows 95/NT Edition**
Pat Coleman, Peter Dyson
ISBN: 0-7821-1991-3, $49.99
CD included

Mastering Lotus Notes 4.5 (2nd Ed)
Kenyon Brown, Kyle Brown,
François Koutchouk, Kevin Brown
ISBN: 0-7821-1996-4, $54.99
CD included

Mastering Visual Basic 5
Evangelos Petroutsos
ISBN: 0-7821-1984-0, $49.99
CD included

Mastering Java 1.1 (2nd Ed)
Laurence Vanhelsuwé, Ivan Phillips,
Goang-Tay Hsu, Eric Ries, John
Zukowski
ISBN: 0-7821-2070-9, $49.99
CD included

Mastering JavaScript
James Jaworski
ISBN: 0-7821-2014-8, $49.99
CD included

Available Now at Bookstores Near You

SYBEX®

© 1997 Sybex Computer Books

PowerPoint Transitional Effects

Effect	Description
No Transition	No transitional effect has been applied to this slide.
Blinds Horizontal	Horizontal strips close, revealing the next slide.
Blinds Vertical	Vertical strips close, revealing the next slide.
Box Out	New slide starts as a small box in center of the former slide and spreads outward.
Box In	New slide spreads inward from the outer edges.
Checkerboard Across	A checkerboard pattern fills in the new slide from left to right.
Checkerboard Down	A checkerboard pattern fills in the new slide from top to bottom.
Cover Left	The new slide slides in from the right.
Cover Up	The new slide slides up from the bottom.
Cover Right	The new slide slides in from the left.
Cover Down	The new slide slides down from the top.
Cover Left-Up	The new slide slides up from the bottom right corner.
Cover Right-Up	The new slide slides up from the bottom left corner.
Cover Left-Down	The new slide slides down from the top right corner.
Cover Right-Down	The new slide slides down from the top left corner.
Cut	A quick exchange inward reveals the new slide.
Cut Through Black	A quick exchange reveals the new slide after a momentary blackout.
Dissolve	The old slide dissolves into the display of the new slide.
Fade Through Black	The old slide fades to black and the new slide appears gradually.
Random Bars Horizontal	Randomly placed bars reveal the new slide.
Random Bars Vertical	Random vertical bars reveal the new slide.
Split Horizontal Out	The new slide begins as a horizontal line in the center of the screen and spreads outward.
Split Horizontal In	The new slide begins along the top and bottom of the screen and spreads inward.